INTERNATIONAL LAW

FIGHTING FOR JUSTICE

INTERNATIONAL LAW

FIGHTING FOR JUSTICE

Common Law and Civil Law Judges: Threats and Challenges

Edited by

ELIZABETH GIBSON-MORGAN

UNIVERSITY OF WALES PRESS
2021

www.uwp.co.uk

British Library CIP Data
A catalogue record for this book is available from the British Library.

ISBN 978-1-78683-746-2
eISBN 978-1-78683-747-9

Typeset by Marie Doherty
Printed by CPI Antony Rowe, Melksham, United Kingdom

In memory of my father

Series Preface

Challenges to the independence of the judiciary have mounted alongside the rise in numerous countries around the world of populism and authoritarianism. Meanwhile, in the United Kingdom and elsewhere, the Covid-19 pandemic has hastened a move towards remote systems of judging and also a call for the reform of jury trials. Concurrently, the global Black Lives Matter movement has brought into sharp focus issues around the lack of representativeness on judicial benches.

In this fraught context, this edited volume could not be more timely. It is a well-placed addition to the *International Law* series, which aims to publish dynamic and cutting-edge research in international law, with a strong focus on legal theory. Elizabeth Gibson-Morgan should be commended for bringing together this collection of essays, in which esteemed contributors from academia, the judiciary, and legal practice analyse important themes of judicial independence, diversity of the bench, access to justice, and judicial training reform. The chapters provide essential comparative insights from five countries: the United Kingdom, Denmark, France, Spain, and Canada. The result, a coherent and well-argued defence of the rule of law internationally, will serve as an important reference work for many years to come.

Professor Diane Marie Amann
University of Georgia
Professor Yvonne McDermott
Swansea University

Contents

Acknowledgements

It all started with a one-day conference devoted to judges in common law and civil law countries organised at the Bordeaux Law School on 16 March 2018. This location was chosen because of its unique legal tradition, as the city of Montesquieu, and the only one outside Paris to have a branch of the National Judicial Training College – the *École Nationale de la Magistrature*. The main objective was to bring would-be judges and senior judges from various countries together to share, for the former their expectations, for the latter their long experience of the practice of the law, in order to understand better what being a judge today means, what the main challenges and potential threats are.

Rather than focusing exclusively on national legal identities and legal traditions, the discussions showed both the importance of and attachment to common values and legal principles, most notably the rule of law. They also revealed shared concerns regarding the future of judicial independence, access to justice, diversity in the judiciary and the reform of justice.

My gratitude first goes to all those who contributed to the success of this event, and in particular Lord Judge. His expertise, accessibility and kindness were greatly appreciated and made it a memorable day. I would also like to thank all those who later added their own expertise and thoughts through their written contributions to this volume, thus prolonging the reflection on those key topical issues. I am truly grateful to Professor Valérie Malabat, the Head of the *Institut de Sciences Criminelles et de la Justice* (ISCJ), my research centre in Bordeaux, and Professor Evelyne Bonis-Garçon, the Head of the Institute of Legal Studies (*Institut d'Études Judiciaires*) for having made the Bordeaux event possible and for their continuous support.

I would also like to thank my students for their enthusiasm for the law and also for the joy they bring me as an academic. This book partly aims at strengthening them in their judicial career choice and in keeping the flame alive.

Last but not least, my thanks go to the University of Wales Press, and in particular Sarah Lewis for her patience, encouragement and professionalism.

I would like to dedicate this book to my late father, Derek Gibson, who attended the Bordeaux conference, then passed away a few months later. He held until the end a passion for justice.

Elizabeth Gibson-Morgan
Oxford, June 2020

List of Abbreviations

ADR	Alternative Dispute Resolution
BAME	Black, Asian, Minority Ethnic
CAB	Citizens Advice Bureau
CETA	Comprehensive Economic and Trade Agreement
CGAE	*Consejo General de la Abogacía Española* (General Council of Spanish Lawyers)
CGPJ	*Consejo General Poder Judicial* (General Council of the Judiciary)
CJC	Canadian Judicial Council
CPS	Crown Prosecution Service
DPP	Director of Public Prosecutions
ECHR	European Convention on Human Rights and Fundamental Freedoms
EEA	European Economic Area
EGA	*Estatuto General de la Abogacía* (the Federal Lawyers' Regulations)
ENM	*École Nationale de la Magistrature*/(French Judicial Training College)
EU	European Union
HMCTS	Her Majesty's Courts and Tribunals Service
HMOC	Her Majesty's Online Court
IEHC	Supreme Court of Ireland
IOJT	International Organisation for Judicial Training
JAAB	Judicial Appointments Advisory Board (Republic of Ireland)

JAP	Judicial Appointments Commission (England and Wales)
QC	Queen's Counsel
LASPO	Legal Aid, Sentencing and Punishment of Offenders Act 2012
LCJ	Lord Chief Justice
LGBTQ2	Lesbian, Gay, Bisexual, Transgender, Queer, Two-Spirit
LOPJ	*Ley de orientación y programación de la justicia* (the Act organising and planning the justice system)
MIAM	Mediation Information and Assessment Meeting
PIMMS	Points Information Mediation Multi-Services/ Multi-Service Mediation Information Points
SCC	Supreme Court of Canada
SIAC	Special Immigration Appeals Commission
TTIP	Transatlantic Trade and Investment Partnership
UKSC	United Kingdom Supreme Court
USM	*Union Syndicale des Magistrats* (French Trade Union of Judges)

Notes on the Contributors

Victor Bailey is a Distinguished Professor of Modern British History at the University of Kansas, who has developed an expertise in the history of crime, policing and punishment. He is a prolific author. His latest book is entitled *The Rise and Fall of the Rehabilitative Ideal, 1895–1970* (London: Routledge, 2019).

Benoît Chamouard is a former French judge and currently the Deputy Director of the French National School for the Judiciary (ENM) and Head of the International Department.

David Jose Soto Diaz is a law graduate of the University of A Coruña, Spain and a member of the Research group on Criminology, Legal Psychology and Criminal Justice in the Twenty-first Century. His research focuses on the European Court of Justice, globalisation and the judiciary, as well as Investor State Dispute Settlement.

Géraldine Gadbin-George is a former *Avocat* at the Paris Bar, a French judge and English solicitor. She is currently Professor-elect in Legal English and English Law at the University of Panthéon-Assas, France.

Elizabeth Gibson-Morgan (editor) is Professor in Law and Languages at the University of Poitiers, and at the Bordeaux Law School. She is a Senior Research Fellow in Constitutional Law at King's College, London. Her current research is on House of Lords reform, devolution, the UK Supreme Court, constitutional change and Brexit. She is the author of *Constitutional Reform in Britain and France: From Human Rights to Brexit* (226pp.) (Cardiff: University of Wales Press, 2017).

Peter Gjørtler is a Danish practising barrister based in Brussels and a Lecturer in Law at the Riga Postgraduate School of Law.

Milwyn Jarman is a Specialist Chancery Judge for Wales. He sits as a judge at the High Court in the Queen's Bench Division, Administrative Court and as an Upper Tribunal Judge. He is an Honorary Fellow of the University of Aberystwyth, where he studied law before practising as a barrister in Cardiff for twenty-seven years, then as a Recorder of the Crown Court.

Igor Judge (Lord Judge) is a former Chief Justice of England and Wales (2008–13). He was born in Malta, read History and Law at Magdalene College, Cambridge (1959). He was appointed Recorder of the Crown Court in 1976 and a Queen's Counsel in 1979. In 1987, he was elected Leader of the Midland and Oxford Circuit and a Bencher of the Middle Temple. In 1988, he was appointed a High Court Judge, Queen's Bench Division and knighted. He became a Life Peer in 2008 and was a member of the Constitution Committee of the House of Lords. He is a Visiting Professor at King's College, London. He is the author of *The Safest Shield*, a collection of lectures and speeches (2015) and the co-author of *Magna Carta Uncovered* (2014).

Matthias Kelly QC, England and Wales, Senior Counsel, Ireland, member of Bar of Northern Ireland, is a former Chairman of the Bar of England and Wales and of the UK Personal Injuries Bar Association. He is a part-time judge in England and Wales, sitting as a Recorder in the Crown Court, the County Court and the Family Court. He is an Examiner of the High Court of England and Wales. He is a Bencher of The Honourable Society of Gray's Inn, London.

Michel Morin is Deputy Dean, Faculty of Law, University of Montreal. He is a former professor in the civil law section of the University of Ottawa's Faculty of Law. He is a specialist in comparative history of law (France, UK, Quebec and Canada) and comparative law. The Humanities and Social Sciences Federation awarded him the

Jean-Charles Falardeau prize for his book, *L'Usurpation de la souveraineté autochtone* (*The Usurpation of Aboriginal Sovereignty*, Montreal: Boréal, 1997) in 1998. In 2012, he co-authored, with Arnaud Decroix and David Gilles, *Les tribunaux et l'arbitrage en Nouvelle-France et au Québec de 1740 à 1784* (*Courts and Arbitration in New France and Quebec, 1740–1784*, Montreal, Éditions Thémis) which was awarded the Rodolphe Fournier 2013 prize (*ex aequo*).

Ana María Neira Pena is Associate Professor in criminal procedure and corporate criminal law, University of A Coruña, Spain. She did her PhD on corporate criminal liability. She is a member of the Research group on Criminology, Legal Psychology and Criminal Justice in the Twenty-first Century. She is the author of a book published in 2017 entitled *La Instrucción de los Procesos Penales Frente a las Persona Jurídicas*.

Winston Roddick QC, First Counsel General for Wales (1998) and Leader of the Wales and Chester Circuit, (former) North Wales Police and Crime Commissioner, Honorary Recorder of the Royal Town of Caernarfon, a Companion of the Order of the Bath (CB), practised as a barrister on the Wales and Chester Circuit for over fifty years in the fields of public law, common law, chancery, and town and country planning.

Introduction: Judges' Common Threats and Challenges

Elizabeth Gibson-Morgan

Justice is a universal value and a shared aspiration of civil and common law countries. It is most certainly the case for the five established democracies covered in this book. Yet, the perceptions and expectations regarding those who deliver justice – judges – tend to vary from one of these five countries to another, influenced by a specific national legal history and culture. The common law is generally defined as a 'judge-made' law where judges – such as in England and Wales[1] – are involved in a creative process through their power of setting binding precedent, whereas civil law judges – as in France or Spain – are expected to be no other than the 'mouth of the law' within clearly defined competences in the name of the principle of separation of powers, essential to judicial independence. As the most influential French jurist, Charles-Louis de Secondat, better known as Montesquieu, underlined in *L'Esprit des lois*, 'When the legislative power is united with the executive power in a simple person or in a single body of the magistracy, there is no Liberty [...] nor is there Liberty if the power of judging is not separate from the legislative power and from the executive power.'[2]

In most constitutional arrangements in common law countries – starting with the oldest fully written constitution, the US Constitution of 1787 – the judicial branch was established as an equal and separate power. However, in a civil law country like France it is only dealt with in Title Eight of the Constitution of the Fifth Republic as a Judicial Authority. Its independence is guaranteed by the President of the Republic assisted by the High Council of the Judiciary under the provisions of article 64. In the French legal culture, this forms part of the legacy of the 1789 Revolution. The suspicion of judges interfering with the affairs of the state driven by political considerations – *le gouvernement des juges*, in the words of Édouard Lambert[3] – has not totally disappeared. As a reaction to the powerful *Parlements* – the name given to royal courts of justice under the *ancien régime* – the French revolutionaries, greatly influenced by the ideas and values of the Enlightenment, drafted the Law of 16–24 August 1790, which stated in its article 13: 'judicial functions are distinct and will always remain separate from administrative functions.' This divided, once and for all, the French legal system into two distinct branches, the administrative and the judicial, with their own supreme court at the summit. In this way the courts from the judicial branch were deliberately deprived of the power of reviewing administrative action, thus deterring judges from ruling outside their remit.

By contrast, describing the common law as a 'judge-made law' might give the impression at first sight that common law judges are all-powerful and that they know no limits to what they can do when interpreting the law. As Matthias Kelly shows in his chapter, rather than making the law as is commonly believed, 'common law judges can clarify the law and develop it incrementally over a period of time.' In England and Wales, judges are well aware of the importance of parliamentary sovereignty as a pillar of the constitution and their need as judges to abide by it. The legal culture to which they belong is very much based on self-restraint, as Lady Hale, the former President of the United Kingdom Supreme Court, explained: 'We [members of the Supreme Court] recognize some important limits. First, we are seeking to identify and apply the underlying principle of the laws, extending and adapting them to meet new situations but not to turning them on their head.' She added that there are some things which are better left to Parliament.[4]

This book considers the current threats to the role of the judiciary, from four major thematic standpoints, independence, diversity, access and reform. It considers five countries, the United Kingdom, France, Spain, Denmark and Canada and does so through a comparative viewpoint. Four are members of the Council of Europe in Strasbourg, starting with the United Kingdom at the origin of the common law and the very first country to ratify the European Convention on Human Rights as early as 1951.

Judicial independence – and its corollary, impartiality – is a common requirement for the nation states that have ratified the European Convention on Human Rights and Fundamental Freedoms, whether they belong to the civil law or the common law legal system. Article 6(1) which guarantees people in court a fair trial states: 'In the determination of his civil rights and obligations or of any criminal charge against him, everyone is entitled to a fair and public hearing within a reasonable time by an independent and impartial tribunal established by law.'

Among these four countries, three are civil law countries – Denmark, France and Spain. As for the last, Canada – a common law country with the exception of Quebec – (although it is a non-member state), it has been an Observer State since 1996. Their judges are guided by the common principles that all the members share, having officially committed themselves to respect and promote democracy, the rule of law, human rights and fundamental freedoms. The interpretation of the Court of Human Rights of the European Convention has provided the Council of Europe member states with essential guidelines defining common standards while leaving a margin of appreciation of the Convention to national courts and a common source of law bringing civil law and common law countries closer. As it is stated in the Cabinet Manual of the UK, 'Each country is given certain latitude in how it gives effect to the Convention rights in order to reflect national circumstances.'[5] Lady Hale for her part noted that via the interpretation of the ECHR by the Court of Human Rights, national courts and judges have acquired a 'common European understanding' of the Convention.[6]

Independence: Threats to the Judiciary

The act of judging is in itself under normal circumstances highly challenging for judges, whether they sit in a national or international court. If they are in charge of protecting individual liberties and personal freedoms, judges also have the huge responsibility of deciding when to deprive an individual found guilty of a serious offence of their liberty as the ultimate (last resort) penalty.[7] In the same way, the Constitution of the French Republic in its article 66 describes the Judicial Authority as 'the guardian of the freedom of the individual', which finds its source of inspiration in the English Habeas Corpus Act of 1679, which preserves people from arbitrary arrest and detention.

'Maintaining the rule of law' and 'serving the community' – in the words of the former Lord Chief Justice of England and Wales, Lord Judge – thus remains a highly demanding and stimulating profession. The judiciary in European countries like the UK, Denmark, France and Spain – EU members or future EU partners – but also Quebec, influenced by both the civil law and common law legal traditions, is well known for its high standards of legal practice and moral integrity. A civil law country like France and a common law country like the UK also have a strong tradition of involving lay people in delivering justice, either as non-professional judges or as jurors – being tried by one's peers being an essential right traditionally associated with the Magna Carta – which is a way of bridging the gap between ordinary citizens and the Bench. Whether professionals or non-professionals they are all driven by the same passion for justice; as Lord Judge – quoted by Winston Roddick, in his chapter – has said, 'the judge must have [. . .] moral courage [. . .] a very important judicial attribute to make decisions that will be unpopular with the politicians or the media and the public.'

Yet contemporary judges, whether they belong to common law or civil law countries, are faced with similar unprecedented challenges under exceptional circumstances. Some of them are likely to have long-lasting consequences on the status of judges that may even seriously affect the way they deliver justice. It is, indeed a challenging time for judges in both civil and common law countries, with drastic cuts in justice ministry budgets affecting legal aid and access to justice, as well as growing threats to their independence.[8] Judges first of all are faced with more immediate practical problems – overburdened courts, low wages and pensions. It is however less the case in a country like Denmark[9] – as Peter Gjørtler points out – where judges are protected from potential financial loss if they retire before the legal retirement age of seventy. The status of Canadian Federal judges is even more unusual as they benefit from a high annual salary while in office, followed by a generous pension when they retire at seventy-five – as Professor Morin explains in his chapter devoted more specifically to the case of Quebec.

Morale was already low among judges in both civil and common law countries due to unfair professional and pension contracts and deteriorating working conditions, but also personal attacks against judges in the media and on social networks.[10] Fierce criticisms of the use of judicial review by judges and its scope have aggravated the malaise in the judiciary, as mentioned above. They may also deter the new generations of law students from joining the Bench. The recruitment process of judges is also often called into question, including in the UK in spite of its long tradition of judicial independence. As Benoît Chamouard, a French judge and Deputy President of the French Judicial Training College (ENM[11]) points out in his chapter, 'in systems where judges are not elected, their legitimacy is based solely on their competence and independence.'

This book provides key information on the functioning of justice, including the practicalities and daily challenges of judges' work. Beyond that, it has three main objectives. The first is to give a better understanding of who judges are, how and why they decide to join the judiciary, and also what motivates them. This is part of 'an attempt to demystify the work of judges', as Judge Jarman describes it in his chapter. If there are threats against judges – too often people are afraid of judges and justice – they see them as highly powerful people, like Balzac, who famously described the French investigating judge as 'the most powerful man in France'. The fear and suspicion of judges – which characterised a country like France at the time of the 1789 Revolution – have not totally disappeared.

Questions have also been raised in Spain – another civil law country – in the last few years about the effective independence, impartiality and self-restraint of Spanish judges, especially in spite of the entrenchment of judicial independence in the Spanish Constitution of 1978, in the handling of Catalonian political independence activists in the wake of the popular consultation on the independence of Catalonia on 7 September 2017. It was ruled unconstitutional by the Constitutional Court of Spain as clearly incompatible with the indivisible unity of the Spanish nation. This contributed to undermining the perception of judges by the people in Spain and, to a degree diminishing their authority.

Another aim of this book is to improve the perception of judges and the trust that people and the community can or should have in the judiciary at a time when they are more and more targeted, whether they sit in a national or a European court. The objective is to go beyond the widespread official rhetoric, which systematically opposes (unelected) judges and implies that they have no legitimacy, to the people, and to reconcile judges with the people. For judges, far from being 'the enemies of the people', serve justice and through justice the people themselves. It is perhaps clearer in a country like France, where judges are civil servants. French judges are sworn-in individuals who have special additional responsibilities that other civil servants do not have.

Finally, the main thread of the book is to examine how the independence of judges is achieved in both civil law and common law countries – what legal safeguards already exist and, even more important, how independence can be better protected. The case of Poland – although an EU member state – illustrates that the survival of democracy and the rule of law lies in maintaining a clear separation of powers and an effective independence of the judiciary. This is currently proving difficult in Hungary.

In the spirit of one of the founding fathers of comparative law, Adhémar Esmein, a comparative approach will be developed here as a means of observation rather than a way of imposing one's views or claiming that one legal system is better than another. In terms of one's differences in law and legal culture, the comparative method used here will aim at neither replicating nor incorporating a legal system from another country, but at trying to learn from it – as a source of inspiration for improving one's own legal system and administration of justice. Lord Judge points out below, 'we need greater care when looking at systems which are not our own.' Even if the countries covered by this book are not all part of the EU, they are part of a wider legal community which shares common legal values and common legal obligations under international law. The French founding fathers of comparative law, Édouard Lambert and Raymond Saleilles, had a highly ambitious project, which was no less than building a law common to mankind. At a much more modest level, the current book is based on a cross-cultural, cross-professional and interdisciplinary approach to better identify those common values and see how similar legal problems can be solved in countries with different legal systems and cultures through a conversation between experts with a different legal experience, background and nationality. Yet this is not just a book written by eminent legal authorities, law practitioners and academics, but by people who, by comparing as well as contrasting their legal systems and cultures, are all eager to share their expertise and common passion for the law and justice with a wider possible audience. Through their rich and complementary contributions, they all make justice and judges more accessible.

Synopsis of the Different Chapters of the Book

Judicial Independence

'However independent we must be, we are servants of the community,' Lord Judge declared about his role as a judge. In chapter 1, Lord Judge, a former Lord Chief Justice of England and Wales – well known for his expertise on judicial review – points out the importance of judicial independence in every sense of the term. He writes that 'judges must be fair-minded and independent of mind', reflecting the two main requirements of section 6(1) of the ECHR. Not only does he show the need for the institutional independence of the judiciary from the potential interference of either the executive or the legislative, but also for judges' 'independence of mind', in other words impartiality.

Early in the book a historical perspective is provided by Professor Victor Bailey in the second chapter entitled 'A Customary Scale of Punishment: Judicial Sentencing in England and Wales'. He offers an insight into the practice of the law and sentencing in the Victorian era. He focuses on a particular aspect of the independence of judges, their independence in sentencing, part of the essence of being a judge. Sentencing is a key power that judges hold, with potential long-lasting effects on offenders as they can ultimately deprive them of their liberty. Today, many governments try to influence their sentencing power – sometimes judges are blamed for being too severe but more often than not they are criticised for being, or rather giving the impression of being, too lenient. They are more than ever under pressure to adopt a more repressive approach, especially towards alleged and/or convicted terrorists under anti-terrorism legislation.[12] The issue of sentencing and judges' leeway in sentencing analysed in the mid-Victorian years by Victor Bailey raises the key question of the level of discretion – and therefore independence – that judges should have in their sentencing power. He shows that the 'vast range of sentencing discretion enjoyed by Victorian courts' led to serious divergences in sentencing – Victorian judges' sentences being both characterised by their disparity and severity. He thus raises a highly topical question: that of 'concerns over divergences in sentencing practice' and therefore the need to introduce more uniformity in sentencing practice while taking into account the individualisation of the sentence so important in French law for example. These can be achieved today through common European and/or international standards and an effective dialogue between judges. After a historical perspective giving readers insight into the evolution of the practice of the law and the independence in judges' sentencing, a second chapter extends the reflection on judicial independence.

In the third chapter, entitled 'National Perceptions of Judges and Lawyers in the UK', Matthias Kelly QC, SC uses his own experience as a lawyer who has practised the law in different countries including in the Republic of Ireland and in North America. He provides a multinational comparative perspective. It is at the same time an interdisciplinary one, as Kelly has practised both as a lawyer and as a Recorder or part-time judge. His chapter covers the main themes that will be developed in more detail by the other contributors, starting with judicial independence, but also judicial diversity. As Kelly suggests in his chapter, guaranteeing the independence of judges starts right at the beginning with the existence of an independent, transparent recruitment process based on merit. He focuses on the progress introduced in England and Wales by the setting up of the Judicial Appointments Commission under the provisions of the Constitutional Reform Act 2005 – and the existence of the same type of recruitment in more than 80 per cent of Commonwealth countries. In a comparative approach, he contrasts the latter with more politicised ways of recruiting judges, such as in the Republic of Ireland and in the United States of America, where the President, a senior politician, is involved – either following the recommendation of the government or with the approval of the Senate. A parallel could be drawn today with proposals made by Geoffrey Cox, the British Prime Minister's senior adviser, the Attorney General, at the beginning of 2020 to review the appointment process of Justices of the United Kingdom Supreme Court. One of the key questions Matthias Kelly raises is how to guarantee an independent recruitment process while avoiding any form of corporatism detrimental to judicial diversity. The latter is often discussed in terms of gender or ethnic balance, notably in the UK, but Matthias Kelly also examines the 'lack of socio-economic diversity' within the judiciary, crucial in so unequal a society as the United Kingdom.

Much importance in his chapter is given to judicial independence, which it is essential to protect throughout a judge's time in judicial office. It includes providing safeguards against the arbitrary removal of judges and, if necessary, sanctions when it does happen. After recalling the key provision of the 1955 Declaration of the International Commission of Jurists at Athens under which 'judges should be guided by the rule of law, protect and enforce it without fear or favour and resist any encroachment by governments or political parties in their independence as judges',[13] Matthias Kelly evokes the cases of both Poland and Hungary, which have both seriously and persistently breached the rule of law and their obligations as EU member states.

Ana María Neira Pena and David Soto Diaz, two Law Lecturers at the University of A Coruña in Spain in their co-written chapter discuss the key importance given by the Spanish constitution of 1978 to the principle of judges' independence. They show that the legal safeguards provided by the Spanish Constitution in its Title VI entirely devoted to the judiciary protects judges' independence – at least institutionally – from any infringement from the other branches of power. Under the same Title VI – article 117 – judges' power and competences are themselves clearly delineated to prevent them from acting beyond what the law requires from them, and especially from any interference with politics or other non-jurisdictional areas. Any attempt to interfere would lead to disciplinary sanctions, as judges' liability is the corollary of their independence. Members of the Spanish legal profession, whether they are lawyers or court representatives, are also subject to the observance of a strict principle of independence. Lawyers and judges are expected to serve the community, and there is a strong attachment to this notion of service. Judicial independence is thus formally entrenched in the Spanish Constitution as a key constitutional principle. Although Spain is still officially a monarchy – the monarch's role is mainly ceremonial – the Constitution explicitly states in its Title VI, article 117.1 that 'justice emanates from the people' and that it is delivered by 'independent irremovable, liable judges, subject only to the rule of law'.

Judicial Diversity

Peter Gjørtler shows that there are still efforts to be made to achieve a broader representation of civil society within the judiciary. Denmark, a constitutional monarchy like the British monarchy, joined the European Economic Community at the same time as the UK, but unlike the latter – except for Greenland, the first country to have left the European Union – Denmark remains a key EU member state. The Danish constitution, exceptionally rigid, or well entrenched, provides Danish judges with highly effective legal safeguards in terms of separation of powers (section 62) and judicial independence (section 64). Thus section 62 states that 'the administration of justice shall always remain independent from the executive'. So the executive is well under control, with strong mechanisms of sanctions in case of any interference with the judiciary, including a Special Court of Impeachment. In addition, Danish judges, like French judges, are protected from arbitrary removal by their status as civil servants under the provisions of section 34 of Denmark's Civil Service Law. In the words of Peter Gjørtler, 'there is little doubt about the independence of the Danish judiciary, both from a legislative and practical point of view, and judicial corruption is not in any manner a current topic in Denmark.'

Yet the question of judicial diversity is more of an issue. It was revived by the setting-up of the Danish Judicial Appointments Council in 1999 in charge of making recommendation for all judicial appointments, except the President of the Supreme Court, to the Minister of Justice. As Dr Gjørtler notes, 'there is some concern in Denmark as to whether the procedure established with the Judicial Appointments Council is suitable for ensuring a broad representation of civil society.'

Professor Morin in the sixth chapter, devoted to Canada, and more precisely the case of Quebec, widely covers the general common theme of judicial independence. Nonetheless, he sheds new light on the sensitive question of judicial diversity. Indeed, far from limiting his analysis to the key question of the necessity of a more gender-balanced diversity, he deals with the 'importance of taking into account indigenous people' (native Canadians) and, more broadly 'visible minority and cultural/ethnic communities'. In addition, he also approaches the issue of judicial diversity in terms of the specific legal and linguistic requirements in an officially bilingual country. Under article 16(1) of the Canadian Charter of Rights and Freedoms, 'English and French are the official languages of Canada and have equality of status and equal rights and privileges as to their use in all institutions [of] the parliament and government of Canada', to which article 19(1) – which applies more specifically to legal matters – adds: 'either English or French may be used by any person in, or in any pleading in or process issuing from, any court established by parliament.' Thus he explains the practical difficulties faced in implementing the right to bilingual trials, especially in criminal cases.

Access to Justice

In the seventh chapter Géraldine Gadbin-George draws on her own experience as a lawyer in England and Wales, but also as a judge in France, to discuss the critical issue of access to justice. This is a key prerequisite to securing people a fair trial under the provisions of article 6(1) of the European Convention on Human Rights. She focuses on the threats to this fundamental right with drastic cuts in legal aid in England and Wales – and to a lesser extent in France – following the controversial Legal Aid, Sentencing and Punishment of Offenders Act 2012 (LASPO) recently under review. Yet far from focusing solely on the negative impact of this statute on the most vulnerable, she also discusses the new challenges for judges in the wake of the report of the British Commission, presided over by Lord Bach, devoted to the modernisation of access to justice with proposals such as on-line justice, whilst pointing out the risk that it could lead to the dehumanisation of justice and judges' work.

Judge Jarman's chapter for its part (chapter 8) on the laws and judges of Wales is both about judicial independence and the accessibility of justice. Yet he discusses those key themes from a different perspective, the Welsh perspective. Wales is a nation with a strong sense of identity based on a long linguistic and legal tradition – law and the language being two fundamental pillars of Welsh identity. This is a point emphasised in a recent lecture by the one Welsh-speaking Supreme Court Justice, David Lloyd-Jones.[14] In this chapter, judicial independence is also to be understood as the judicial independence of Wales from England, and justice accessibility as linguistic accessibility – the language(s) used by the courts and their understanding by court-users. So, the question of accessibility of justice is raised not only in financial and technical terms but also political, reflecting Wales's own specific needs and challenges.

Beyond the question of the accessibility of Welsh law, Judge Jarman also discusses the key question of how to face growing divergences between different types of law since the advent of Welsh devolution and the rapid expansion of specifically Welsh legislation. He focuses on English and Welsh law, yet the challenges mentioned are highly enlightening too, regarding the divergences between continental civil law and English common law. There are also informative similarities between the specific needs encountered by Wales and Quebec, which were both greatly influenced by Roman civil law, and also the Catholic Church in the latter case. Finally, a key issue in Wales today is not so much the potential independence of Wales but the importance of giving Wales its own separate jurisdiction, as powerfully advocated by the Report of the Commission on Justice for the people in Wales presided over by Lord Thomas of Cwmgiedd, the first Welsh holder of the office of Lord Chief Justice of England and Wales. If this issue is not resolved as powerfully argued in this report, the application of the process of devolution will remain uncertain and incomplete.

Judicial Training Reform

In France, on 18 February 2020 Frédéric Thiriez,[15] a lawyer, officially submitted the report he was requested to produce by the French prime minister, Édouard Philippe, in 2019 on the reform of the training of would-be top civil servants – as part of their recruitment process before joining their respective state, territorial or hospital administration – which proposed a controversial common training period of six months for the three administrations. This led to angry reactions among judges starting with the Chairman of the ENM, a former judge, Olivier Leurent, being concerned about losing the specialised training of future judges more adapted to the specific needs and requirements of the judiciary.[16] The eighth and ninth chapters therefore deal with another kind of challenge in two very different nations involving the future – the challenge and responsibility of training judges 'or delivering judicial education', as Benoît Chamouard calls it, taking into account judges' specific needs and type of work.

In chapter 9, entitled 'The Status and Influence of Judges of France and of Common Law Jurisdictions: Recruitment, Training and Reform', Winston Roddick QC provides a Welsh perspective – different from, and complementary to that of Judge Jarman – based on his unique experience as the first Counsel General for Wales (1998–2003), then as Police Commissioner for North Wales (2012–16). This chapter is also based on a (British) comparative approach between France on the one hand, England and Wales on the other. In this chapter, the book's dominant theme of judicial independence is again examined, but Winston Roddick focuses not so much on the independence of judges as on the importance of the independence of the Bar – as a key requirement for guaranteeing the independence of judges in the prolongation of a significant practice of the law as a barrister or what Winston Roddick calls 'a self-selection process', as opposed to the French-style career judiciary. Beyond the analysis of the selection process and training of judges in England, Wales and France, what is really at stake is what kind of reforms should be introduced to improve the quality of justice. On that front, Roddick recommends devolving the responsibility and administration of justice to Wales, showing that a distinct legal jurisdiction for Wales is the natural corollary of a more and more productive Welsh legislature whose laws increasingly diverge from those of England. It is also a consequential development from Welsh devolution and the recent Wales Act of 2017.

In his final chapter Benoît Chamouard, a French judge and Deputy President of the French Judicial Training College (ENM), adopts a European perspective, widening the discussion of judicial independence to the European and international levels. He argues that 'only a properly trained judiciary will have the ability and strength to act independently and impartially' along the lines of the European Convention on Human Rights. In his concluding remarks he rightly insists on the importance of asserting common values in spite of the significant divergences between common law and civil law countries. He notes that they have succeeded in reaching unanimity around a Declaration of Judicial Training Principles on 8 November 2017 under the aegis of the International Organisation for Judicial Training (IOJT), which he describes as 'the largest network of judicial training institutions in the world'. He highlights the benefits of collective efforts and judicial cooperation for all countries. Amid a rich diversity of legal systems and structures, all are united by a similarity of challenges and a unity of principles and values. Thus Chamouard, in the final chapter, provides a unique perspective from someone who has a long practice of the law as a judge and who can reflect on it with some hindsight. He now works at improving the training of his fellow judges as a member of the Board of the International Organisation for Judicial Training. This international body, which has seventy-nine civil law and common law countries as members, focuses on judicial education, including revisiting national curricula and teaching methods not only to guarantee the best possible standards within the judiciary but also to better protect 'the rights of all people'. The Declaration of Judicial Training Principles is not just a document about judges and the training of judges. It also has a universal dimension since its ultimate objective is 'to promote the rule of law' in all societies.

Under the rule of law, a key requirement for both decision-makers, and for those they govern, is that no one is above the law. A. V. Dicey, himself greatly inspired by the writings of de Tocqueville,[17] insisted on the paramount importance of the 'supremacy' or 'predominance' of the law. He understood this essentially as legal certainty and legal equality.[18] According to him, the latter was to be understood as both absolute and permanent, thus suffering no exception.[19] Today more than ever judges should not be the sole custodians of the rule of law; we can all do our part to protect it as the essential component of a civilised society.

Oxford, June 2020.

Notes

1. At least as far as judges sitting in Higher Courts are concerned.
2. *Montesquieu, the Spirit of the Laws*, ed. Anne M. Cohler, Basia C. Miller and Harold S. Stone (New York: Cambridge University Press, 1989), book XI, chapter 6.
3. Édouard Lambert, *Le gouvernement des juges*, foreword by Franck Moderne, reprint of the 1921 edn (Paris: Dalloz, 2005).
4. Lady Hale, 'Beanstalk or living instrument? How tall can the ECHR grow?', Barnard's Inn Reading, London, Gresham College, 16 June 2011.
5. *The Cabinet Manual: A Guide to Laws, Conventions and Rules on the Operation of Government*, first edn (London: Cabinet Office, 2011), p. 52.
6. Hale, 'Beanstalk or living instrument? How tall can the ECHR grow?'
7. All the countries covered in this book – being signatories of the European Convention on Human Rights – have abolished the death penalty.
8. It is however less acute in a country like Denmark.
9. Under section 64 of the Danish Constitution devoted to the independence of judges, a judge who has completed his sixty-fifth year may retire, but without loss of income up to the time when he is due for retirement on account of age.

10. Most notably in the wake of the 2017 Miller v. Secretary of State for Exiting the European Union in the UK
11. *L'École Nationale de la Magistrature* in French.
12. An emergency Terrorist Offenders (Restriction of Early Release) Bill to end the automatic half-way release of people convicted of terrorism was introduced in the House of Commons on 11 February 2020 and was due to be discussed for a second reading in the House of Lords on 24 February 2020.
13. Matthias Kelly in his chapter quotes Lord Bingham in *The Rule of Law* (2011), p. 173.
14. United Kingdom Supreme Court ten-year anniversary lecture series (2009–19), 'Wales: Law in a Small Nation', Lord Lloyd-Jones, Justice of the Supreme Court, 26 November 2019; text published in *The UK Supreme Court Yearbook*, Vol. 10, 44 (forthcoming).
15. Baptiste Jacquin, 'Les objections des magistrats au rapport Thiriez', *Le Monde*, 23 and 24 February 2020.
16. A slightly less controversial aspect of the Thiriez report concerns proposals of reform to introduce more judicial diversity including more social and geographic diversity.
17. De Tocqueville, *Oeuvres Complètes*, edn of 1864–6 (Paris: Hachette, 2012), VIII, pp. 455–7.
18. A.V. Dicey, *Introduction to the Study of the Law of the Constitution*, eighth edn (London: Macmillan and Co., 1915), p. 180.
19. Dicey, *Introduction to the Study of the Law*, p. 283.

PART I

Judicial Independence

1

Reflections on Judges in Civil Law and Common Law Countries

Lord Judge

We have different systems for the administration of justice. Although we can always learn from each other, neither is a better or worse system than the other. They are just, well, different. I have little doubt that both systems need to be alert to the possibility of greater efficiency, and in particular should look to welcome new technology. After all, our ancestors worked by candlelight: electricity was once new technology; so was the telephone. We embraced them; so with today's technology. However, we need greater care when looking at systems which are not our own, and liking bits of another system, and transplanting them into our own. Indeed, a plant that flourishes in the Sahara desert is unlikely to do very well in the wet misty fogs of England. Our systems are different because our national histories are different, and although you can reinterpret history, you cannot change it. We are where we are because of where we have come from. So we must listen to each other and respectfully exchange views and knowledge. New fresh insights will enable us to improve our own systems.

What we do share, however, is that, in the public interest and for the benefit of the communities we as judges serve (and however independent we must be, we are servants of the community), our systems should be directed to two major objectives, indeed immutable objectives. The first is that our systems must provide for justice to be done according to the law; that surely is immutable. The second is that the men and women vested with responsibility for achieving justice according to law must be highly intelligent, modest and humble, without airs and graces, aware of our human fallibility but nonetheless decisive, that is willing to make uncomfortable decisions, expert in the law, alive to the needs and developments of the society in which we live, fair-minded and independent of mind.

Without those two principles the administration of justice, such a necessity in every society, cannot succeed.

So when I describe some aspects of the system in England and Wales I am not, emphatically not, suggesting that our system is better than the French system. I am simply seeking to identify features of our system, which strives to achieve the same objectives, but does so differently.

Perhaps the first, stemming from our Anglo-Saxon past, is the deep involvement of non-lawyers. At home you cannot be convicted of a serious crime unless twelve citizens are convinced by the evidence that you are guilty of it. In a serious criminal trial the judge, although directing those twelve citizens about the relevant law, has no part to play in their discussions or their decisions. When they are considering their verdict, the judge is not there. They organise themselves. They choose their own foreman. They deliver the verdict. No one can challenge a verdict of 'Not Guilty'. And if the verdict is 'Guilty', the defendant can challenge it if the judge has interfered too much. This process is a direct link and involvement of the citizen in his or her own judicial processes. You cannot avoid jury service, although you may ask for it to be postponed if it would be inconvenient for some good reason, like, for example, that you have a hospital operation. What is more, we also have what you may regard as a fairly quixotic sentiment about the jury system. Many judges who try criminal cases will tell you that they sense (sense just because they are not themselves in the jury room) that juries will sometimes acquit in the face of apparently clear evidence if it would lead to injustice, as they see it. For example an individual who has revealed evidence of ministerial wrongdoing, which the government of the day wished to keep hidden, might be acquitted of a charge of contravening Official Secrets provisions. Maybe it is quixotic. We like to think that juries will not convict of what they themselves would regard as unjust laws, for example, making it a criminal offence to have red hair, and whether that is right or wrong, in its turn even the perception that it might be true is a discouragement to the executive to pass laws which are in conflict with the conscience of the nation.

The second feature, this time stemming from our Plantagenet kings, and every single one of our Plantagenet kings was descended from Eleanor of Aquitaine, as she is known to us, arguably the most remarkable woman of medieval Europe, is our form of magistrates, Justices of the Peace. Sitting in benches of three, men and women who are not lawyers, but volunteers, contributing in different ways to the community, for example, as a local trade union official, or nurse or doctor or farmer, provided with legal advice by a qualified clerk, decide the overwhelming majority of criminal cases, with power to impose short sentences of imprisonment. Again, this is community involvement in the administration of criminal justice, and the maintenance of the peace, that most precious gift that is the fervent wish of every citizen in every country.

In summary, for us any ordinary adult citizen may be called upon to administer justice. We like that and it has served us well, not perfectly of course, but no human system yet devised is perfect. As we shall see it has consequences for our judicial system.

In direct contrast to the French legal system, the British system is adversarial. Whether in a criminal or civil or family law case, we try and achieve justice on the basis that in each case, whether criminal or civil, we try to establish the truth and achieve justice by leaving it to each side to offer the evidence and arguments which will sustain its own case and demonstrate the weakness of the other side's case. This is not an inquisitorial process at all. Dealing with it broadly, a judge or magistrate only becomes involved when both sides are ready to present their evidence, or, where one side is holding up the process for its own reasons, the other side asks the judge to intervene, not to investigate the case, but to put a rocket behind the slow party. The judge can interfere to order the parties to be ready, and give them the date for the hearing, but that is the extent of it. Evidence gathering is not a judicial responsibility. Decisions whether to prosecute or not are made by the independent Crown Prosecution Service, without any judicial involvement. If Social Services are concerned about the welfare of a child, they bring all the evidence to the judge for decision, but they are responsible for submitting the evidence, and answering the evidence put forward by the other side.

This has a number of consequences, or if not direct consequences, certainly linked features. The professional integrity of the advocates is an essential ingredient of our processes. There are times when the professional duty of the advocate may require him or her to act in a way which the client would find disagreeable. For example, if the argument is about a principle of law, and you know of a legal decision which contradicts you, if your opponent has not relied on it or drawn it to the attention of the judge, it is your duty to do so. When doing so, of course, you can argue that it is not strictly relevant, or that your case is different in some way, but you cannot keep it hidden. Your client will not like it, but nevertheless it would be professional misconduct to do so. So the day-to-day working relationship between the judicial bench and the advocates, who are, of course, independent of the judge and of each other, must involve mutual trust.

And that leads to this further feature, of specific interest to this book. Our judges are appointed from those who have had practice as lawyers, usually something like twenty to twenty-five years in practice. No one joins the judiciary soon after leaving university, and indeed, once you have been appointed as a judge, the expectation is that you will never return to practice as a lawyer. Once a judge you remain a judge until you retire. Just because our processes are not inquisitorial, and of civilian involvement in the judicial process, we do not need the numbers of judges needed by an inquisitorial system. And however much you would like to be appointed as a judge, our general approach is that you should only ascend the judicial bench as a man or woman of proved experience in the law and in the operation of the system, with time to have demonstrated that you are possessed of essential judicial qualities. So there is no judicial career path, and very few are appointed as full-time judges until their late forties or early fifties.

Before appointment as a full-time judge, a candidate is expected to sit as a part-time judge for a few weeks every year, whether in criminal or civil or family cases, but continuing in ordinary practice as a barrister or solicitor. In other words, before full-time appointment as a judge, the process is that you should understand the true nature of judicial responsibilities, and the burdens of judicial office, and how they should be approached and handled by sitting as a judge. This process enables a number of men and women who are thought to be of the requisite quality to realise that the judicial life will not suit them. Not every lawyer, however brilliant, is temperamentally suited to judicial office. There is a separate purpose, of course, which is that the process helps to reveal whether the particular individual has true judicial quality. Is the candidate too impatient? Does the candidate have that crucial judicial quality, the ability to give a decision, and with appropriate speed, and with sound, understandable reasons?

I should like to claim that the system is infallible. Of course it is not. But it certainly helps the appointment process. So, in essence, those appointed to full-time judicial office are mature lawyers with many years of practical experience. But now, instead of advancing the case for one side or the other, they are committed to holding the balance between the two sides in the adversarial process, and ready to give an appropriate judgment or summarise the law and direct the jury accordingly.

Before about 1980 it was thought that your years of legal practice provided a sufficient level of training for the office. When such training was first proposed, many serving judges were deeply suspicious of the introduction of a system which looked as though it might give the executive power to influence the judicial process. That concern was addressed by the creation of a body to run judicial training which was itself led by judges. Serving as I did on the Judicial Studies Board, I know that it very quickly became possible to assert, without the slightest contradiction, that this was indeed a process designed to assist judges to do their jobs, and that there was no executive interference or involvement in the process.

So now, before you sit even as a part-time judge, you must have attended an appropriate seminar: you must visit a prison, and see how non-custodial sentences like community service or probation actually work. Once you have become a full-time judge you are required to attend on a regular basis, and there are, in addition, specialist courses, for example for judges who are required to try serious sexual crime, or in the use of language, which if deployed insensitively, can cause offence to individuals of a particular faith or colour or sexual orientation. It is not enough just to be polite. You need to know, for example, that for some individuals it would be disrespectful to look someone in authority, like a judge, directly in the eye. That does not mean that they are being shifty or untruthful. It is just their culture. Your attention is drawn to things you are unlikely to know. I still remember the shock, indeed horror, of a judicial seminar some twenty-five years ago, as we listened to a respectable citizen, who happened to be black-skinned, telling us that at thirty-eight years old he had been stopped by the police while driving his car no less than thirty-seven times. That was his life experience. We needed to appreciate it.

The change in my professional lifetime is remarkable. Judges want continuous training. They want to be updated. Our legislature never seems to stop enacting new provisions. You could say that we are deluged with them. Judges have to keep up, and a man or woman who does not, has ceased to understand what is required of him or her. But in the meantime the process continues to be, in our words, 'judge-led'. Although, of course, the Ministry of Justice has to provide the funds, the courses are organised by senior judges. As well as participating themselves, they choose the academic experts to speak and the topics which must be addressed. The ready acceptance of continuing training by the judiciary is one of the great successes of my time.

That leads me to perhaps the final question. How are judges appointed? It is bound to be a different system from the French one. Our system has to cater not for the post-university young man or woman who has been good enough to pass the examination, but rather for selection among – dare I say it? – middle-aged men and women with many years of practice behind them as lawyers, who are willing to give up professional practice and assume judicial responsibilities.

The appointment system used to be the ultimate responsibility of the Lord Chancellor, one of our ancient historic offices, who to everyone's surprise except our own was a member of the cabinet and a member of the legislature, in the House of Lords, and a judge and indeed head of the judiciary. So he embodied a negation of the principle of the separation of powers. But in the present context he was the head of a department which was responsible for finding men and women of the appropriate quality, so that they could be offered a judicial appointment. That has all changed.

We now have an independent Judicial Appointments Commission in which neither the Lord Chancellor nor any minister or politician is represented. At present there are fifteen members, seven non-judges and seven judges from all levels, with a non-judge chairman. If you wish to be considered for appointment, you make a formal application to this body, and after sifting through all the appointments, making the inquiries that are thought necessary, taking account of the evidence with which the Commission is provided, including what may have been revealed during your years of practice of the presence or absence of judicial qualities, and an interview process in which at least one member (usually two) of the three-person panel, is not a judge, they recommend or do not recommend your appointment. The two features to highlight are that you nowadays apply, whereas before you waited to be invited, and the second is that there is no actual or apparent political involvement in the process. I should perhaps add that in my professional lifetime I do not know of any appointment in which political considerations were thought to play any part. But as I am sure you already appreciate, perception, even if completely wrong, is itself a fact, and no fact can be ignored. So we have got rid of the perception of possible political interference or influence in the process.

Our real problem at home is a different one. The attraction of judicial office has diminished. For a variety of reasons, many of our very best lawyers, apparently well qualified for judicial appointment, are no longer interested in making this huge change in their lives.

Perhaps I should end by underlining one simple message. No country, no society can do without men and women who are prepared to take on these responsibilities. Those who are thinking of it, or are about to enter the judicial arm of the administration of justice are going one day to be absolutely critical to the maintenance of the rule of law: that is quite a responsibility, but it is simultaneously a fantastic challenge both as a lawyer and as a human being.

2

'A Customary Scale of Punishment': Judicial Sentencing in England and Wales

Victor Bailey

> *Probably no system in the world leaves so wide a discretion to the judges in the matter of punishment.*
>
> SIR JAMES FITZJAMES STEPHEN,
> 'The Punishment of Convicts', *Cornhill Magazine*, 7 (1863)

Victor Bailey shows, from a historical perspective, how judicial independence, primarily as judges' discretion in their sentencing power, evolved from an almost unconstrained practice in the Victorian era – leading to disparity and inequality – to strict sentencing guidelines that potentially challenged judicial independence.

1. Sentencing as a Unique Decision-making Process

Sentencing is a unique decision-making process. Judgments of great importance are made quickly by justices who, while possessing a wide discretion when it comes to choice of sentencing aim, to the assessment of the gravity of the offence, to the admission of factors of aggravation and mitigation, and to choice of penalty, have no explicit principles to determine the object of the sentencing exercise, nor any clear rules, until very recently, to guide the exercise of their discretion. Such discretion, as Lucia Zedner states,

> is founded upon the immensely powerful, though arguably mythical, notion of judicial independence ... In England it has been inflated, at least in the minds of the judiciary, to suggest that any attempt by government to influence sentencing is unconstitutional. Despite the doubtful validity of this extreme interpretation of judicial independence, it has acted as an important bulwark against legislative attempts to limit or structure judicial powers of sentencing.[1]

The present essay seeks to trace the history of English sentencing from the mid-Victorian years to the present day, and in particular the wide discretion of judges – the central principle of the English sentencing system – and the emergence of a normal range of penalties, or a judge-configured 'tariff', to guide sentencing practice.

To begin with, we need to describe the sentencing courts and the backgrounds of the sentencers. Of the two levels of criminal court in England and Wales – the magistrates' courts and the Crown Court – the former deal with the largest number of cases by far. This is not a new trend. As far back as the eighteenth century, summary jurisdiction of lay justices was predominant and expanding.[2] By 1999, counting all types of offence and all ages of offender, 1,331,000 or 95 per cent were sentenced in magistrates' courts. Only 77,000 offenders were sentenced in the Crown Court.[3] The latter sits as a trial court with judge and jury – although approximately two-thirds of Crown Court cases involve a guilty plea, and are dealt with by judge alone. A High Court judge on circuit hears the most serious Crown Court cases; the majority of cases, however, are heard by a circuit judge or by a Recorder (a part-time circuit judge). The statutory maximum sentence available to the magistrates' courts is six months' imprisonment, or a total of twelve months' imprisonment if there are two or more convictions. In the Crown Court, the judge's power of imprisonment is limited only by the maximum penalty prescribed by Parliament for the specific crime. It is the Crown

Court which passes the larger number of prison sentences (especially in cases of robbery, sexual offences and burglary). Out of approximately 35,000 sentences of immediate imprisonment in 1994, 67 per cent were imposed by the Crown Court, and most of the 33 per cent of sentences of immediate imprisonment imposed by magistrates' courts were, by definition, the shorter ones.[4] It is the Crown Court judges, moreover, who have historically set the conventions of sentencing, guided since 1907 by the senior High Court judges who compose the Court of Criminal Appeal (since 1966 the Court of Appeal Criminal Division). We are talking about a very small number of judges. As late as 1890, there were 15 judges of the Queen's Bench Division conducting assize courts. Only in modern times has the number expanded. Between 1970 and 1990 the number of professional judges quadrupled. By the later date, there were 29 Lords Justice in the Court of Appeal, 85 High Court judges, and 420 circuit judges.[5] The present essay, it should be noted, is primarily concerned with sentencing by judges in the Crown Court.[6]

It is useful also to present the political, social and educational background of these legal men – and until recently they were all men – since it shows judges as coming, in the past and present, from a narrow upper-class, professional stratum. In the recruitment of Victorian judges, legal and professional qualifications were less important than their politics. In a celebrated essay, the Labour politician Harold Laski revealed that between 1832 and 1906, 80 of the 139 judges appointed were Members of the House of Commons at the time of nomination, and 11 others had been parliamentary candidates; 63 of the 80 had been appointed whilst their party was in office.[7] Lord Halsbury, Conservative Lord Chancellor for seventeen years between 1885 and 1905, appointed 30 judges to the High Court, of whom 14 were politicians, 10 being Conservatives. Barrister-politicians declined in number from this point forward. The *Economist*'s 1956 survey recorded that only 23 per cent of their 69 judges (of the Supreme Court, the House of Lords, and the Judicial Committee of the Privy Council) had been MPs or parliamentary candidates.[8] As for social-class origins, to judge from the occupations of the fathers of judges, studies indicate that between the late eighteenth and the mid-nineteenth centuries, the proportion of judges from landed families fell sharply, while professionals (including barristers and solicitors) became the predominant group. Moreover, almost half of the sons of judges followed in their father's professional footsteps by becoming barristers. Not one Victorian judge hailed from a working-class background.[9] A study of the longer period between 1820 and 1968, with class status assigned according to father's occupation, again reveals the dominance of the upper-middle class.[10] Educational history reflects these origins. Over 60 per cent of judges were educated at public (for which read 'private') schools (with Eton and Winchester the pre-eminent judge-providers), and three-quarters of judges attended a university, with Oxbridge colleges the dominant educational experience.[11]

It remains only to say that judges have always tended to be middle-aged or older, white, wealthy and male. As late as 2003, a Labour Member of Parliament, Keith Vaz, claimed that 78 per cent of senior judges in England and Wales achieved the 'full house' of being white, male, public school- and Oxbridge-educated. The appointments system has long been secretive and elitist. In 2011, 1 in 20 judges was non-white, and fewer than 1 in 4 was female (though among strictly High Court judges, only 16 per cent – or 17 out of 108 – were female).[12] It is still unclear – thanks to a paucity of research – how the attitudes and reasoning practices of judges have been influenced by their recruitment from and into the close professional society of barrister and judge. One imagines it has some impact on their approach to sentencing people whose life experience is typically beyond their ken. One thing is clearer: judges have held fast to the belief in the offender's capacity to make moral choices. As Lucia Zedner concluded: 'At the point of sentence, perhaps more than at any other in the criminal process, the offender is held up as an autonomous agent whose assumed free will and moral responsibility legitimate, even demand, this calling into account.'[13]

2. The Development of Conventions in English Sentencing

With this sketch of the courts and judicial personnel as backcloth, we turn to an extended account of the development of conventions in English sentencing. The decisive moment for our purposes was the passage of the five criminal law statutes or Consolidating Acts of 1861, dealing with offences against the person, larceny, malicious damage, forgery and coinage offences. This legislation provided the basic materials upon which the principles of judicial sentencing were to develop. First, the Acts were constructed on the principle of high maximum penalties with few restraints on the judge's choice of sentence length. A judge was free to fix a custodial term in non-capital felony cases, reflecting his view of the offender's culpability, between one day's imprisonment and a maximum term of penal servitude. Secondly, the penalties prescribed in the five statutes emerged directly from three strands of penal thought and practice. One strand was the reform activity of the 1820s and 1830s, when capital punishment was gradually replaced by transportation. With transportation, unlike the death penalty, the gravity of offences was measured in units of time, units which, significantly, retained their influence when transportation transitioned into penal confinement. The second strand was the reports of the criminal law commissioners, which appeared between 1833 and 1849, and which tried to construct a single scale of penalties, and to restrict judicial discretion in awarding punishment. The commissioners' dismal failure to do any such thing served to deter the 1861 draftsmen from attempting to rationalise the structure of penalties. The third strand was the Penal Servitude Acts of 1853 and 1857, which enacted that a person should be liable to penal servitude for the same period, subject to remission and licence, as the term of transportation to which formerly he would have been liable.[14]

Guided by these ideas and practices, the 1861 Acts, enacted within four years of the demise of transportation, merely consolidated the existing criminal law and the maximum punishments prescribed there. As the Advisory Council on the Penal System concluded over a century later,

> The statutory maxima established in 1861 as the foundation of the modern sentencing structure were thus based on an incongruous analogy with the periods of transportation fixed in the 18th century, as adapted to terms of penal servitude fixed in the middle of the 19th century.[15]

Maintaining the *status quo* also meant broad offence definitions, embracing different degrees of crime and moral culpability, subject to wide latitude in sentencing. It was a long way from the Benthamite template of proportioned punishment. All legislation since 1861 has built upon the irrational and incoherent penalty system of the Consolidating Acts. Today, for offences triable on indictment, there are nine maximum terms, though the majority are punishable with imprisonment for two, five, seven, ten or fourteen years or life – all terms to be found in the 1861 Acts, and most of which are distant echoes of the transportation system.

This legislative consolidation ensured, above all, that the judiciary were left with extensive discretion, but few guidelines to regulate its exercise. The structure of maximum penalties, for sure, provided little or no influence on sentencing practice. The penalties were too high, too much of a distant long-stop, to affect the practice of the courts.[16] The consequence was disparity in sentences, made more visible by the fact that imprisonment, measured in publicly declared units of time, was now the principal form of punishment. There was the disparity between the severity with which crimes against property were punished, and the leniency with which offences against the person were punished. There was the disparity caused by the cumulative principle, or the practice of passing a longer sentence on an offender on each succeeding conviction. Some judges acted on this principle, others did not. The impact of this principle was further aggravated between 1864 and 1891 by the large gap that existed between the longest sentence of simple 'imprisonment', which was by law and convention two years, and the shortest possible sentence of 'penal servitude', which, if there was a prior felony conviction, was seven years from 1864 to 1879, and five years from 1879 until 1891. Once deemed to be a recidivist, an offender might well fall foul of an immoderate leap from two years to five or seven years of incarceration (though the habit of passing long terms of penal servitude after previous convictions was said to be true more of magistrates at Quarter Sessions than judges at the Assizes).[17] And, finally, there was the disparity in the sentencing practices of different judges, sufficient for the accusation to be heard that different economies of punishment, 'distinct codes of criminal jurisprudence', were in play. Charles Hopwood, Recorder of Liverpool, who mounted a personal campaign to mitigate the severity of sentences, described how in the 1860s in Manchester, presided over by a Recorder, the second offence was invariably punished with penal servitude, while at Salford Quarter Sessions, a stone's throw away, the punishment for like offences was a sentence of two or three months' imprisonment. In 1883, the Home Secretary, Sir William Harcourt, branded the inequality of sentences given by different judges for the same offence as 'one of the great scandals of our criminal jurisprudence'. Public, parliamentary and judicial concern over idiosyncratic sentencing became so insistent from the 1870s that three major debates on the subject were held in the House of Lords (in 1870 and 1890) and in the House of Commons (in 1889).[18]

3. Devising Sentencing Standards

The most direct attempt to lessen disparity in sentencing and to devise sentencing standards came from the hand of Sir Edmund Du Cane, Chairman of the Prison Commission, in an article in the *Fortnightly Review* in 1883, and in an unusually forthright correspondence in 1884 with Home Secretary Harcourt and Lord Chief Justice Coleridge.[19] Du Cane believed he had uncovered arbitrariness and illogicality in the distribution of sentences, which he laid at the door of the judiciary.[20] Sentences of penal servitude were almost always for certain lengths – namely five, seven, ten, twelve, fourteen or fifteen years, or life – and rarely for the intermediate lengths. Du Cane could only presume that 'the sentence pronounced by the court is much affected by the law, practice and tradition of the old transportation times ...' Harcourt forwarded Du Cane's letter and his own reading of the evidence to Lord Chancellor Selbourne, who in turn sent it to the judges. Harcourt's letter to Selbourne hoped the Lord Chancellor might find it possible, in consultation with the judges, to lay down 'general rules in this matter ... so as to lead to greater uniformity of practice'. While the Lord Chancellor agreed that the figures revealed unacceptable disparities, the judges themselves thought it 'inexpedient to pass any formal resolutions attempting to determine the amount of the sentences, allowed by law, which ought to be imposed for any specified offences'.[21] Clearly, their discretion was not to be fettered. One judge in particular took up the cudgels for judicial independence. James Fitzjames Stephen believed that the level of disparity was exaggerated, that frequent informal judicial discussions on sentencing took place (especially when two judges travelled on Assize together), and that tacit norms of sentencing already existed. These beliefs guided the rest of his critique of the notion that general rules could be formulated to ensure greater uniformity. Any system of general rules would require the reintroduction of minimum penalties, and also the lowering of maximum penalties, though the latter step would serve no practical purpose, 'for the maximum punishment authorized by law for any given offence is in practice very rarely inflicted'.[22] Moreover, a rigid code of minimum and maximum sentences for every offence, in every variety of circumstances, would be a more arbitrary system than the existing one. For Stephen, then, neither formal legislation nor judicial rule-making would remove the defects of the present system. Since the other judges were of like mind, there is little wonder that Du Cane's and Harcourt's proposals were unanimously rejected.

Even so, these discussions uncovered the important straw in the wind: what Stephen called 'an unwritten scale of punishments', or agreement among the judges on some basic norms to be applied to each type of offence. In short, a 'tariff' system. There were harbingers of this approach to sentencing. In 1856, Stephen had spoken of a judicial review of sentences as follows: 'Judgments would be delivered, laying down the principles upon which punishment ought to be allotted; and by degrees the discretion which the judges exercise would be guided and regulated by a sort of tariff formed by the ablest men in the country.'[23] In 1876, the term was used by Lush J in reply to a Home Office circular on the adequacy of penalties for wife-beating. The power to order flogging, Lush argued *inter alia*, should not be given to Recorders, since they 'have not the opportunity, as we have, of consulting with each other, and forming a conventional tariff'.[24] By the mid-1880s, Stephen was willing to put flesh on the tariff, at least in relation to burglaries:

> As almost anything – the opening of a door or window – amounts to a breaking, a considerable number of burglaries are little more than thefts, not very greatly aggravated; and as such they are usually punished with terms of imprisonment varying from six, or even three, months to a year or eighteen months. In some cases, however, burglary is an extremely bad offence. If a lonely house is broken into by a gang of armed men, the house ransacked and the inmates put in bodily fear, I should not consider fifteen years penal servitude at all exceptionally severe, though in such cases distinctions would have to be made according to the prominence of the part taken by different offenders.[25]

Stephen rested his case: among High Court judges, there was 'a nearer approach to a customary scale of punishment than is often supposed to be the case'.

The scent goes cold until 1900 when the International Congress of Comparative Law, which met in Paris, appointed a commission charged, according to the English member of the commission, 'with the duty of investigating the principles which should guide the judiciary when pronouncing a criminal sentence'.[26] While the Commission revealed heightened judicial concern over divergences in sentencing practice, it was possibly more influential as the inspiration (though no strong evidence for the trace exists) for the High Court judges' 'Memorandum on Normal Punishments' of 1901. This Memorandum indicated the range of penalties that should be passed for a core group of offences against the person and property. So, for example, for cases of indecent assault, the scheme proposed imprisonment for a period of between one and twelve months. Attempted murder in which life was endangered carried a range of penal servitude for a period of between seven and twelve years.[27] These guidelines had little practical impact, since the Home Office thought the 'normal' standard of punishment was insufficiently severe, particularly for violent and sexual crimes, and for recidivist or habitual offenders (for whom the department had indeterminate sentences in mind), and hence the guidelines were never communicated to Quarter Sessions, where the bulk of indictable crimes were tried, and where sentencing inequalities were most prevalent. Even so, as the Advisory Council on the Penal System stated in its 1978 report, the Judges' Memorandum was 'the first, and only, emergence in public of the tacit tariff'.[28] Thereafter, the starting point of the sentencing process was no longer the maximum penalty (if it ever was) but the tariff itself. The judges followed, after a fashion, their own sentencing guidelines from 1901; and the Court of Criminal Appeal, set up in 1907 to review sentences and set standards for other courts to follow, acted on the basis that there existed a set of informal conventions the like of which Stephen had described in the mid-1880s.[29]

In the last forty years of the nineteenth century, then, the vast range of sentencing discretion enjoyed by the Victorian courts abated to a small degree, in part from executive pressure, in part from the decisions of the Court of Criminal Appeal, and in the main from the development by the judges of their own sentencing conventions. Judges reached a modicum of agreement on a normal range of penalties of imprisonment which an individual offence should attract, in an attempt both to reduce disparities in sentencing and, the subject to which we now turn, excessively long prison sentences.

4. Last Half of the Nineteenth Century: Reducing the Length of Prison Sentences

The last half of the nineteenth century marked a concern not only with sentencing inequality but also with sentences that were on average too long. Once more, we begin with Du Cane's 1884 correspondence.[30] Du Cane recommended a reduction in the length of prison sentences by the fuller use of the complete scale of penalties available to the courts. It was evident, from the table he provided of the sentences of prisoners in convict prisons on 31 March 1883, that out of 10,196 sentences of penal servitude, no fewer than 7,579 were for five, seven, and ten years, while only 434 were for six, eight, and nine years. The periods chosen derived from transportation days, yet a person sentenced to transportation spent a shorter time in prison than one sentenced to penal servitude, as he explained:

> For instance, fifteen years penal servitude involves at least eleven years five months and eight days in prison, whereas a person sentenced to fifteen years transportation, if not sent to Australia, would ordinarily be released at the end of six years two months and eight days, and, if sent to Australia, even earlier, and so on with other periods of sentence.

'It is impossible not to feel', said Du Cane, 'that some more exact measurement is possible than is exhibited in the above figures, and, if it is possible, that the present arbitrary practice is incapable of justification.' A similar picture emerged from the figures of the range of sentences undergone by local prisoners, within the limit of two years' imprisonment. Home Secretary Harcourt's letter to the Lord Chancellor, ten months later, emphasised the marked fall in crime and the prison population between 1854 and 1883, and fully endorsed Du Cane's conclusion,

> that the time has come when a sensible mitigation of punishment may be safely introduced into the administration of our Criminal Law by materially shortening the length of sentences imposed in ordinary cases ... I must ... ask you [the Lord Chancellor] to communicate to the Judges in the most respectful manner my concurrence in the opinion of Sir E. Du Cane, that the deterring and reformatory effect of imprisonment ... would be as well and even more effectually accomplished if the average length of sentences were materially shortened.

Once again, the executive had a lusty opponent in Stephen J. He had set out his stall in *A General View of the Criminal Law of England*, published in 1863, and *A History of the Criminal Law of England*, published in three volumes in 1883, in both of which he stressed the moral significance of the criminal law, and declared that retribution was the primary object of punishment. As he said in the preface to his *General View*, the book was intended to give an account of 'an important part of our institutions, of which surely none can have a greater moral significance ... than those by which men rightfully, deliberately, and in cold blood, kill, enslave, and otherwise torment their fellow-creatures'. In the *History*, he wrote: 'A man may disbelieve in God, heaven, and hell ... let him at least be plainly told what are the acts which will stamp him with infamy, hold him up to public execration, and bring him to the gallows, the gaol, or the lash.'[31]

Not surprisingly, Stephen J disagreed with Harcourt that the *quid pro quo* of a decline in the amount of crime was a reduction in the severity of sentences. The preventive effect of punishment could not be dismissed lightly

> The sudden adoption of a great change in the severity of sentences without any other reason for it than diminution of crime would, I should think, operate as an invitation to all persons hesitating on the brink of dishonesty or violence to take courage and sin vigorously, as it would be understood as an official announcement of the doctrine that the objections to crime have been overrated, and that it is not after all such a serious matter as it has hitherto been supposed to be.

For Stephen the judge had one essential task,

> to ratify and approve as far as a judicial sentence can the feeling and disgust which great crimes produce in the public mind ... it is unavoidable that the judge should have his attention more strongly directed to the crime, and that the officials of the prison department [here Stephen was surely twitting Du Cane] should think more of the criminals.[32]

On this issue, however, Fitzjames Stephen was swimming against the tide. The trend was unmistakably towards the mitigation of punishment, and against lengthy detention. Indeed, Stephen's intervention coincided with the start of a remarkable sixty-year abatement of imprisonment between 1880 and 1940 – an era of decarceration, a de-centring of the prison. To this we now turn, though not before adding the side-note that the reduction in the scale of punishments which we are anticipating, had the knock-on effect of narrowing the range of sentencing diversity and inequality.

5. The Decline of Prison Population for Sixty Years

First, let us mark the scale of the declining prison population. In 1876–7, when local prisons were nationalised, the daily average population was 20,000; by 1913–14 (the year before the First World War broke out) it was 14,300; by 1918–19 it was down to 7,000. The decrease in the number of female prisoners was proportionally greater than with males. The daily average populations for convict prisons for the same years were 10,000; 2,700; and 1,200. The fall in prison population was precipitous during the First World War, notably of those committed for short prison sentences. And the trend continued beyond the war. In the early part of the twentieth century, the daily average population in all prisons exceeded 20,000; between 1920 and 1932, the figure rarely exceeded 12,000.[33] At the back of these figures was a decline in the courts' custody rates; or the proportion of offenders convicted of indictable offences who were sent to prison; and a marked fall in the length of sentences. In the 1860s, close to 90 per cent of those convicted of indictable larcenies were sentenced to imprisonment. By 1881–5, this figure had fallen to 65 per cent, by 1896–1900 to less than 50 per cent, and by 1911–14 the figure was down to 35 per cent. Prison sentences increasingly made way for non-custodial penalties, as courts were given powers, via the Probation of Offenders Act (1907) and the Prevention of Crime Act (1908), to individualise sentences. As for sentence lengths, the number of penal servitude sentences per 100,000 of population fell from 5.86 in 1881 to 2.64 in 1895; and the number of sentences of imprisonment for one year and upward per 100,000 of population fell from 4.73 in 1881 to 2.51 in 1895. Moreover, by 1896, only 2 per cent of those convicted of indictable offences were being awarded penal servitude, and nine-tenths of these sentences were for five years or less. The decreasing severity is evident from the percentage distribution of penal servitude sentences:

Length of term in years	1880	1913
Above 10 years	5.1	1.0
10 years and above 7 years	14.5	1.3
7 years	23.1	3.3
Below 7 years	57.3	94.5

By the exercise of their discretion whether to send offenders to prison or not, and for how long, the courts changed the size and shape of the late Victorian and Edwardian prison population.[34]

Secondly, how do we explain this remarkable abatement of imprisonment? There is space for only a bare-bones explanation, so let us reveal our hand straight away.[35] While a multi-factorial analysis is required to explain fully such a dramatic drop in the prison population, the factor that has attracted too little attention, in our view, is judicial sentencing. The entire subject poses the question: why did the judiciary, both high and low, alter their sentencing practices, without which decarceration would have been stillborn? Imprisonment appealed to a tariff-minded judiciary, since it could be measured out in periods of prison time, marking and denouncing the seriousness of the offence. Yet judges and magistrates scaled back the sentencing tariff to an inordinate degree over the sixty years in question. One feature of this judicial activism was the unwillingness to accept those parts of the rehabilitative programme that required long preventive or indeterminate sentences. Let us put a bit more flesh on this judicial activism.

One influence on the judiciary was the sharp fall in the incidence of property and violent offences in the second half of the nineteenth century, which helped to reduce anxiety about crime, and encouraged mitigation of punishment.[36] The decline in serious crime was more than sufficient to convince Victorians that the war against crime was being won. 'The knowledge that crime is diminishing', declared the criminal registrar in 1894, 'encourages judges and magistrates to deal with crimes more leniently.'[37] Another influence was the expansion in the criminal jurisdiction of the magistrates' courts, and the devaluation of the gravity of many offences by transferring them to summary jurisdiction. Shifting more and more of the criminal caseload from jury trials to summary jurisdiction automatically lowered the scale of punishment by shortening the length of prison sentences and by greater use of non-custodial penalties. A third influence was the transition in the ways of seeing criminals. They were seen less as rational, responsible human beings and more as victims of social deprivation or mental impairment. The courts began to divert a proportion of the delinquent group away from the prison system, offenders for whom regular prison discipline was deemed unsuitable: juveniles, young adults, women, vagrants, inebriates and mentally or physically disabled offenders. We can also witness in these years three more influences: a growing disenchantment with the prison paradigm among both prison administrators and the judiciary; an increasing rejection of the cumulative principle in sentencing, in particular for petty property offenders; and the arrival of an appellate court which set lower benchmarks for certain punishments, imposed some retributive limits to the sentence of preventive detention and generally confirmed the recalibration of the tariff of punishment that the judiciary had installed between 1880 and 1914.

By 1914, if the tariff of punishment was considerably more lenient with regard to the most serious crimes, the lower courts were still sending a large number of offenders to prison on short sentences for petty crimes. Yet radical change was imminent. The war years would do what Winston Churchill had wanted, which was to 'break in upon this volume of petty sentences for trifling offences from several different directions with a view to effecting a substantial and permanent reduction in them'.[38] The First World War proved to be a major watershed in the country's penal profile. The socio-economic changes prompted by the demands of total war included a buoyant labour market, a reduction in primary poverty, and greater regulation of drinking hours. This in turn led to a reduction in the volume of crime, especially of minor offences like drunkenness, and an enormous drop in the number of short prison sentences. To the impact of war, the Criminal Justice Administration Act 1914 added the provision to require courts to give offenders time to pay fines, leading to a large fall in the number of people imprisoned in default of fine payment. Finally, in the two decades following the First World War, judicial activism (including a more effective intervention of the Court of Criminal Appeal) again lessened the tariff of punishment, leading to a continued abatement of penal servitude and imprisonment.

Between 1880 and 1940, then, the judiciary, with little executive or legislative guidance, converted the severe Victorian tariff of punishment, erected in the immediate post-transportation years – in which minor property offenders regularly received long sentences of penal servitude in convict prisons – into a sentencing structure that relied, at first, on sentences of imprisonment that were by law and common consent no more than two years in length and typically shorter, and increasingly on the non-custodial penalties of discharge, fine and probation. Almost single-handedly, though with no high strategy behind it, the judges reduced the severity of sentencing for indictable crimes, encouraging magistrates at Quarter Sessions to follow suit. They did so because they believed that the sentences handed down in the 1860s and 1870s were out of all proportion to the incidence and gravity of crime. It took the war years, however, to rid the prisons of the stage army of vagrants, drunks and petty thieves. The change was a function less of judicial action than of social and economic intervention and improvement, but at least the courts never again sought refuge in the kind of sentencing that characterised the pre-war years. Living in an age when penologists deride the judiciary for filling the prisons beyond capacity by their sentencing decisions, it is salutary to discover that this was not always the case.

6. The Shaping of Sentencing Policy since 1945

As for developments in the conventions of English sentencing since 1945, the storyline is very much that of business as usual. The shaping of sentencing policy remained firmly in the hands of the judiciary. As we have seen, the system of maximum penalties played no role in most sentencing decisions; the judiciary eyed the maxima as the final limit placed by Parliament on the court's discretion. In the absence of any more precise guidance from Parliament, the tariff system prevailed, providing rough benchmarks for awarding sentences of imprisonment, with the maximum reserved for the worst examples of any particular crime. Rape, for example, carried a maximum of life imprisonment; most of the rapists sent to prison received no more than seven years. A tariff sentence was, of course, one that gave the offender his 'just deserts' by way of a punishment proportionate to the gravity of the offence and to his own culpability. Adjustments were made to this economy of punishment by the Court of Criminal Appeal and its successor, the Court of Appeal, Criminal Division – adjustments that were meant to be followed by Crown Court judges.[39]

In these post-war decades, too, the judicial voice was as resonant as ever, and notably in the matter of capital and corporal punishment.[40] In the house of Lords debates on the Criminal Justice Act 1948, the Lord Chief Justice, Lord Goddard (or 'Lord God-damn', as Churchill styled him), delivered a furious assault on those who believed 'that punishment should never be punitive, only reformative'. He continued:

> If the criminal law of this country is to be respected, it must be in accordance with public opinion ... I cannot believe that the public opinion (or I would rather call it the public conscience) of this country will tolerate that persons who deliberately condemn others to painful and, it may be, lingering deaths should be allowed to live.

The conclusion was foregone: 'I believe that there are many, many cases where the murderer should be destroyed.'[41] The senior judges, Lord Justice Denning and Goddard LCJ, gave evidence to the Royal Commission on Capital Punishment 1949–53 calling for a limit to the number of death sentences and executions, but only as a means of reinforcing the denunciatory effect of capital punishment. By reserving death for the more heinous murder cases in which no extenuating circumstances sufficient to justify clemency could be found, they hoped to make capital punishment morally more acceptable, and less prone to the ignominy of reprieve.[42] Her Majesty's judges were also adept at keeping the pot boiling in relation to corporal punishment, particularly Goddard and his successor as Lord Chief Justice, Lord Parker, who advocated reintroducing what they insisted was a deterrent penalty. At the annual Lord Mayor's banquet in 1952, Goddard spoke about the increase in crimes of violence, suggesting that the remedy for 'gangsterism' was to restore corporal punishment. In 1959, in an injudicious speech in Canada, Lord Parker put his judicial authority behind the return of corporal punishment, to combat the vast increase in crime since the war.[43]

However, in the post-war era, new challenges faced the sentencer. In response to socio-psychiatric ways of explaining crime, and to new reformative forms of penalty, sentencers were frequently confronted with a 'primary' decision between a tariff sentence where the aim was deterrent-cum-retributive, and an 'individualised' measure whose aim was largely rehabilitative.[44] At the same time, penal reformers and the Home Office sought to persuade judges that a principal role of imprisonment was to reform the prisoner. Short prison sentences were said to be unhelpful for this purpose, and judges were advised to avoid passing them. A sentence had to be long enough to do some good, or so the theory went. The belief in the prospect of rehabilitation within prison surely contributed, along with changes in the incidence and seriousness of criminal activity, to an increase in the length of prison sentences, which an analysis of receptions into prison by effective length of sentence reveals. The proportion of long sentences of over two years (including life sentences) increased between 1951 and 1971.[45] By the mid-1970s, the Advisory Council on the Penal System, appointed to complete a review of maximum penalties, was motivated to issue a short interim report, *The Length of Prison Sentences*, in which they asserted that 'many sentences of imprisonment in the lower and middle ranges are too long', and urged courts 'to stop at the point where a sentence had been decided upon and consider whether a shorter one would not do just as well' – especially since research showed that, if reconviction rates were used to measure the efficacy of sentencing policy, there was nothing to choose between different lengths of custodial sentence.[46] In their main report, *Sentences of Imprisonment*, the Council insisted that 'the case for a reduction in the length of prison sentences passed on the ordinary offender is as strong today as it was in the late 19th century'.[47] The Home Office sent a copy of the interim report to every judge and bench of magistrates.

It is unclear what impact the interim report had on sentencing practice, but there is no doubt that the main report, which put forward a scheme proposing that new maximum penalties should be imposed at the level below which 90 per cent of sentences passed by the Crown Court for the particular offence had fallen in recent years, did no more than endorse and adopt the scale of penalties which courts were then imposing. From the Council's point of view, there were advantages to this approach. The device of looking at what was currently being done avoided the need for them to make fresh and controversial value judgements about every individual offence. The Council also believed that their proposals involved a stricter limitation upon the judge's sentencing discretion for the vast majority of ordinary offenders. But it is surely remarkable that in what the Council claimed was 'the first comprehensive review of the [sentencing] system since the 1840s', the outcome should be little more than a formalising of the tariff.[48]

Nothing came of the Advisory Council's proposals, despite the support for them from the Parliamentary All-Party Penal Affairs Group.[49] A more effective way of changing the tariff, it turned out, was the guideline judgments pioneered in the Court of Appeal by Lord Justice Lawton in the 1970s, and taken up by Lord Lane as Lord Chief Justice in the 1980s – judgments which considered sentences for all the main varieties of particular crimes, or particular sentencing factors, giving indications of the 'proper range' of sentences. In *Turner* (1975) 61 Cr. App. R. 67, for example, Lawton considered the logic of the upper echelons of the tariff, confronting the difficulty of comparing fixed-term sentences for armed robbery with the periods typically served by persons sentenced to life imprisonment for murder. More significantly, in *Upton* (reported in *The Times* for 25 April 1980), Lord Lane stated that 'the time has come to appreciate that non-violent petty offenders should not be allowed to take up what has become valuable space in prison. If there really is no alternative to an immediate prison sentence, then it should be as short as possible.' Lane also handed down a series of judgments – *Bibi (1980) Crim. Law Rev. 732*; *McCann (1980) Crim. Law Rev. 734* – designed as a guide to the lower courts of the type of cases which ought to receive more lenient treatment. Critics of such tampering with the tariff believe that the Court of Appeal was too reluctant to formulate guideline judgments for those offences – theft, burglary, handling stolen goods – which occupy most sentencers' time. Guideline judgments had the distinct advantage, however, that they were guidance *by* judges *for* judges, and as such more acceptable to a judiciary that prides itself on independence from executive or legislative interference.

7. The Sentencing Framework of the Past Thirty Years

In the past thirty years, the sentencing framework has been muddled, though not as yet profoundly changed, by legislative interference. The Criminal Justice Act 1991 installed 'just deserts' as the primary rationale for English sentencing, or the calculation of offence seriousness and a proportionate sentence. It also laid down restrictions on the use of custodial sentences, and on the way previous convictions could be taken into account.[50] Judges were hostile to the imposition of this framework, but their vatic utterances were premature. Judges were left with considerable latitude for discretion in the length of custodial sentences, and eventually in the sentencing of repeat and multiple offenders. As such, the new law did nothing to disturb the tariff or 'going rate'. In the Crime (Sentences) Act 1997, despite the opposition of Lord Taylor LCJ, a strictly desert-based system was modified by a mandatory life sentence for those who repeat serious sexual or violent offences, and mandatory minimum sentences for persistent burglars and drug dealers.[51] At the same time, there emerged a drumbeat of calls from press and populist politicians for tougher sentences. In response to this legislative and political intervention, the courts imposed custody in a higher proportion of cases (from 44.3 per cent in 1992 to 55.7 per cent in 1995 in the Crown Court), and for longer terms. They also handed down a larger number of indeterminate sentences; 19 per cent of prisoners are currently serving indeterminate sentences. The impact was devastating on the prison system. Between 1993 and 2015, the prison population almost doubled from 44,200 to 86,000. At 148 per 100,000 of population, the imprisonment rate has outdistanced the early Victorian peak of 120 per 100,000, and is much larger than in Germany (79), the

Nordic countries (70) and France (98). The principal causes of this twenty-year increase were a more serious mix of offenders appearing for sentence, and harsher sentencing, including higher custody rates and longer prison sentences.

In the early twenty-first century, in the face of this burgeoning prison population, it was finally decided to give judges much firmer guidance on sentencing. Indeed, the most striking development in English sentencing in the past ten years has been the inception of structured sentencing. An independent Sentencing Advisory Panel was created by the Crime and Disorder Act 1998 to assist and advise the Court of Appeal. In the Criminal Justice Act 2003, the Sentencing Guidelines Council (SGC) was established. With judicial and lay members, and chaired by the Lord Chief Justice, the Council took over the Court of Appeal's responsibility for issuing guidelines. Finally, the Coroners and Justice Act 2009 provided for the new Sentencing Council, with a judicial majority among its fourteen members, with the role of issuing a comprehensive sentencing guideline scheme. Now courts 'must, in sentencing an offender, follow any sentencing guideline which is relevant to the offender's case'.[52] It is unclear what impact the guidelines will have upon either the consistency of sentencing or the size of the prison population. It is presumed that the involvement of the judiciary in the development of the guidelines, and the fact that the guidelines cleave closely to Court of Appeal judgments, will lead to judicial acceptance of structured sentencing. We shall see.

8. No Sentencing Variety without a Modicum of Judicial Discretion

It is time to recap what we have discovered. With the abandonment of the death penalty (except for murder) and the end of transportation, the prison bulked supreme in the realm of punishment. In the wake of the Consolidating Acts of 1861, which installed high maximum penalties for almost all the main felonies, the judiciary claimed the right to calculate the custodial penalty for each discrete offence. Parliament and the executive rarely sought to trench upon this wide judicial discretion.

In July 1889, in preparation for a House of Lords debate on sentencing diversity, Godfrey Lushington, Permanent Under-Secretary of State at the Home Office, wrote this internal minute: 'Discretion must be left to the Judges. Nothing could be more unfair or unequal than a hard and fast rule of certain punishments for certain offences. But wherever there is discretion of course there is variety.'[53] This opinion was a staple of departmental lore from this time forth. And if ever the legislature or the executive overstepped their bounds, their hands were slapped by the Lord Chief Justice. The judges' pleasure was not to be fettered by law or administrative directive. In fact, judicial discretion was attenuated by the formulation of a normal range of penalties in the Alverstone Memorandum of 1901, and by the establishment of the Court of Criminal Appeal in 1907, but these changes did little more than prescribe the 'going rate' or 'tariff' that the judges had informally fixed in the last forty years of the nineteenth century – a tariff that was gradually curtailed in severity by comparison with mid-Victorian days. The striking abatement of imprisonment between 1880 and 1940 indicates that judicial discretion is not invariably unwelcome. As Evelyn Ruggles-Brise, Chairman of the Prison Commission, wrote in 1901, judicial discretion was 'practically unlimited in the direction of lenity'.[54] Judges mitigated the tariff, and resisted the use of long, preventive sentences of imprisonment for habitual offenders. From the 1940s onwards, however, judicial discretion moved in the direction of severity, including a stubborn resistance to the abrogation of corporal and capital punishment. While the range of types of sentence expanded, giving courts a greater level of sentencing refinement in matching punishments and offenders, judges responded to the post-war crime increase and to press and political criticism of leniency, with proportionately more and longer prison sentences. Prison numbers climbed inexorably. In the past ten years, Parliament has tried to rein in judicial discretion by the imposition of new sentencing guidelines. Yet the range of sentence within which courts must sentence still leaves judges with more than a modicum of discretion, which is the essence of the story of sentencing for the past century and a half.

Notes

1. Lucia Zedner, *Criminal Justice* (Oxford, Clarendon Press, 2010), p. 186.
2. Douglas Hay, 'Legislation, magistrates, and judges: High law and low law in England and the empire', in David Lemmings (ed.), *The British and Their Laws in the Eighteenth Century* (Woodbridge: The Boydell Press, 2005), pp. 59–65.
3. Home Office, *Making Punishments Work: Report of a Review of the Sentencing Framework for England and Wales* (London: Home Office, 2001), p. 79.
4. Home Office, *Digest: Information on the Criminal Justice System in England and Wales* (London: Home Office, 1995, p. 37.
5. Robert Stevens, *The Independence of the Judiciary* (Oxford, Clarendon Press, 1997), p. 164.
6. The Crown Court system was installed in 1971. Before that date, the principal jurisdictions (at least outside London) were as follows: High Court judges on circuit at county assizes hearing jury trials; magistrates at county quarter sessions, also with juries; magistrates without juries hearing summary offences under statutory authority.
7. Cited in J. A. G. Griffith, *The Politics of the Judiciary* (London, Fontana, 1977), p. 20.
8. Griffith, *The Politics of the Judiciary*, p. 27.
9. Daniel Duman, 'A Social and Occupational Analysis of the English Judiciary: 1770–1790 and 1855–1875', *The American Journal of Legal History*, 17 (1973), 353–64. For the social origins of the county magistracy, see Carl H. E. Zangerl, 'The Social Composition of the County Magistracy in England and Wales, 1831–1887', *Journal of British Studies*, 11 (1971), 113–25.
10. Griffith, *The Politics of the Judiciary*, p. 25.
11. Patrick Polden, 'The Judiciary', in *The Oxford History of the Laws of England*, XI: *1820–1914*, Part Four: *The Legal Professions* (Oxford: Oxford University Press, 2010), pp. 967–8. See also Brian Abel-Smith and Robert Stevens, *Lawyers and the Courts: A Sociological Study of the English Legal System 1750–1965* (London, Heinemann, 1970), p. 299.
12. *Guardian*, 3 April 2003, 28 March 2012.
13. Zedner, *Criminal Justice*, p. 173.
14. See D. A. Thomas, *The Penal Equation: Derivations of the Penalty Structure of English Criminal Law* (Cambridge: Institute of Criminology, 1978), p. 1; Home Office, *Sentences of Imprisonment: A Review of Maximum Penalties*, Report of the Advisory Council on the Penal System (London: HMSO, 1978), pp. 20–3; Keith Smith, 'Sentencing and Review', in *The Oxford*

History of the Laws of England, XIII: *1820–1914: Fields of Development* (Oxford: Oxford University Press, 2010), pp. 122–3; Leon Radzinowicz and Roger Hood, 'Judicial Discretion and Sentencing Standards: Victorian Attempts to Solve a Perennial Problem', *University of Pennsylvania Law Review*, 127 (1979), 1288–1349 at 1304.

15. Home Office, *Sentences of Imprisonment*, p. 24.
16. Moreover, executive review by way of the Royal Prerogative of Mercy provided only intermittent guidance to sentencers. See Victor Bailey, *The Rise and Fall of the Rehabilitative Ideal, 1895–1970* (London: Routledge, 2019), pp. 66–7.
17. D. A. Thomas, *Constraints on Judgment: The Search for Structured Discretion in Sentencing, 1860–1910* (Cambridge: Institute of Criminology, 1979), pp. 12–13.
18. Radzinowicz and Hood, 'Judicial Discretion and Sentencing Standards', 1288–1349 at 1307; C. H. Hopwood, 'Crime and Punishment', *The New Review*, VIII (1893), 620–6, at 626; Home Office, *Sentences of Imprisonment*, pp. 187–9. For the Harcourt quotation, see Smith, 'Sentencing and Review', in *The Oxford History of the Laws of England*, p. 125. According to his biographer, Harcourt 'was always thundering against judges and magistrates who were harsh or inconsiderate'. He was especially critical of the long periods prisoners were held in prison before being put on trial. A. G. Gardiner, *The Life of Sir William Harcourt*, 2 vols, vol. 1: *1827–1886* (London, Constable and Co., 1923), p. 391.
19. Edmund Du Cane, 'The Duration of Penal Sentences', *Fortnightly Review*, 33 (1883), 856–63. For the full correspondence, see Home Office, *Sentences of Imprisonment*, Appendix D, pp. 173–86.
20. See Thomas, *Constraints on Judgment*, p. 25.
21. Thomas, *Constraints on Judgment*, pp. 60–1. See also Radzinowicz and Hood, 'Judicial Discretion', 1313–15.
22. James Fitzjames Stephen, 'Variations in the Punishment of Crime', *Nineteenth Century*, 17 (1885), 755–76, at 763. See also Thomas, *Constraints on Judgment*, pp. 61–4; Radzinowicz and Hood, 'Judicial Discretion', 1317–18.
23. Quoted in Home Office, *Sentences of Imprisonment*, note 2, p. 29.
24. Quoted in Thomas, *Principles of Sentencing*, note 1, p. 29. Since judges differed on the wisdom of flogging, however, it seems evident that informal discussions had failed to produce general agreement.
25. Thomas, *Constraints on Judgment*, pp. 64–5.
26. Montague Crackanthorpe, 'The Criminal Sentences Commission up to Date', *The Nineteenth Century*, LII (1902), 847–63, at 847.

27. For the Memorandum, see R. M. Jackson, *Enforcing the Law* (London: Macmillan, 1967), p. 250.
28. *Sentences of Imprisonment*, p. 30. Radzinowicz and Hood wrote: 'Never before had the judges of England made such a concerted effort to lay the foundations for a consistent sentencing policy', 'Judicial Discretion and Sentencing Standards', 1288–1349 at 1323.
29. Thomas, *Principles of Sentencing*, p. 7. The question of sentencing norms and uniformity was revived once more by Home Secretary Winston Churchill in 1910–11, who was dissatisfied with the Court of Criminal Appeal's limited interventions. He suggested the enactment of smaller maxima, and a Royal Commission to explore the subject. Nothing came of either idea. See Victor Bailey, 'Churchill as Home Secretary: Prison Reform', *History Today*, 35 (1985), 10–13; Smith, 'Sentencing and Review', 137.
30. For the full correspondence, and the quotations that follow, see Home Office, *Sentences of Imprisonment*, Appendix D, pp. 173–86. See also Francis Galton, 'Terms of Imprisonment', *Nature*, 20 (June 1895), 174–6.
31. Quoted in Stefan Collini, *Public Moralists: Political Thought and Intellectual Life in Britain 1850–1930* (Oxford: Clarendon Press, 2006), p. 285. See also C. H. S. Fifoot, *Judge and Jurist in the Reign of Victoria* (London: Stevens & Sons, 1959), pp. 112–24.
32. Quoted in Thomas, *Constraints on Judgment*, p. 62.
33. See Nigel Walker, 'Crime and Penal Measures', in A. H. Halsey (ed.), *Trends in British Society since 1900* (London, 1972); Edwin H. Sutherland, 'The Decreasing Prison Population of England', *Journal of Criminal Law & Criminology*, XXIV (1933), 880–96.
34. For this entire paragraph, see Victor Bailey, *The Rise and Fall*, pp. 51–7.
35. A fuller treatment of the next four paragraphs appears in Bailey, *The Rise and Fall*, chs 2 and 3.
36. See V. A. C. Gatrell, 'The Decline of Theft and Violence in Victorian and Edwardian England', in Gatrell et al. (eds), *Crime and the Law* (London: Europa, 1980).
37. Quoted in Martin Wiener, *Reconstructing the Criminal: Culture, Law, and Policy in England, 1830–1914* (Cambridge: Cambridge University Press, 1990), p. 258.
38. Quoted in Randolph Churchill, *Winston Churchill: Companion Volume*, vol. 2, part 2: *1907–1911* (London, Heinemann, 1969), p. 1199.
39. See Thomas, *Principles of Sentencing*, chs 1 and 2.
40. For an extended treatment of the subject of this paragraph, see Bailey, *The Rise and Fall*, chs 7 and 10.
41. Hansard, *Lords*, 155/27 (April 1948), cols 490–4

42. Royal Commission on Capital Punishment, 1949–53, Report (Cmd. 8932), 1953; *Mins. of Evidence*, 5 January 1950: q. 3111, p. 248; q. 3219, p. 255; qq. 3251–3, p. 258; q. 3212, p. 255.
43. See Bailey, *The Rise and Fall*, pp. 379–80, 383. See also Fenton Bresler, *Lord Goddard: A Biography of Rayner Goddard, Lord Chief Justice of England* (London, 1977); Home Office, *Corporal Punishment*, Report of the Advisory Council on the Treatment of Offenders (Cmnd 1213), 1961.
44. See S. R. Brody, *The Effectiveness of Sentencing: A Review of the Literature*, Home Office Research Unit Report (London: HMSO, 1976), pp. 1–3.
45. See Home Office, *Sentences of Imprisonment*, Appendix J, p. 206.
46. Home Office, *The Length of Prison Sentences*, Interim Report of the Advisory Council on the Penal System (London: HMSO, 1977).
47. Home Office, *Sentences of Imprisonment*, p. 8.
48. Introductory letter by Lady Serota to the Home Secretary.
49. See *Crim. Law Rev.* (November 1980), 675.
50. See Andrew Ashworth, 'Sentencing', in M. Maguire, R. Morgan and R. Reiner (eds), *The Oxford Handbook of Criminology* (Oxford: Clarendon Press, 1997), pp. 1101, 1107, 1112–14, 1129.
51. Ashworth, 'Sentencing', pp. 1095, 1118–19.
52. See Julian V. Roberts, 'Sentencing Guidelines and Judicial Discretion', *British Journal of Criminology*, 51 (2011), 997–1013; Julian V. Roberts, 'Structured sentencing: Lessons from England and Wales for common law jurisdictions', *Punishment and Society*, 14 (2012), 267–88.
53. The National Archives, HO45/9699/A50087/4.
54. My emphasis. See Thomas, *Constraints on Judgment*, p. 26. Ruggles-Brise was informing the Home Office of the Proceedings of the 5th and 6th International Penitentiary Congress.

3

National Perceptions of Judges and Lawyers in Common Law and Civil Law Countries

Matthias Kelly QC

Matthias Kelly sets out to show through a comparison between the United Kingdom, the Republic of Ireland and the United States that a transparent, merit-based, politically neutral judges' recruitment process is one of the best means of achieving judicial independence while advancing gender and socio-economic diversity.

One of the most sensitive, fraught and indeed often controversial tasks in any constitutional democracy is the selection and appointment of judges. In contrast to the frequently confrontational US processes, or the 'tap on the shoulder' by a government minister that was the norm for so long in the UK and its former colonies, a 'third way' of appointing judges has gained traction in many common law countries. This alternative procedure is to entrust the task to an independent Judicial Service Commission or Judicial Appointment Commission with a broad membership that typically includes judges, lawyers and lay representatives. By 2015, more than 80 per cent of Commonwealth member states had established such bodies, according to research by the Bingham Centre for the Rule of Law[1].

In its report 'The Appointment, Tenure and Removal of Judges under Commonwealth Principles, a Compendium and Analysis of

Best Practice'[2] the Bingham Centre for the rule of law recorded the consensus that in order to uphold the rule of law and dispense justice, the judiciary must be 'independent, impartial, honest and competent'. It identified the aim of the appointment process as being 'to provide a reliable means of identifying persons who possess these qualities, and to do so in a manner that is legitimate, in order to sustain public confidence in the judiciary'.[3] The report concluded that 'it is now relatively uncommon for judicial appointments to be in the hands of the executive alone, without the involvement of any other public body in selecting or shortlisting candidates'.[4]

The report noted the need for the involvement of lay people, the conducting of an open and transparent process, the advertisement of vacancies, the need for interviewing candidates, in some cases in public. The report pointed to the desirability of a lay Chair of the selection body, noting that the Venice Commission[5] recorded in its conclusion that with election from amongst non-judicial members a lay Chair could 'bring about a balance between the necessary independence of the Chair and the need to avoid possible corporatist tendencies within the council'.[6] The report also considered judicial tenure of office, removal from office and disciplinary issues.

The report was clear that there was a role for lay representatives in addition to lawyers and judges, as well as a positive case to be made for a lay Chair of a judicial appointments body. The report recorded that the Venice Commission[7] recommended that not all members of the body responsible for judicial appointments should be judges in order to avoid a situation of 'corporatism' in which the existing judiciary may make appointments that further its own interests or develop an unduly narrow view of the qualities that are desirable in a judge.[8] It is also worth noting that the Dublin Declaration on Standards in the Recruitment and Appointment of members of the Judiciary, by the European Network of Councils for the Judiciary which met on 9–11 May 2012 in Dublin, noted the view that in some countries even a majority of judges creates this danger.[9] There is, in fact, much to be said for a lay majority, provided the lay members are representative of wider society and that the executive does not pack it with lay members who are political appointees.

1. England and Wales

In England and Wales there currently are 16,500 barristers, 13,076 of whom are self-employed, the remainder being employed in the Government Legal Service, NGOs, local government, companies or law firms. There are 140,000 solicitors regulated by the Solicitors Regulation Authority. In terms of judges there are approximately 1,900 full-time judges in England and Wales.[10] There are currently 100 High Court judges, 39 Court of Appeal judges, 12 Supreme Court judges and over 600 circuit judges.

In the United Kingdom, the Constitutional Reform Act of 2005 enshrined in law the independence of the judiciary and changed the way judges are appointed. As a result of this legislation, the Judicial Appointments Commission (JAC) was established on 3 April 2006. It has a statutory duty to select candidates solely on merit, select only people of good character and have regard to the need to encourage diversity in the range of persons available for judicial selection.

Before the establishment of the Judicial Appointments Commission, judges at all levels up to and including the High Court were appointed by the monarch acting upon the recommendation[11] of the Lord Chancellor. In the case of the Court of Appeal and the Judicial Committee of the House of Lords,[12] whilst the appointment was by the Queen, they were recommended for appointment by the Prime Minister acting on the recommendation of the Lord Chancellor. This was a procedure which had been in operation for hundreds of years. However, it was not a procedure which met with universal acclaim. In his book *The Judge*[13] Lord Devlin, one of the UK's most eminent judges, said that judges were chosen for their office because they did not seriously question the *status quo*. He said: 'No doubt judges, like any other body of elderly men who have lived on the whole unadventurous lives, tend to be old fashioned in their ideas.' It was, he said, 'a simple fact of nature which reformers must accept'.

Clare McGlynn in her book *The Woman Lawyer: Making the Difference*[14] quoted Lord Bridge (a law lord) in 1992 to the effect that when selecting new members of the Court he and other senior judges looked for 'chaps' like themselves.

Whilst the JAC is committed to diversity in terms of gender and race, there is still an enormous amount to be done to achieve socio-economic diversity amongst the judiciary, a task made more difficult by the imposition of tuition fees in the Teaching and Higher Education Act 1998, introduced by the Blair government in spite of a commitment in its 1997 manifesto that 'the costs of student maintenance should be repaid by graduates on an income-related basis'. This was stated to be directed towards parental means testing with only students from higher-income families being liable for any tuition fees. Set beside the ever-decreasing availability of maintenance grants, the deterrent effect of such an expensive education is likely to have a long-term chilling effect on social mobility in the professions in England and Wales, because fewer working-class students are willing to take on enormous debts to finance their education. The fees levels are strikingly large especially when compared to fee levels in most other EU countries.

2. Judicial Appointment in the Republic of Ireland

The Republic of Ireland, which in 1921,inherited the then prevailing English way of appointing judges, has not substantially changed the way in which it appoints judges. Appointments to the judiciary in Ireland are made by the President on the recommendation of the government. It is the government which, in effect, appoints judges. The Courts and Court Officers Act 1995, by section 13, established a Judicial Appointments Advisory Board (JAAB) to assist in the appointments process. Its remit is quite clearly set out in section 13, which reads: 'For the purposes of identifying persons and informing the government of the suitability of those persons for appointment to judicial office there shall be established a body to be known as the Judicial Appointments Advisory Board.'

Its task is to 'identify' candidates, not to choose judges. It is made up of the Chief Justice, the President of the High Court, the President of the Circuit Court, the President of the District Court, the Attorney General, one practising barrister and one practising solicitor. In addition, there are three additional members appointed who are not lawyers.

There is, thus, a clear majority of lawyers. Out of ten members, four are full-time judges, one is the Chief Legal Adviser to the government,[16] another is a practising barrister and yet another is a practising solicitor. Out of a membership of ten, three are lay people and the Chair is the Chief Justice. The government are not obliged to accept the advice of the Judicial Appointments Advisory Board. Indeed, in the past the government have appointed people who were not even on the list submitted by JAAB. To many observers, the role of the Board appears to be no more than eliminating candidates who clearly are not qualified for appointment, whilst the real power to make appointments rests solely with the government, in other words with politicians.

There has been much recent criticism of the appointments system in Ireland. One criticism has been that there is a lack of transparency, with even those who apply not being told whether they were or were not included on the list submitted by JAAB to the government. Since 2011 the criticism has increased. In an interview in 2012 published in the journal of the Law Society, *The Parchment*, Mr Justice Peter Kelly, then the Senior Judge of the Commercial Court and now the President of the Irish High Court, said that appointments to the Supreme Court in Ireland were 'purely political'. He also said that the creation of the Judicial Appointments Advisory Board in 1996 'was done to create the semblance of independence as to how judges were appointed' but 'the Judicial Appointments Advisory Board by common consent does not really work'. He is also reported in the same article as saying: 'we all know of cases of people who would have been excellent judicial appointments and are passed over in favour of people who are not so well qualified.'

In an article in *The Irish Times* on 14 November 2011 it was reported that just a few months into its tenure, the government had nominated six judges and that five of those had a personal, family or funding link to parties then forming the government, Fine Gael or the Labour Party. In the Oireachtas (the Irish Parliament) on 14 June 2017, the leader of the opposition Mícheál Martin TD said:

> Yesterday's appointment to the Court of Appeal was the first time in nearly a quarter of a century that an appointment such

> as this was made in this manner. It directly bypassed established procedures and the excuse that there were no qualified applicants is clearly false given that the last application process closed nearly six months ago and there was no public advertisement of this vacancy. Given the controversies in which the outgoing Attorney General has been involved and the findings of the Fennelly Report, the rushed and unusual manner of the appointment to which Deputy Varadkar and all of his colleagues were subject is, at best, squalid. Added to this is the behaviour of the Minister for Transport, Tourism and Sport, Deputy Shane Ross. Where once he insisted on removing politics completely from such appointments, he has now agreed to the most directly political appointment in nearly a quarter of a century. It is essential that Deputy Varadkar addresses this controversy. We expect them to explain what he knew and outlined his discussions with the Minister, Deputy Ross on this matter and the highly unusual decision to take one partial recommendation of an incomplete report from the Garda Commissioner and announce it with a banner on a south Dublin road.

This was a reference to the appointment of Marie Whelan, the then Attorney General,[17] directly from her post as Attorney General to the Irish Court of Appeal. The appointment had not been publicly advertised nor does it appear to have gone through the Judicial Appointments Advisory Board, of which she was a member. It was widely criticised as purely political, made by the outgoing Taoiseach (Prime Minister) Enda Kenny. The Irish Parliament has for the last two years spoken of reforming judicial appointments but so far, whilst publishing a bill, which has been changed several times, has not yet made any meaningful progress in reforming the process.

There has been some resistance from the Irish judges to reform of the judicial appointments process in Ireland. Whilst the judges recognise the need for reform in creating a system that is not perceived as one where candidates for judicial posts are appointed on the basis of their political allegiance, the judges have nevertheless shown resistance to a majority of lay people on any new appointments body, and resistance to its Chair being an appropriately qualified lay person.[18] In a press release of 26 June 2017, the Association of Judges in Ireland (AJI) said that any proposal to have a lay Chair would mean that

> the Office of Chief Justice is diminished by the requirement that he or she should be an Ordinary Member of the Commission but should be statutorily precluded from being its Chairman. The AJI is concerned that the present proposals may damage the judiciary as an institution.

This view was expressed despite the fact that many jurisdictions close to Ireland have such an arrangement, including Scotland and England and Wales, without the rule of law imploding or the world ending.

3. The United States

In the US there is yet another model of judicial appointment. Its legal system is divided into the federal system, where judges are appointed by the president in office at the time and confirmed by Congress. In the case of the US Supreme Court the process is often seen as overtly political with some presidential nominees attracting political controversy, for example, Brett Kavanaugh in September 2018 and before him Clarence Thomas in 1991. In the case of state judges, their method of appointment varies from direct appointment by the state governor and legislature to direct election by the electorate.

In Alabama in 2001 Judge Roy Moore was elected by the electorate as Chief Justice of the State's Supreme Court. The Alabama media later reported[19]

> After taking office, Moore installed a 5,280-pound granite block that featured Constitutional quotes and two large tablets with the 10 Commandments[20] outside the state Judicial Building. The move prompted a lawsuit from the ACLU and the Southern Poverty

Law Center, among other groups, which Moore dismissed saying the 10 Commandments were the 'moral foundation of U.S. law' and therefore appropriate in a judicial setting.

Court rulings later ordered Moore to remove the monument, though he remained defiant. Alabama's Supreme Court voted to overrule Moore's decision to disobey the court order and a complaint against him was filed with the Alabama Court of Judiciary. The COJ issued a unanimous ruling that Moore had violated the Canons of Judicial Ethics by defying the ruling and ordered the Chief Justice be removed from office in November 2003. The decision was upheld through several appeals.

Judge Roy Moore was re-elected Chief Justice of the State of Alabama in November 2012 but was suspended on charges that included disregarding Federal Injunctions, interfering in Probate Court business, substituting his own judgment for that of the entire Alabama Supreme Court. He was ultimately suspended from office as Chief Justice in September 2016 by the Alabama Court of Judiciary for the remainder of his term which ran to 2019. Judge Roy Moore later ran for election to the US Senate to fill the Senate seat vacated by Senator Jeff Sessions upon his appointment by Donald Trump as US Attorney-General. Roy Moore was defeated in the election on 12 December 2017 by Senator Doug Jones.

4. Canada

A recent Canadian case provides a good example of a court acting to protect itself as well as upholding the law. In *Reference re Supreme Court Act, ss. 5 and 6 [2014] 1 SCR 433 [Neutral citation 2014 SCC 21]* the Supreme Court of Canada, by a 6–1 majority[21] blocked the appointment of a serving judicial officer, Marc Nadon to the Canadian Supreme Court. He had been nominated by the government of Canada led by the then Canadian Prime Minister Stephen Harper pursuant to section 6 of the Supreme Court Act 1985. That section provided that 'at least three of the nine judges appointed to the Court shall be appointed from among the judges of the Court of Appeal or of the Superior Court of the Province of Quebec or from among the advocates of that Province'. Marc Nadon was a supernumerary judge of the Federal Court of Appeal and formerly a member of the Quebec bar for more than ten years.

The government had introduced changes in the Economic Action Plan Act 2013 (a taxation measure) which purported to amend the Supreme Court Act and would have had the effect of making Marc Nadon eligible for appointment to the Canadian Supreme Court. The Governor-General of Canada referred two questions, directly bearing on the appointment to the Supreme Court, pursuant to section 53 of the Supreme Court Act 1984:

1. Can a person who was, at any time, an advocate of at least ten years standing at the *Barreau du Québec* be appointed to the Supreme Court of Canada as a member of the Supreme Court from Quebec pursuant to sections 5 and 6 of the Supreme Court Act?
2. Can Parliament enact legislation that requires that a person be or has previously been a barrister or advocate of at least ten years standing at the bar of a province as a condition of appointment as a judge of the Supreme Court of Canada or enact the annexed declaratory provisions as set out in clauses 471 and 472 of the Bill entitled Economic Action Plan 2013 Act, no. 2?

The majority held that the answer to both questions was 'No' and that the challenged provision of the 2013 Act was unconstitutional on the basis that section 41 of the Constitution Act 1982 set out a procedure which had to be followed before any changes to the court's constitution could be made, namely that any such proposal as was contained in the 2013 Act would require the consent of the Federal Parliament and the provincial legislatures. That procedure had not been followed in this case. McLachlin CJ said

> The plain meaning of s. 6 has remained consistent since the original version of that provision was enacted in 1875, and it has

> always excluded former advocates. By specifying that three judges shall be appointed 'from among' the judges and advocates (i.e. members) of the identified institutions, s. 6 impliedly excludes former members of those institutions and imposes a requirement of current membership. Reading ss. 5 and 6 together, the requirement of at least ten years standing at the Bar applies to appointments from Quebec.
>
> This textual analysis is consistent with the underlying purpose of s. 6 and reflects the historical compromise that led to the creation of the Supreme Court as a general court of appeal for Canada and as a federal and bijural institution. Section 6 seeks (i) to ensure civil law expertise and the representation of Quebec's legal traditions and social values on the Court, and (ii) to enhance the confidence of Quebec in the Court. This interpretation is also consistent with the broader scheme of the Act for the appointment of *ad hoc* judges, which excludes judges of the federal courts as *ad hoc* judges for Quebec cases.

Thus the court ruled that its composition was constitutionally protected, and Parliament's attempt to amend the Supreme Court Act through a budget bill was unconstitutional. Accordingly, Marc Nadon's appointment to the Canadian Supreme Court was declared void retrospectively, and he was deemed to have never been sworn in. In addition the court ruled that the relevant provision of the 2013 Act was outside the power of Parliament and thus null and void.

5. Diversity: Does it Exist?

The remit of the Judicial Appointments Commission in England and Wales[22] extends to encouraging diversity in the range of people available for judicial selection. The Judicial Diversity Statistics 2017, published 20 July 2017, recorded that 28 per cent of court judges and 45 per cent of tribunal judges were female. It noted: 'among court judges, senior roles showed lower representation of female judges than in less senior roles.' This was less evident among tribunal judges, with more variation in female representation across tribunal appointments. It also recorded that 7 per cent of court and 10 per cent of tribunal judges were BAME,[23] and non-legal tribunal members were 16 per cent. It also recorded that more than half of all magistrates (lay) were female, at 54 per cent. It recorded that 11 per cent of magistrates declared themselves as BAME.

6. Impact of the Commercialisation of Education

Whilst the JAC is committed to diversity in terms of gender and race, there is still an enormous amount to be done to achieve socio-economic diversity amongst the judiciary, a task made more difficult by the imposition of tuition fees in the Teaching and Higher Education Act 1998, introduced by the Blair government in spite of an earlier commitment not to impose tuition fees. The position was made worse by the raising of the cap on tuition fees from £1,000 imposed in 1998 to £3,000[24] with effect from 2006, and then in 2010 by the Cameron government to £9,000 per annum. Set beside the ever-decreasing availability of maintenance grants, the deterrent effect of such an expensive education is likely to have a long-term chilling effect on social mobility in the professions in England and Wales, because fewer working-class students are willing to take on enormous debts to finance their education. The fees levels are strikingly large especially when compared to fee levels in most other EU countries.

7. Full-time and Part-time Judges

In England and Wales, with a part-time as well as a full-time judiciary, the jurisdiction of the judge can be varied. For those who sit in specialist tribunals such as those dealing with tax, land etc., the jurisdiction is highly specialised. However, for those sitting in the courts, be they at Circuit Court level or High Court level, the jurisdiction is wide. It covers civil matters, criminal matters[25] and family matters. The existence of a part-time judiciary does, in my view, help to encourage diversity as it enables practitioners to determine whether a full-time appointment is or is not something that they personally would want. It also has the effect of enabling practitioners to experience 'the other side' in seeing the case from a judge's point of view and understanding what it is that the judge needs in order to reach a decision in any given case. In addition the reality, in England and Wales, is that without the existence of a part-time judiciary the judicial system would have enormous difficulty in functioning at all.

8. Brexit and its Impact on the Law

In the UK our legal system faces many challenges, not least those substantial challenges posed by Brexit. There is still a great deal of uncertainty as to what role, if any, European law will play in England and Wales after the United Kingdom leaves the European Union. It is also unclear how decisions of the Court of Justice of the European Union are to be treated in the courts of England and Wales, Scotland and Northern Ireland post-Brexit. These are matters about which there is a great deal of debate but very little in the way of clarity at present.

9. The Judge as Law Maker?

In the common law system, judges are not law makers since that role is exclusively for Parliament. However, common law judges can clarify the law and develop it incrementally over a period of time. For example, in the case of *R. v. R. (1992) 1 AC 599*, the House of Lords (the predecessor of the Supreme Court) held that a husband could rape his wife and that marriage was neither a bar nor a defence to a charge of rape. That is a very significant development over what had been understood to be the law for many, many decades. Up to then it was the law that a wife must be taken, by virtue of her marriage, to have given an enduring consent to having sex with her husband.

In *Wells v. Wells (1999) 1 AC 345*, the House of Lords also held that the way in which damages in tort were calculated should be developed to reflect the needs of those who were seriously injured and to develop fully the long-established principle that English tort law seeks to deliver full compensation (the 100 per cent principle) for the person injured by the wrongful act of another. It did this by declaring that claimants in serious injury cases should be treated as in the same position as a risk-averse investor. Thus in calculating the capital sum needed to meet a proven loss of future earnings and proven future reasonable expenses the claimant should be entitled to invest his/her damages in index linked government stock, which is regarded as a risk-free investment. That in turn had the effect of driving up the multiplier used to calculate the annual loss and expense and thus increasing the total damages awarded to the seriously injured. However, following long periods of low interest rates, indeed negative interest rates, Parliament is now proposing to intervene so as to change that underlying assumption that the injured party is entitled to a risk-free investment, ensuring a continuous stream of income to meet proven loss and expense. That may well have dramatic consequences in the event that the fund awarded by the court does not in fact deliver the compensation it was intended to.

10. What Makes a Good Judge?

A good judge, in my view, should be a good lawyer, humane, and aware of the community he or she serves, particularly in a diverse multicultural society. A good judge should also be efficient in court, and ever mindful that his/her effectiveness is enhanced by a fair, well-run court where the respect he/she enjoys is earned and not commanded. Above all, a good judge is someone who is capable of making a reasoned, transparent judgment driven by logic and the law. He or she must also be wholly independent of the state and the parties as well as alive to and averse to imposing upon others any social values shared by his or her class or social group. The good judge should possess professional integrity and be able to rely upon the integrity of those professional lawyers appearing before them. Finally, the good judge must be someone who has the patience to listen. The ability to really listen and understand is an extremely important judicial attribute.

In contrast to this, the bad judge may well be someone who is pompous, bullying, self-opinionated, prone to arbitrary decisions, prone to unfairness, ignorant of people and more than willing to impose his or her social values and laws upon everyone else. There is no need or benefit to be had from such a judge and much to be lost.

11. Training, Knowledge Enhancement and Experience

Judging is one of the most important functions a lawyer can perform in a liberal western democracy. To that end, ability, humanity and independence must also be reinforced with regular training. The training does not have to take the form of lectures. It can also be more imaginative. In England and Wales, His Honour Judge Keith Hornby[26] introduced the concept of theatre to judicial training in family law. Under that model, a theatre company enacted a not untypical relationship between a man, a woman and their child. The actors played out the all too recognisable scenario in which over the years the relationship degenerated as the man became more and more controlling, dominating and undermining. The experience of most who have attended one of those sessions has been to transform the way in which they view domestic abuse and its evolution. By such means, the gradual evolution of the controlling and dominating partner can be clearly demonstrated together with the effects not only on the person's partner but also on the children. Such training is now more common in England and Wales, with actors playing roles in recruitment exercises to the Bench where real-life courtroom scenarios are acted out to test the candidates, and in ongoing judicial training in coping with difficult but realistic courtroom scenarios.

12. The International Challenge

For judges there will be many challenges in the future. One example may well be in the growth of international tribunals to reflect the multinational and global nature of trade and human movement. The European Union had spent many years negotiating with the United States of America the Transatlantic Trade and Investment Partnership (TTIP). With the election of Donald Trump as President, that was swept aside, as he withdrew the United States from the negotiations. However, similar deals have been agreed with Canada (CETA), Japan, with an economic partnership agreement announced on 8 December 2017, as well as agreements with the European Economic Area (EEA). One of the features of the CETA Agreement and that which was proposed in the TTIP Agreement was the creation of a dispute resolution mechanism. Hitherto, such disputes were resolved by international mediation. However, in TTIP, it was proposed that an entirely new mechanism be established whereby there would be a tribunal of first instance which would consist of five members drawn from the European Union, five members from the United States of America and five from other parts of the world. They would all be appointed for a six-year period. Sitting above those in the draft TTIP Agreement was the establishment of an appeals tribunal which was to consist of six members, with two drawn from the European Union, two from the United States of America and two from the rest of the world. It was proposed that such tribunals would be able to resolve disputes which arose out of employment rights, labour relations, environmental rights, social protection, social dialogue, rights at work, gender issues, equality issues, fiscal policy as well as intellectual property.

Such agreements[27] attracted widespread criticism and opposition, not least within the European Union, because they had the potential to create a dispute resolutions mechanism which was available only to investors and global corporations. That was seen by many as detracting from the legal systems that currently operate in the European Union. Whilst TTIP did not in fact occur, CETA has been provisionally implemented[28] since 21 September 2017. That agreement anticipated its dispute resolution mechanism being replaced when TTIP came on stream with the dispute resolution mechanism set out in TTIP. That was clearly envisaged by Article 8.29 of the CETA Agreement which envisaged the establishment of a multilateral investment tribunal to replace the mechanism established in CETA.

These will be amongst the future challenges for lawyers and national courts throughout the European Union as well as for the European Union's own institutional disputes mechanism namely the Court of Justice of the European Union.

13. The Role of Law in Controlling the Executive Arm of Government

There is, very often, a tension between the courts and politicians. Politicians tend to assume that when they are elected to office, they are there to 'rule' over the people, as opposed to being the elected representatives of the people in government. In that mind frame, law and the courts are often seen by the politicians as tedious obstructions. This tension has a long history. In *Liversidge v. Anderson (1942) AC 206*, the Judicial Committee of the House of Lords (the predecessor of the present Supreme Court) was called upon to decide the meaning of Regulation 18B of the Defence (General) Regulations 1939 which empowered the Home Secretary to detain any person whom he had reasonable cause to believe to be of 'hostile origin or association or to have been recently concerned in acts prejudicial to the public safety of defence of the realm'.

This regulation permitted internment (that is detention without trial) during the Second World War. Mr Liversidge was so detained. He wished to know the reason for his detention. In order to do so, he brought an action against the Home Secretary in the hope that a court case would force the Home Secretary to say in a public court why he had been detained. He was unsuccessful. A majority of the House of Lords held that if the Home Secretary claimed to have reasonable cause to believe that Mr Liversidge was a person of hostile associations then that belief of the Home Secretary was enough in itself. In a famous dissenting judgment which has now become one of the most famous dissenting judgments in the common law world,[29] Lord Atkin, a member of the Judicial Committee, said:

> In this country, amid the clash of arms, the laws are not silent. They may be changed but they speak the same language in war as in peace. It has always been one of the pillars of freedom, one of the principles of liberty for which on recent authority we are now fighting that the judges are no respecters of persons and stand between the subject and any attempted encroachment on his liberty by the executive, alert to see that any coercive action is justified in law. In this

case I have listened to arguments which might have been addressed acceptably to the Court of the King's Bench in the time of Charles I.

In his view the phrase 'reasonable cause' in the statute in question meant that the actions of the Home Secretary should be evaluated by an objective standard as opposed to the Home Secretary's subjective view that he had reasonable cause. In short, the courts should be obliged to examine whether the Home Secretary in fact had reasonable cause by using an objective, not a subjective standard.

In modern times this conflict has manifested itself in the desire of the executive arm of government to use 'secret evidence' against those it wishes to detain, coerce or restrain. The situation usually arises where the government believes that a particular person has terrorist links and is a potential danger to public safety. However, the government is usually not willing to produce the evidence upon which it bases its belief. The government will then wish to rely and act upon its belief and detain the person or otherwise place severe restrictions upon their liberty. The principle of a fair trial dictates that the case against ought to be put to the person so that they may have an opportunity to answer the allegations. Such a situation arose in *A and Others v. UK*, App. No. 3455/05 on 19 February 2009. The Grand Chamber of the European Court of Human Rights considered the detention aspects of the system then in operation in the United Kingdom. The applicants were terrorist suspects detained at Belmarsh Prison. The Grand Chamber determined that procedural fairness required that a suspect be provided with the gist of the secret evidence supporting the allegations made against him. Without sufficient information, the suspect would not be able to challenge the allegations effectively, or at all. At paragraph 220 of its judgment, the court said:

> While this question must be decided on a case by case basis the Court observes generally that, where the evidence was to a large extent disclosed and the open material played the predominant role in the determination, it could not be said that the applicant was denied an opportunity effectively to challenge the reasonableness of the Secretary of State's belief and suspicions about him.

> In other cases even where all or most of the underlying evidence remained undisclosed, if the allegations contained in the open material were sufficiently specific, it should be possible for the applicant to provide his representatives and the special advocate with information with which to refute them, if such information existed, without his having to know the detail or sources of the evidence which formed the basis of the allegations.

This was a reference to the United Kingdom's use of a specially constituted tribunal known as SIAC (Special Immigration Appeals Commission). Under the UK system a judge hears all the evidence, the accused hears only part, that which is not classified as 'secret' or 'confidential'. His interests are said to be protected by having a court-appointed special advocate. That is a barrister who has been 'security cleared' or vetted by the executive and its intelligence agencies. In most cases it is the same agencies that have produced the secret evidence. It is a system which has attracted criticism for a number of reasons. Firstly, there is no relationship between the advocate and the accused. Amongst the fundamental principles of the Bar of England and Wales are the principles that the advocate acts on behalf of his/her client, acts upon the client's instructions, within the Bar's code of ethics, and does not hold evidence back from his/her client. Once the special advocate has seen the evidence he or she cannot speak about it to the accused. Secondly, it destroys the basis upon which the Bar in England and Wales operates, whereby all advocates must accept a case whether they believe in it or not. In SIAC only barristers cleared by the intelligence agencies are able to act as special advocates. Thirdly, it leaves the United Kingdom open to the charge of 'closed courts' and the use of 'secret evidence'. Fourthly, the accused cannot give his version since he does not know what has been said about him.

In *A v. Secretary of State for the Home Department (2004) UKHL 56 and (2005) 2 AC 69*, the House of Lords Judicial Committee gave judgment in the case of nine detainees held in Belmarsh High Security Prison. They had challenged the lawfulness of their detention. The House of Lords held that it was incompatible with article 4 of the

European Convention on Human Rights and Fundamental Freedoms to detain without charge or trial non-nationals suspected of international terrorism, whilst exempting UK nationals similarly suspected from that same detention.

One shining example of an impartial judge was Lord Bingham, the former Lord Chief Justice of England and a member of the Judicial Committee of the House of Lords. In his book *The Rule of Law* published in 2011, Lord Bingham quoted the 1955 declaration of the International Commission of Jurists at Athens as to what constituted the rule of law:

> The State is subject to the law;
>
> Government should respect the rights of individuals under the rule of law and provide effective means for their enforcement;
>
> Judges should be guided by the rule of law, protect and enforce it without fear or favour and resist any encroachment by governments or political parties in their independence as judges;
>
> Lawyers of the world should preserve the independence of their profession, assert the rights of an individual under the rule of law and insist that every accused is accorded a fair trial.

The fourth point in that definition of the rule of law is one that all lawyers and judges would do well to bear in mind. The European Union prides itself on a

> respect for human rights, freedom, democracy, equality, the rule of law and respect for human rights including the rights of persons belonging to minorities. These values are common to the member states in a society in which pluralism, non-discrimination, tolerance, justice, solidarity and equality between men and women prevail.[30]

Article 7 of the Lisbon Treaty provides that the Council of the European Union acting by a majority of four-fifths of its members, after obtaining the consent of the European Parliament, may determine that there is a clear risk of a serious breach by a member state of the values referred to in article 2. Before making such a determination, the Council is obliged to hear what the member state in question has to say and may address recommendations to it acting in accordance with the same procedure. The Council is then obliged to regularly verify that the grounds on which such a determination is made continue to apply. Article 7.2 of the same Treaty

> Permits the European Council acting by unanimity on a proposal by one-third of the member states or by the European Commission and after obtaining the consent of the European Parliament to determine the existence of a serious and persistent breach by a member state of the values referred to in article 2 after inviting the member state in question to submit its observations.

This is the procedure that has recently been employed by the European Commission against Poland in respect of its changes and proposed changes to its judicial system. The EU has now not only begun article 7 proceedings; it has, in addition, begun infringement proceedings under article 19(1) of the Treaty on European Union. In a statement at the beginning of June 2018, the Commission said it was 'of the opinion that these measures undermine the principle of judicial independence, including the irremovability of judges, and thereby Poland fails to fulfil its obligations under Article 19(1) of the Treaty on European Union'. Poland was suspended from the European Network of Councils for the Judiciary on 17 September 2018, because the body in Poland which nominates the country's judges is no longer seen as being independent of political control. The Polish Government, at the time of writing, shows no sign of a willingness to change course.

The issue of genuine judicial independence in the EU also extends to Hungary. On 12 September 2018 the European Parliament voted by 448 to 197 to support a report to the Parliament, written by Judith Sargentini, a Dutch MEP, which accused Hungary of threatening the rule of law by hampering press and academic freedoms, cracking down on the funding of NGOs and denying rights to minorities and migrants. This was an unprecedented step that appears to have left Hungary unmoved. Poland was reported to have said that it would veto any infringement proceedings brought against Hungary.[31] This gives rise to a concern that not all may be well with the established European democratic value and belief that essential to the functioning of a democratic society is the rule of law with a genuinely independent judiciary at its heart.

The concern over judicial appointments and judicial independence are a salutary reminder that we must be vigilant to ensure that the rule of law operates and that our judiciary is in fact wholly independent. In the Irish case of *The Minister of Justice and Equality v. Artur Celmer (2018) IEHC 119*, Ms Justice Donnelly, in a judgment delivered on 12 March 2018, dealt with a European arrest warrant case in which the surrender of the person to Poland was challenged on the grounds of a potential breach of article 6 of the ECHR. The challenge was founded upon recent changes in Polish legislation concerning the judiciary, the courts and the public prosecutor. The respondent, Mr Celmer argued that recent legislative changes and proposed legislative changes in Poland created a real risk of a denial of justice if he were surrendered for trial in Poland. That, he argued, fundamentally undermined the basis of mutual trust between the issuing and executing judicial authorities, and as a result the operation of the European arrest warrant system was called into question. Having heard evidence concerning the legislative changes and the proposed legislative changes, and having considered the European Commission's reasoned proposal pursuant to Article 7 of the Treaty of the European Union, the Irish High Court decided to refer the case to the Court of Justice of the European Union pursuant to article 267 of the treaty on the functioning of the European Union which provides for the Court of Justice of the European Union to have jurisdiction to give a preliminary ruling concerning issues. The question she has referred to the court[32] is

> Is the Aranyosi and Caldararu test, which relies upon principles of mutual trust and mutual recognition, the correct test to apply where the High Court, as an executing judicial authority under

> the framework decision, has found the common values of the rule of law set out in article 2 of TEU has been breached in Poland;
>
> If the test to be applied is whether the requested person is at real risk of a flagrant denial of justice, does the High Court, as an executing judicial authority, have to revert to the issuing judicial authority for any further necessary information about the trial that this requested person will face, where the High Court has found that there is a systemic breach to the rule of law in Poland?

This is a reminder that within the European Union, Courts can be, are and should be alive to challenges to the rule of law.

In another Irish High Court case, *AP v. The Minister for Justice and Equality (2016) IEHC 408*, the judge, Ms Justice Stewart, dealt with a case in which a man who had been granted refugee status in Ireland in 1991 and had repeatedly sought thereafter nationalisation (citizenship) but had his applications refused on the ground that material before the Minister was secret and could not be disclosed to him on the grounds of 'National Security'. That had the inevitable effect that he could not address the case against him as he did not know what was being held against him, and could not address whatever the concern was. Nor could he give any explanation as he did not know what the material contained. He argued that fair procedures dictated that the reason for his rejection or, at least, the gist of the reasons should be disclosed to him. He also argued that the State had a duty[33] pursuant to article 34 of the Geneva Convention on the Status of Refugees 1951. That Article provides that

> The contracting state shall as far as possible facilitate the assimilation and naturalisation of refugees. They shall in particular make every effort to expedite naturalisation proceedings and to reduce as far as possible the charges and costs of such proceedings.

That Convention is part of European Union law[34] and citizenship of the European Union, of course, depends upon citizenship of a member state. The judge dismissed AP's application, finding that the applicant had no right to know the reasons why he was refused citizenship on the basis that a judge in a previous challenge to the refusal of his application for citizenship had decided that to disclose the document containing the reasons placed national security at risk. The state's position was that it could rely upon the undisclosed material as the sole reason for refusal. The judge agreed. AP argued that the assertion by the state that it should not be compelled to disclose the material (or the gist of it) as such disclosure would put national security at risk was itself a conclusion, not a reason. He argued that if there were reasons, those could only be found in the secret material contained in the undisclosed document. That argument was summarily rejected.

In the subsequent appeal *XP v. The Minister for Justice and Equality [2018] IECA 112* Hogan J in the Court of Appeal agreed with the view that it was unfair that the relevant Minister should be able to rely on material touching on national security of which the applicant knew nothing and could not address in any realistic way. Hogan J in dismissing the appeal said

> It gives me no pleasure to have to reach this conclusion because I agree entirely with Gilligan J that it is in many respects unfair that the Minister should rely on material which is said to involve highly sensitive matters touching on national security of which the applicant, Mr X., has not had sight and in respect of which he knows nothing. Mr X. cannot accordingly address these national security concerns in any realistic way so far as his application for naturalisation pursuant to s. 15 of the Irish Nationality and Citizenship Act 1956 (as amended) is concerned.
>
> This state of affairs cuts across the basic constitutional value of fair procedures since it is elementary law that a decision-maker exercising statutory powers cannot generally rely on material not disclosed to the applicant, at least absent exceptional circumstances: see, e.g., *Kiely v. Minister for Social Welfare (No.2) [1977] I.R. 287*. The circumstances here are, however, quite exceptional and touch directly on national security concerns and, it seems, sensitive diplomatic channels involving foreign states. It is already clear from the separate (and unappealed) decision of McDermott J

> in the High Court on the issue of privilege that he has reviewed the relevant documentation on which the Minister relies. He accordingly has ruled that the Minister may properly claim a public interest immunity from disclosure in respects of key parts of these documents. It must therefore be accepted that there is a judicial finding to the effect that the material which was not disclosed to Mr X. in the course of his naturalisation application presents real and pressing national security concerns.
>
> In these circumstances, like Gilligan J, I feel compelled to hold that the present case is one where this Court's capacity, in the words of article 40.3 of the Constitution, to defend and vindicate the fair procedure rights of the applicant 'as far as practicable' is constrained by these same national security concerns. While I accept that this is in many respects unsatisfactory, the only other step presently open to this Court – namely, to order the release of the material on even a redacted or summary basis to Mr X. – is simply not a practicable one.

His view as to the unfair result was shared by Gilligan J who said

> It has to be accepted that the situation from the applicant's perspective appears to be unfair. The reality is that there is no other better solution available. There is not, as such, any formal procedure in place in this jurisdiction whereby an independent body or person, such as a retired or current judge of the High Court or a senior barrister, can examine a particular document over which privilege is claimed in the interest of national security so as to consider whether or not the document should be released, or alternatively, that perhaps the gist of the document in some way can be released to an unsuccessful applicant seeking Irish citizenship.

Gilligan J went on to hold:

> The interests of national security in my view outweigh the position of the applicant who finds himself in an unfair situation whereby

> he does not know the basis of the reason for the respondent coming to a conclusion that national security interests result in him not being given the basis of the conclusion arrived at by the respondent Minister.

It is, however, worth recalling that in *A and Others v. UK, App. No. 3455/05* the Grand Chamber of the European Court of Human Rights pointed out, at paragraph 220:

> In other cases, even where all or most of the underlying evidence remained undisclosed, if the allegations contained in the open material were sufficiently specific, it should have been possible for the applicant to provide his representatives and the special advocate with information with which to refute them, if such information existed, without his having to know the detail or sources of the evidence which formed the basis of the allegations. An example would be the allegation made against several of the applicants that they had attended a terrorist training camp at a stated location between stated dates; given the precise nature of the allegation, it would have been possible for the applicant to provide the special advocate with exonerating evidence, for example of an alibi or of an alternative explanation for his presence there, sufficient to permit the advocate effectively to challenge the allegation. Where, however, the open material consisted purely of general assertions and SIAC's decision to uphold the certification and maintain the detention was based solely or to a decisive degree on closed material, the procedural requirements of art. 5(4) would not be satisfied.

It may be that this is an example that much has still to be done[35] to ensure recognition that an important part of the fundamental right to a fair hearing, and central to western ideas of democracy and fairness, is the right to know the case against you in order that you may answer the charge. In the XP case the Minister relied upon undisclosed material as justification for the challenged decision, and further relied upon the fact that in prior litigation a High Court Judge had ruled that the documents were immune from disclosure on grounds of public interest immunity. As the UK Supreme Court put it in *Al Rawi and others v. The Security Service and others [2011] UKSC 34*, per Lord Dyson at paragraph 41,

> If documents are disclosed as a result of the process, they are available to both parties and to the court. If they are not disclosed, they are available neither to the other parties nor to the court. Both parties are entitled to full participation in all aspects of the litigation. There is no unfairness or inequality of arms.

And Lord Kerr at paragraph 89: 'The right to be informed of the case made against you is not merely a feature of the adversarial system of trial, it is an elementary and essential prerequisite of fairness.' Lord Kerr continued at paragraph 93:

> The appellants' second argument proceeds on the premise that placing before a judge all relevant material is, in every instance, preferable to having to withhold potentially pivotal evidence. This proposition is deceptively attractive – for what, the appellants imply, could be fairer than an independent arbiter having access to all the evidence germane to the dispute between the parties? The central fallacy of the argument, however, lies in the unspoken assumption that, because the judge sees everything, he is bound to be in a better position to reach a fair result. That assumption is misplaced. To be truly valuable, evidence must be capable of withstanding challenge. I go further. Evidence which has been insulated from challenge may positively mislead. It is precisely because of this that the right to know the case that one's opponent makes and to have the opportunity to challenge it occupies such a central place in the concept of a fair trial. However astute and assiduous the judge, the proposed procedure hands over to one party considerable control over the production of relevant material and the manner in which it is to be presented. The peril that such a

procedure presents to the fair trial of contentious litigation is both obvious and undeniable.

Notes

1. In 81 per cent of Commonwealth Jurisdictions there is a Judicial Appointments Commission which plays some part in the selection or shortlisting of candidates for judicial appointment; see paragraph 1.6 of the report.
2. Published by The British Institute of International and Comparative Law, 2015.
3. See paragraph 1.1.2 of the report.
4. Paragraph 1.4 of the report.
5. Judicial Appointments CDL-AD (2007), paragraph 35.
6. In England and Wales, Scotland and Northern Ireland each Judicial Appointments Commission has a lay Chair.
7. The Venice Commission – Judicial Appointments, paragraphs 27–8, CDL-AD (2007) 028.
8. See paragraph 1.6.16 of the report *The Appointment, Tenure and Removal of Judges under Commonwealth Principles*, a compendium and analysis of best practice by the Bingham Centre for the Rule of Law (London: British Institute of International and Comparative Law, 2015).
9. See II(2), p. 8 of the Declaration available at *https://www.encj.eu/images/stories/pdf/GA/Dublin/encj_dublin_declaration_def_dclaration_de_dublin_recj_def.pdf*
10. Judicial Diversity Statistics, 2017. This figure relates to the courts. When part-time judges are included, the figure rises to 3,134.
11. Often described as 'the tap on the shoulder system', in which the individual's appointment was due to his/her being known to the Lord Chancellor and/or a member of the senior judiciary, leaving the system open to allegations of cronyism and the appointment of people in the image of those who already were in post, and creating a judiciary often criticised for its lack of diversity.
12. The predecessor of the present Supreme Court.
13. Oxford: Oxford University Press, 1979.
14. Butterworths, 1998, p. 178,
15. The Higher Education Act 2004
16. A purely political appointment, the appointee holding office at the pleasure of the Taoiseach (Prime Minister).
17. The chief legal adviser to the government.

18. See paragraph 4 above. For a reasonable explanation of the need for lay members and a lay Chair see paragraph 1.6.16 of the report *The Appointment, Tenure and Removal of Judges under Commonwealth Principles.*
19. *https://www.al.com/news/index.ssf/2017/09/who_is_roy_moore_former_alabam.html*
20. Author's note: thus violating the First Amendment of the US Constitution which separates Church and State.
21. McLachlin CJ and LeBel, Abella, Cromwell, Karakatsanis and Wagner JJ, in the majority, Moldaver J dissenting.
22. Established by the Constitutional Reform Act of 2005.
23. Black, Asian, Minority Ethnic.
24. The Higher Education Act 2004.
25. Where all indictable crime is tried by a jury drawn at random from the ranks of ordinary citizens, a highly valued tradition of the common law going back for many centuries.
26. Through the Judicial College.
27. TTIP in particular.
28. And therefore will need to be ratified by the national parliaments of all member states, something which has not yet been achieved as of the date of writing.
29. And reflects the current legal standards and principles in public law; see *Inland Revenue Commissioners v. Rossminister Ltd (1980) AC 952 at 1011*, where Lord Diplock said that 'the time has come' for the Law Lords to acknowledge that the majority 'were expediently and, at that time, perhaps, excusably, wrong and the dissenting speech of Lord Atkin was right'.
30. See article 2 of the Lisbon Treaty.
31. According to a report in the *Financial Times* of 12 September 2018
32. As recorded in the Judgement (2018) IEHC 119.
33. Ireland is a signatory to the Geneva Convention on the status of Refugees, having first signed in 1962 and then having signed succeeding protocols in 1999.
34. Council Directive 2004/83/EC of 29 April 2004 on minimum standards for the qualification and status of third country nationals or stateless persons as refugees or as persons who otherwise need international protection and the content of the protection granted, OJ 2004 L 304, p. 12.
35. The case is currently under appeal to the Supreme Court.

4

Judicial Independence in Spain

Ana María Neira Pena and David Soto Díaz

In their co-written chapter Ana María Neira Pena and David Soto Díaz deal with institutional judicial independence, which in Spain, is enshrined in the Constitution of 1978. It goes along with a strict regulation of the judicial profession, judges being held accountable for their acts and subject to the rule of law, with potential disciplinary sanctions. There is no judicial independence without liability.

1. Constitutional Principles concerning the Judiciary

Any study of the judiciary in Spain must start with the text of the Spanish Constitution of 1978.[1] The provision that includes the definition and main characteristics of the judiciary is article 117 of the SC – more specifically article 117.3, which defines the essence of this state power – at the beginning of Title VI, dedicated entirely to the judiciary, reading:

> The exercise of judicial authority in any kind of action, both in passing judgment and having judgments executed, lies exclusively within the competence of the courts and tribunals established by the law, in accordance with the rules of jurisdiction and procedure which may be established therein.

In turn, paragraphs 1, 2 and 4 of the same precept include the main characteristics, which are: independence, irremovability, liability and exclusivity.

Independence is the most important of all the constitutional requisites of the judiciary, as it defines its essence. In order to exercise the function entrusted to him by the Constitution, the judge must act subject only to the rule of law,[2] aside from pressures coming from other powers of the state, from established powers and even from the other judges, while among the members of the judiciary there are no relations of hierarchical dependence. Each judge must develop the jurisdictional function in a sovereign manner and subject only to the legislation in force. Therefore, this guarantee is not only institutional, predicable of the judiciary compared to the rest of the state powers, but also a personal guarantee of each member of the judiciary.[3]

The guarantee of irremovability, which prohibits judges from being dismissed, suspended, transferred or retired for reasons other than those provided for in law (article 117.3 of the SC), is also an instrumental guarantee of independence, as it prevents decisions relating to assignments, as well as sanctions of suspension or dismissal, from being taken arbitrarily or discretionally, exerting undue pressure on judges and magistrates.

The guarantee of exclusivity ultimately serves the same purpose, which is to protect the independence of members of the Judiciary. Exclusivity implies that the courts and tribunals may not, as a general rule, exercise functions other than the jurisdictional function (article 117.4),[4] which is intended to prevent them from acting motivated by interests aside from or contrary to those of their function.

The constitutional guarantee of exclusivity is legally reflected in articles 389 to 397 of the Organic Law of the Judiciary,[5] which establish a strict regime of incompatibilities and prohibitions for members of the judiciary. The main incompatibilities include the impossibility for active judges and magistrates to exercise any jurisdiction other than that of the judiciary, occupy positions of popular election or political designation, hold jobs, positions or paid professions, as well as any type of commercial activity, advocacy or legal representation or legal advice, not even if free of charge. The only occupation compatible with the exercise of the jurisdictional function is legal teaching or research, as well as the production of literary, artistic, scientific and technical creation, and publications arising from such works.

Another essential guarantee of the independence of the judiciary lies in the existence of an autonomous governing body, like the General Council of the Judiciary.[6] The constitutional provision of this body[7] and its subsequent creation by law[8] allowed the Ministry of Justice to divest itself of key competences related to the selection and appointment of judges, in line with strengthening the independence of the judiciary compared to the executive authority.[9]

The other side of independence that guides the actions of judges and magistrates is liability, which is also referred to in article 117.1 of the SC. The system of liability of judges and magistrates is regulated in the LOPJ, specifically, in Title III ('Liability of Judges and Magistrates') of Book IV ('Magistrates and Judges'). The aforementioned precepts regulate certain procedural specialities regarding the requirement of criminal liability for crimes committed in the performance of their judicial duties (articles 405 to 410 of the LOPJ) and also disciplinary liability for infringements of this nature committed in the performance of their profession (articles 414 to 427 of the LOPJ).

The direct civil liability of judges and magistrates was abolished by the Organic Law 7/2015 of 21 July, which amended the LOPJ. The amendment law justified this disappearance in its preamble because this type of liability is 'very rarely used in practice'. The aforementioned law also indicated that this abolition 'aligns the liability of judges with that of other civil servants and complies with the recommendations of the Council of Europe on this matter'. At present, therefore, any party injured by a fraudulent or wrongful judicial act may not directly approach the judge or magistrate, but must rather address their claim to the Ministry of Justice for it to be processed in accordance with the rules regulating the state's patrimonial liability. However,

> if the damages and detriment are the result of wilful misconduct or gross negligence on the part of the judge or magistrate, the general administration of the state, having issued compensation to the injured party, may demand, via administrative channels [...] that the responsible judge or magistrate reimburse the payment

that was made, notwithstanding any disciplinary responsibility that might have been incurred. (Article 296.1 of the LOPJ).

2. Recruitment, Training and Promotion of Judges and Magistrates

A. The Judicial Career

Jurisdictional functions may only be exercised by professional judges and magistrates who are members of the judicial profession (article 298.1 of the LOPJ).

As an exception to this general rule, it should be noted that substitute magistrates and judges, as well as justices of the peace and their surrogates also exercise jurisdictional functions, without belonging to the judicial profession, although not as 'gazetted judges but as provisional tenured offices' (article 298.2 of the LOPJ).

Substitute judges and magistrates shall only be used in exceptional circumstances, where substitution by a member of the judiciary or by a trainee judge proves impossible (article 213 of the LOPJ). Substitutes and surrogates are appointed directly by the General Council of the Judiciary, on the proposal of the Governing Chambers, from among law graduates (articles 152, 200 and 201 of the LOPJ).

There are also justices of the peace, who are regulated in articles 99 to 103 of the LOPJ, as well as in Regulation 3/1995, of 7 June, of justices of the peace. These judges exist only in small municipalities, where there is no Court of First Instance and Preliminary Investigation. They have minimum powers, such as claims for sums of less than ninety euros and attempts at preliminary conciliation in specific private offences which, such as libel and slander, require this procedural step as a condition for filing a complaint and initiating criminal proceedings.

Justices of the peace are appointed for a period of four years by the Governing Chamber of the corresponding High Court of Justice (in Spanish, *Tribunal Superior de Justicia*) on the proposal of a plenary session of the Town Council, which must elect them by an absolute majority (article 101 of the LOPJ). This form of appointment calls into question their independence, since they are elected by a body of the Executive Authority.[10] In addition, as they are not required to have a degree in law (article 102) it can be questioned whether the training they have for the post is adequate. For these and other reasons it is advocated that they should be phased out.

Aside from these exceptions, the judicial profession consists of three categories: from the highest to the lowers rank, they are the Senior Judge of the Supreme Court (in Spanish, *Magistrado del Tribunal Supremo*), the Senior Judge (in Spanish, *Magistrado*) and the Judge (in Spanish, *Juez*).

B. Systems of Accessing the Judicial Profession

The system of accessing the judicial profession is one of the key elements of the legal status of judges and magistrates. However, such a system of access is not defined by the constitutional norm, which is limited to referring the matter back to the legislator to establish it, with the constitutional norm stating only: 'The Organic Law of the judiciary shall determine […] the legal status of professional Judges and Magistrates, who shall form a single body' (article 122.1 of the SC).

Under Article 301 of the LOPJ, entry into the judicial profession shall be based on the principles of merit and capacity to perform judicial duties. The assessment of these attributes tries to be objective, as far as possible, in the different forms of access provided by the law and which are detailed below. Specifically, three systems of accessing the judicial profession can be distinguished: public entrance examination, examination of merit and discretionary appointment.[11]

(i) Public Entrance Examination

The public entrance examination system is the ordinary system of accessing the judicial profession. Passing the public entrance examination, followed by the theory-practical selection course at the Judicial School, allows admission to the category of Judge, combining, as will be seen below, two systems of promotion: seniority and selective examinations. The requirements for sitting the public entrance examinations are: to be Spanish, of legal age, and with a degree in law, as well as not being involved in any causes for disqualification as established by law.

This access system consists in passing a series of highly competitive examinations in which the theoretical knowledge, as well as the rote learning and expository skills, of the candidates are valued above all. Once the examinations, both oral and written, have been passed, the candidates must pass a theory-practical course at the Judicial School, belonging to the General Council of the Judiciary. Both phases are selective in nature, although, in reality, the first phase is much more competitive than the second, in the sense that practically all the candidates who pass the public entrance examination also pass the theory-practical course, although it is true that the evaluation carried out in the second phase may cause changes in the classification order resulting from the public entrance examination phase.[12]

The public entrance examination consists of three theory exercises, all of an eliminatory nature. The first consists of responding in writing to a multiple-choice test comprising one hundred questions relating to the subjects of constitutional law, civil law, criminal law and procedural law, both civil and criminal. The second and third exercises are oral examinations, which consist in presenting orally, and in a limited period of time, before a panel,[13] several topics chosen at random from among those that make up the syllabus. The subjects of civil law, criminal law and procedural law are particularly important at this point, although subjects such as constitutional law, commercial law, administrative law and labour law are also examined.

Once the theory phase has been passed, the candidate enters the Judicial School, which is a selection and training centre for judges and magistrates belonging to the General Council of the Judiciary. During this phase, the candidate will undertake a selection course that must include: a multidisciplinary theoretical training programme; a tutored work experience period in different bodies in all judicial spheres; and a period in which the trainee judges act as substitutes and support personnel. Only by successfully completing each stage will candidates be allowed to progress to the next (article 307.2 of the LOPJ).

The candidates who successfully complete the theoretical course and the work experience will be appointed as judges in the order proposed by the Judicial School (article 307.6 of the LOPJ). Those who do not pass the course may repeat it once. But, if they fail to pass the course on the second attempt, they will be definitively excluded and any rights to access the judicial profession by virtue of the entrance examinations they have passed will lapse (article 309 of the LOPJ).

The duration of the work experience, its nature, the assigned post and the duties of the trainee judges will be regulated by the General Council of the Judiciary, in accordance with the programme drawn up by the Judicial School. The theoretical training programme cannot, under any circumstances, last for less than nine months. The tutored work experience has a minimum duration of four months; the same minimum duration applied to the period during which the trainee judge will carry our substitution or support duties (article 307.5 of the LOPJ).

Trainee judges, who will be referred to as assistant judges, will have a tutor, who will be the presiding judge of the jurisdictional body at which the candidate undertakes this training course. During the tutored work experience period, the assistant judges will carry out duties to support and collaborate with their tutors. In accordance with the LOPJ, these duties cannot extend beyond drawing up drafts of rulings that the judge or rapporteur may, where appropriate, adopt, with any amendments that are deemed apposite. They may also oversee hearings and proceedings, but always under the supervision and guidance of the presiding judge (article 307.3 of the LOPJ).

Having successfully completed the phase of tutored work experience, there will be a compulsory period in which trainee judges will carry out duties as substitutes and support personnel, affording priority to substitute judges in any calls for candidates to perform such roles. During this final phase, they will hold jurisdiction with the same scope as those presiding over the judicial body and will be in the service of the President of the respective High Court of Justice, who will draw up a report on their level of commitment and performance whilst carrying out duties, which will be evaluated by the Judicial School (article 307.4 of the LOPJ).

After successfully completing this period of work experience, the candidate will participate in the choice of destinations to which he will gain access on the basis of the final grade achieved, omni-comprehensive, in the entrance examination phase, the theory-practical course at the Judicial School and the assistant judge phase. At this point the candidate will be appointed as a judge and will enter, for all intents and purposes, the judicial profession, to which he will probably devote the rest of his professional life.

The system described is, without doubt, by far the most common one, since more than 90 per cent of active judges and magistrates have entered the judicial career via this route. The main advantage of the model is, without doubt, its greater respectability and legitimacy in the eyes of the public, as it is a system in which access is based on recruitment by competition or public entrance examination.[14]

However, the system also has certain disadvantages, especially in comparison with others in which practical experience is valued as a form of access, and in which the legitimacy of the system is based, above all, on the social recognition of candidates.[15] It is criticised above all for focusing too much, or almost exclusively, on legal knowledge and the ability to memorise things by heart, leaving out other attributes such as maturity, general culture or the practical experience of the candidate.

Of course, we can only agree with Jiménez Asensio that, in an access system such as the Spanish one, with recruits from among young law graduates without any practical experience, it is the obligation of the state to train them appropriately, either in the access phase, or through suitable continuous training programmes.

It is also criticised because no psycho-technical and/or psychological test is carried out to access the judicial profession, which would make it possible to determine, beyond legal knowledge, whether the person possesses the emotional balance and mental aptitudes required to exercise jurisdictional duties.[16]

This bureaucratic system, prevailing in Spain, tries to be tempered, as will be seen, with some accessory forms of access reserved for jurists of established prestige.

(ii) Merit-based Competition

This modality of admission, colloquially named 'fourth turn' (in Spanish, *cuarto turno*) has been devised for filling one in four vacancies in the category of Senior Judge; that is, the category above that of judges. The other three vacancies are filled by judges through advancement and promotion.

Candidates must be renowned lawyers, and have at least ten years of professional experience (article 311.1 IV of the LOPJ). Their curricula will be assessed (such procedure is known in Spanish as *concurso de méritos*). Candidates are usually lawyers, *procuradores*, civil servants in the Justice Administration and university professors. One in each three fourth-turn vacancies is reserved for senior officers of the court (in Spanish, *Letrados de la Administración de Justicia*; a similar profession to that of court clerks in other jurisdictions). The rationale behind this modality of admission into the Judiciary is to open windows and build bridges between the judiciary and other legal professions, in an attempt to outweigh what is perceived as the memorisation overload that prevails in the open competition for the selection of judges.

Candidates' selection is based, firstly, on their *curriculum vitae*, which is assessed in accordance with the terms, which are approved by the CGPJ. In any case, such terms shall comply with the scale of assessment as set in article 313 of the LOPJ. Such scales make reference to the candidate's academic record, the possession of a doctoral degree, the years of professional experience, scientific publications and lectures or papers presented at academic events or courses, among others.

Those candidates with the best scores undertake a number of case studies and write an expert opinion proposing solutions to the problems advanced in such case studies (article 313.3 of the LOPJ). Finally, those who pass the test undergo a personal interview whose objective is to ensure that the claimed merits are real. In accordance with article 313.7 of the LOPJ, this interview must not turn into an examination of legal knowledge.

Selected candidates undergo a legal training course at the Judicial Training College (in Spanish, *Escuela Judicial*). This course lasts one month and, after that, candidates undertake a professional training internship which may last as much as three months (article 301.5 of the LOPJ).

In relation to this modality of admission, it is important to bear in mind the legislative reform performed through Organic Law 16/1994 (8 November), which empowered the CGPJ to launch merit-based competitions for the filling of Senior Judge vacancies within each judicial speciality among respected lawyers. This reform has permitted the CGPJ to devise specific competitions for specialised branches, focusing on lawyers with a proven track record of expertise in civil law, labour law, trade law, criminal law and administrative law.

(iii) Discretionary Appointment

This system is restricted to lawyers of established prestige. According to Nieva Fenoll, this does not mean that the lawyer shall be well known, although they must be known as brilliant in their field.[17] The assessment of such prestige is to be done by the Plenary of the Judicial Council. One in three vacant positions at the High Courts of Justice is filled through this method, as well as one in five vacant positions in the category of Senior Judge of the Supreme Court.

For the High Courts of Justice, applicants must have more than ten years of professional experience within the limits of the Autonomous Community (in Spanish, *Comunidad Autónoma*). The General Judiciary Council appoints the chosen judge from a slate of three candidates, which is proposed by the Regional Parliament (article 330.4 of the LOPJ). This modality of admission does not imply becoming a member of the judiciary. It only entitles applicants to perform the judicial activity in the scope of the High Court of Justice. That is the reason why the LOPJ states that those who are admitted to the High Court of Justice following this modality cannot be appointed to a different court, unless their possible career is advancement to the Supreme Court (article 331 of the LOPJ). This system has been labelled as a kind of federalisation of the judiciary, since its design seems to be directed at allowing the opening of the judicial system to political sensibilities stemming from the scope of the Autonomous Community.[18]

At the Supreme Court, the highest court in every legal field in Spain, one in five vacancies will be filled by counsel/advocates and other lawyers with established prestige (article 343 of the LOPJ). These lawyers must have more than fifteen years of experience, preferably in the field of law of the branch in which they are going to develop their duties (article 345 of the LOPJ).

Some of these discretionary appointments have been criticised. For this reason, there has been an attempt to make these selection criteria more objective, through the issue of a Regulation.[19] This legal norm is based partly on the case law stemming from the third chamber of the Supreme Court. Such case law deals with certain legal actions against previous discretionary appointments made by the CGPJ.[20] In accordance with the Preamble of this Regulation, three basic principles are to guide the appointment process: (1) The CGPJ acts freely when evaluating the merits of the candidates; (2) in spite of this, the CGPJ decision must comply with the principles of merits and capability; and (3) the decision has to be motivated.

Regulation 1/2010 sets the merits that shall be taken into account for the vacancies, but it also regulates the public notice required for applications, the content of such applications and the motivated proposals of the Qualification Commission of the CGPJ and the proceedings before the Plenary of the CGPJ in order to reach a final decision.

In accordance with the aforementioned Regulation, once the application has been submitted by the candidates, the qualification Commission shall make a provisional assessment of the merits, and they shall exclude those candidates who do not fulfil the legal or statutory requirements. After that, the spokespersons of the CGPJ are summoned to a public appearance of the candidates. At this stage, the candidates shall defend and give explanations about their *curriculum vitae*. Afterwards, the Qualification Commission will deliver its definitive proposal. This proposal is submitted to the Plenary of the CGPJ, who will take the final decision.

C. Promotion and Advancement in the Judicial Career

As already indicated, there are three different categories in the Spanish judicial career: Judge, Senior Judge and Senior Judge of the Supreme Court.

The main system of promotion is based on the seniority of the members of the judiciary. For instance, two out of four vacancies in the category of Senior Judge shall be filled by Judges with three years of tenure (articles 311.1 and 2 of the LOPJ). The third vacancy in the category of Senior Judge shall be filled with members of the judiciary coming from the lower category of Judges, through selective tests if the candidates operate within the field of civil or criminal law. If the candidates operate in the realms of administrative law, labour law and trade law or violence-against-women courts, they must pass specialisation tests. In order to take the test, candidates must have a seniority of two years.

In accordance with article 312 of the LOPJ, selective tests for fields of civil and criminal law shall be aimed at evaluating the skills and legal training of the candidates, as well as their knowledge in the different fields of the legal science. Such tests may require previous courses and may consist in drawing up opinions and reports to be defended before a selection board, or expounding and debating a specific issue before the board. Moreover, if the candidate chooses to operate within the fields of administrative law, labour law or trade law, or in the violence-against-women courts, selective tests must assess specific competences related to those specialities. The CGPJ is the competent body for setting out the regulation of the selective tests and the academic curricula regarding the aforementioned specialities. To this end, the CGPJ issued Regulation 2/2011 on the judicial career.[21]

To be promoted to the Supreme Court as a Senior Judge, three different ways are available: discretionary appointment from among members of the judiciary, selective tests for members of the judiciary and discretionary appointment by the plenary of the CGPJ among respected lawyers with more than fifteen years of professional experience.

Among all the vacancies in each division of the Supreme Court, three of five shall be filled through discretionary appointment by the CGPJ, while two out of five vacancies shall be filled by Senior Judges that have passed selective tests. In the first case, the plenary has to fill one vacancy with one candidate that fulfils the requirement of being a respected lawyer, and two vacancies with candidates from among members of the judiciary, with more than fifteen years of experience, ten serving in the category of Senior Judge (article 343 of the LOPJ). In the second case, candidates must have completed specialisation courses and, also, must have passed selective tests. In the latter case, candidates must also have more than fifteen years of experience and at least five years serving in the category of Senior Judge (article 344 of the LOPJ).

In relation to the chambers of civil and criminal law in the High Courts of Justice, two of three vacancies shall be filled by candidates proposed by the CGPJ from members of the judiciary with the category of Senior Judge and at least ten years of professional experience in this category. In these cases, expertise in the rules of the Autonomous Community's *fueros*[22] is required (article 334.0 LOPJ).

D. Continuous Training

The CGPJ also has competences in the legal training of the members of the judiciary. In this respect, article 433 *bis* 1 of the LOPJ states that the CGPJ must guarantee that members of the judiciary receive high-quality continuous training, which shall be individualised and specialised. Continuous training must be available throughout the entire career of the judges. Therefore, in accordance with the LOPJ, training objectives shall be designed for five-year periods meeting the particular needs of each member of the judiciary (article 433 *bis* 3 of the LOPJ). Nevertheless, the CGPJ barely complies with this provision and so, in practice, judges choose the training courses that they prefer among those which are offered for all members of the judiciary.[23]

As well as the lack of individualisation, a periodic assessment system for members of judiciary is also lacking.[24] In this sense, the LOPJ foresees only an assessment that is seldom done by the CGPJ for the purpose of promotion and advancement (article 433 *bis* 3 LOPJ). The Judicial School is the institution in charge of developing training programmes and implementing formation courses within the Plan for Continuous Training of the Judicial Career. It must also prepare collaboration agreements with entities and organisations that hold expertise in training plans. It specifically develops these tasks through its continuous training service, which is regulated in articles 22 to 30 of

Regulation 2/199 of the Judicial School. Besides this, the LOPJ states that the Plan for Continuous Training of the Judicial Career will hold specific training courses with a multidisciplinary perspective on judicial protection of the principle of equality between men and women, sex discrimination, violence against women and gender perspective applied to legal interpretation and law enforcement (article 433 *bis* 5 of the LOPJ).

3. Spanish Lawyers

A. Spanish Bar Governing Authorities

The governing bodies of the Spanish Bar – in their respective areas – are: the General Council of the Spanish Bar (in Spanish, *Consejo General de la Abogacía Española*), the Bar Councils of the Autonomous Communities and the Bar Associations.

The Bar General Statute (in Spanish, *Estatuto General de la Abogacía*) states:

> the CGAE is the representative body of the Bar associations in Spain. It also performs coordinative and executive tasks. The CGAE is also a legal person governed by public law and enjoys separate legal personality, as well as full capacity to act within the limits of its social purpose. (article 67.1 EGA)

Among its main tasks are the following: to represent the Spanish Bar; to act as the institutional voice of the constellation of Spanish Bar associations; to approve the creation of any School of Legal Practice (in Spanish, *Escuela de Práctica Jurídica*) affiliated to a Bar association; to draft the EGA and submit it to the government for its approval; to respond to any queries that may arise during the application of by-laws or statutory law; to create, regulate and award prizes for the recognition of outstanding achievements in the legal profession; to rule on remedies against decisions of the Bar associations; to give accounts on draft legislation concerning Bar associations; to compile and update the census of Spanish barristers; to avoid the entry of unqualified people into the Bar; and to prosecute illegal or unfair competition. (article 68 EGA).

The Bar Councils of the Autonomous Communities may be incorporated by proposal of the 75 per cent of the Bar associations acting within such territory. They are governed by autonomous (that is, regional) law and may take on certain tasks of the CGAE through delegation (article 66 of the EGA). There are currently ten autonomous Bar Councils.

For their part, Bar Associations are public law legal entities that enjoy full capacity to act within the limits of its social purpose (article 2.1 of the EGA). Among its aims are: the regulation of the activities of the profession; the representation of the profession; the defence of the rights and professional interests of its members; the continuous legal training of attorneys in law; the oversight of professional ethics; the application of the disciplinary regime as a guarantee for society; and the collaboration, promotion and improvement of the functioning of the justice system (article 3 of the EGA).

The territorial scope of Bar Associations may cover a judicial district (in Spanish, *partido judicial*) or even a province. Within their territorial scope, Bar Associations are entitled to organise and promote activities and services – such as to contract civil liability insurance to cover lawyers – of common interest for their members, to act as arbitral institutions and to propose guiding scales of fees. They shall also look after the professional ethics, exercise the disciplinary authority, manage legal aid services and resolve divergences on the legal fees (article 4 of the EGA).

B. The Two-headed Representation before Spanish Courts: Abogado *and* Procurador

As a general rule, any litigant before Spanish courts needs the assistance of two different professionals: Counsel or (the) lawyer (in Spanish, *abogado*) and the (court representative) *procurador*. There is no parallel with the British distinction between solicitor and barrister, which follows the ancient Roman scheme, according to Nieva.[25] Actually, in the Spanish system, the lawyer takes on advocacy both before lower and high courts, limiting the work of the *procurador* to that of bureaucratic representation of clients, particularly deadline monitoring and the receipt and submissions of legal documents.

(i) Lawyers/Counsel

The basic legal norm that regulates advocacy in Spain is the Royal Decree 658/2001 (22 June), which enacts the Spanish Bar General Statute. Its article 1 states:

> The Bar is a free and independent profession, which provides a service to society following the public interest. It is developed within the limits of free and fair competition. It consists in legal counselling and the defence of rights, as well as public and private interests, through the application of legal techniques and legal science, in order to achieve social harmony, and the effectiveness of fundamental rights and liberties and justice.

Lawyers are subject both to legal and statutory law and the rules of ethics of the profession, which are enforced through the disciplinary regime of the Bar Association (article 1.2 of the EGA). This disciplinary regime is enshrined in articles 80 to 93 of the EGA.[26] The rules of ethics are contained in the code of ethics of the Spanish Bar, enacted by the Plenary of CGAE on 6 March 2019. The following issues are regulated in the latter: the independence of the members of the Bar; their obligation to keep professional secrecy; as well as their obligations when engaging with Bar Associations, courts, other members of the Bar, clients and their counterparts. Certain aspects regarding the payment of professional fees are also regulated, and also the obligation of the lawyer to be covered by civil liability insurance.

For many years in Spain, unlike in the rest of Europe, in order to work as a lawyer, it was only necessary to hold a degree in law and join the Bar. Nowadays, both requirements are still compulsory (article 11 of the EGA). But currently it is also necessary to attend certain specialisation courses and to pass the Bar examination. Such courses are additional to the degree in law and are regulated in Act 34/2006 (30 October), on access to the professions of lawyer/advocate/counsel and *procurador* of the courts, as well as in the Royal Decree 775/2011 on access to the professions of counsel and *procurador*. This legislation states that candidates, who must hold a degree in law, shall first attend specialisation courses with a total workload of sixty European Credit Transfer System (ECTS) credits and, after that, shall perform compulsory external internships with a total workload of thirty ECTS credits. These internships are developed in legal firms, under the supervision of a lawyer with at least five years of experience.

Public and private universities and legal practice schools are entitled to organise and deliver the specialisation courses for candidates for the Spanish Bar. When organised by a university, at least a half of the teaching board must be composed of practising lawyers (article 4.3 of Act 34/2006). In the case of legal practice schools, for their courses to be accredited and recognised (that is, valid), they must have concluded previous collaboration agreements with universities (article 5.2 of Act 34/2006).

After having attended specialisation courses and undertaken external internships, candidates must take a written examination which has been conceived for the assessment of their professional suitability. In this examination, both their practice skills and their knowledge of professional ethics are evaluated (article 7.1 of Act 34/2006). The call for examinations shall have a minimum periodicity of one year and cannot set a limitation on the number of candidates (article 7.6 of Act 34/2006). The examination consists in a test of seventy multiple-choice questions that combine both practical and theoretical questions. It is focused on professional ethics, free legal aid, procedural law and certain issues appertaining to the organisational level of the Bar.

Once they have passed the examination, candidates must join a Bar Association which should be the one existing in their province or judicial district. In spite of this, the new member of the Bar will be able to provide their professional services throughout the entire Spanish territory (article 11 of the EGA). In order to join a Bar Association, the following requirements are compulsory: (a) to be a national of Spain, or of an EU member state or a member state of the European Economic Area; (b) to be of legal age and not be under legal incapacity; (c) to hold a degree in law in accordance with Spanish law or hold a degree in law from another country, as far as such degree has been recognised in conformity with Spanish norms, once the additional training has been passed; (d) to pay the admission fee and other periodical membership fees stablished by the Bar Association (article 13.1 of the EGA).

Members of the Bar may be registered as practising or non-practising. In the first case, it is also necessary for the members: (a) to have no previous criminal records that disqualify the candidate for the performance of legal professions; (b) not to be disqualified due to incompatibility, disqualification or legal prohibition for the performance of the legal professions; (c) to formalise incorporation to the Bar Mutual Insurance Company (in Spanish, *Mutua General de la Abogacía*) or to join the social security system in accordance with the appropriate regime (article 13.2 of the EGA).

(ii) Procuradores *(Court Representatives)*

The *procurador* is in charge of the representation of the litigant in the procedure. The legal framework is set up by the Royal Decree 1281/2002 (5 December), which enacts the General Statute of the courts' *Procuradores*. In its article 1, it defines the profession as 'a free, independent and collegiate [one], whose main duty is the technical representation of those who are a party to any kind of legal procedure'.

The rationale behind the existence of this profession is to ensure that the parties and their counsellors take on their judicial duties in an active and efficient manner, and also to decrease the managing workload of the courts. In this sense, the role of the *procurador* is a key one. As stated in the civil procedure Act (article 276), the *procurador* must hand any legal writ and document over to the counterparts of their client, and must do it before submitting such documents to the court. If not, their omission provokes the non-admission of such writ or document. Apart from that, in every civil court in Spain there operates a joint reception service. This service is organised and managed by the Association of *Procuradores* (in Spanish, *Colegio de Procuradores*).

In an analogous way to what has been set out for lawyers, the professional organisation of the *procuradores* comprises the General Council of Courts' *Procuradores* (in Spanish, *Consejo General de Procuradores de los Tribunales*), which operates throughout Spain, the Councils of

Procuradores' Professional Associations of the Autonomous Community and the *Procuradores'* Professional Associations.

The path to admission to the *Procuradores'* Professional Associations is the same as the one for the Bar.[27] Therefore, it is necessary to hold a degree in law and to have attended training courses with a workload of sixty ECTS credits, and, after that, candidates must perform external internships with a workload of thirty ECTS credits. These external internships are developed under the oversight of a practising *procurador* with no less than five years of professional experience. Once the training course and the internship are finished, candidates have to pass an examination to assess their professional suitability.

Their remuneration is established through a legal tariff. This means that their fees must fit certain amounts of money that are set up by the Ministry of Justice through Royal Decree.[28] Despite this, the Royal Decree allows that the fees can be increased or decreased as much as 12 per cent if the *procurador* so agrees with the client. Therefore, the tariffs are in fact approximate prices.

(iii) State Counsel Corps or the Corps of State Lawyers and Other Lawyers of Public Administrations

Finally, when the state is a party to a procedure, the State Counsel Corps (in Spanish, *Cuerpo de Abogados del Estado*) will deal with its representation and counselling before courts, as established in article 551.1 of the LOPJ. State lawyers also deal with the representation and counselling of autonomous bodies, public entities, state-owned trading companies and state-owned charities. The State Lawyers' Corps is integrated in the State Legal Service. The basic norm regulating its profession is Act 52/1992 (27 November) of Legal Assistance to the State and Public Institutions. This act regulates the admission to this profession, which is carried out through public competition among candidates with a degree in law.

The representation and counselling of the Social Security Administration, as well as its managing bodies, joint services and other organisations or entities of a public nature integrated in this administration, are in the charge of the Lawyers of the Social Security/the Corps of Lawyers in the Social Security Administration (in Spanish, *Letrados de la Seguridad Social*). In spite of this, in certain cases, it is allowed to hire particular lawyers in order to deal with these cases (article 552.1, II of the LOPJ).

The representation and counselling of the State Parliament and Senate (in Spanish, *Cortes Generales*), the Central Election Board (in Spanish, *Junta electoral Central*) and other bodies and institutions related to these are in the charge of the legal advisers of the Parliament and Senate (in Spanish, *Letrados de las Cortes Generales*).

Lastly, the representation and counselling of the Autonomous Communities and the local entities are in the charge of their own lawyers, although, as in the case of the Social Security, it is possible to hire particular lawyers to deal with their cases. Also state lawyers are allowed to represent these entities and give them legal advice when there are cooperation agreements between the central state and such entities (article 552.3 of the LOPJ).

Notes

1. Published in the Official State Gazette of Spain, no. 311 (29 December 1978; hereafter, the SC).
2. As established in art. 117.1 of the SC, 'Justice emanates from the people and is administered on behalf of the King by judges and magistrates of the judiciary who shall be independent, irremovable, liable and subject only to the rule of law.'
3. Manuel Ortells Ramos (ed.), *Introducción al Derecho Procesal*, fourth edn (Cizur Menor: Aranzadi, 2014), p. 62.
4. According to this precept 'The courts and tribunals shall exercise only the powers indicated in the foregoing clause and those which are expressly allocated to them by law as a guarantee of some right.'
5. Organic Law 6/1985 (1 July), on the judiciary, published in the *Official State Gazette of Spain*, 157 (2 July 1985) (hereafter, LOPJ).
6. The General Council of the Judiciary is the governing body of the judiciary (hereafter, the CGPJ)
7. In this regard, art. 122 of the SC states: 'The Organic Law of the Judiciary shall determine the setting up, operation and control of the courts and tribunals [...] as well as the statutes and the system of incompatibilities

applicable to its members of the General Council of the Judiciary and their functions, especially in connection with appointments, promotions, inspection and the disciplinary system.'

8. Initially, the CGPJ was created by the Organic Law 1/1980 (10 January), of the General Council of the Judiciary, currently repealed. At present, the responsibilities and composition of this body are regulated in book VIII of the LOPJ, specifically in articles 558–642.
9. Rafael Jiménez Asensio, 'El acceso a la judicatura en España: evolución histórica, situación actual y propuestas de cambio', in Rafael Jiménez Asensio (ed.) *El acceso a la función judicia. Estudio comparado* (Madrid: Consejo General del Poder Judicial, 2001), pp. 115–249, at p. 191.
10. Jordi Nieva Fenoll, *Derecho Procesal I. Introducción* (Madrid: Marcial Pons, 2014), p. 198
11. Nieva Fenoll, *Derecho Procesal I*, p. 192.
12. Jiménez Asensio,'El acceso a la judicatura en España, pp. 115–249, at p. 208.
13. 'The panel that will evaluate the access tests to the judicial profession for the rank of magistrate [...] will be presided over by a judge from the Supreme Court, from the High Court of Justice or from a Division Senior Prosecutor of the Supreme Court or from the High Court of Justice, and the other members will be two judges, two prosecutors, one department chair from the Faculty of Law specialising in the areas covered by the examination, a state counsel, a legal practitioner with more than ten years' experience in the profession and a first- or second-rank court registrar who will act as the secretary' (art. 304 of the LOPJ)
14. Jiménez Asensio, *El acceso a la judicatura en España*, pp. 115–249, at p. 225.
15. Jiménez Asensio, *El acceso a la función judicial*, p. 225.
16. Jiménez Asensio, *El acceso a la función judicial*, p. 201.
17. Juan Fernando López Aguilar, *Justicia y Estado autonómico. Orden competencia y administración de justicia en el Estado compuesto de la Constitución de 1978* (Madrid: Civitas, 1993), p. 160.
18. Autonomous Communities are the different regions of Spain. Spain is not a federation, but the SC establishes a regime of shared competences between the state and the regions. The judiciary is a state competence, but the auxiliary administration that acts within the judicial system is the competence of those Autonomous Communities that have requested it.
19. Regulation 1/2010 (25 February), which regulates discretionary appointments in the judicial bodies.
20. Such case law starts with the judgments of 29 May and 27 November 2006. This doctrine can be considered to be consolidated after two judgments issued on 12 June 2008.

21. Passed on 28 April 2011 by agreement of the Plenary of the CGPJ.
22. The rules of the *fueros* (ordinances, charters) are those that stem from the customary civil law of a given Autonomous Community. They may differ from the general rules of the Kingdom and may be applied by those who have resided for a certain period of time within the territory of the Autonomous Community.
23. Nieva Fenoll, *Derecho Procesal I*, p. 197.
24. Nieva Fenoll, *Derecho Procesal I*, p. 197
25. Nieva Fenoll, *Derecho Procesal I*, p. 218.
26. This rule is complemented by the Regulation of disciplinary proceedings, passed by the Plenary of the CGAE on 8 May 2009.
27. Act 34/2006 (30 October) and Royal Decree 775/2011 on admission to the Bar and the profession of court *procurador*.
28. Royal Decree 1373/2003 (7 November) passing the tariffs for *procuradores'* fees, modified by Royal Decree 1/2006 (13 January).

PART II

Judicial Diversity

5

Diversity and Judicial Independence in Denmark

Peter Gjørtler

> In the second part of the book, devoted to judicial diversity, Peter Gjørtler explains that while judicial independence is now firmly entrenched in the Danish Constitution, the judiciary in Denmark, his country of origin, is still not sufficiently representative of society as a whole.

The Danish judicial system is mainly regulated by the law that constitutes the Procedural Code (*Retsplejeloven*), as adopted by the Danish Parliament (*Folketinget*), which must comply with a limited number of provisions on the judicial system in the Danish Constitution (*Grundloven*).[1]

In accordance with Danish legislative tradition, a law will be reissued by Parliament as a Restatement Law (*Lovbekendtgørelse*) when the number of amendments made to the law warrants codification in the interest of legal certainty. A similar approach has subsequently been adopted by the European Union (EU) in relation to frequently amended legislation, although such EU codifications have informational value only and do not constitute formal reissuing of the legislation.

The current version of the Procedural Code was issued in 2017,[2] and it has received ten amendments,[3] which implies that it may soon become subject to a further reissue. There is no authorised translation of the Code into the English language, although previous versions of the

Code have been translated, and although selected parts of the current Code are available in English from private publishers.[4]

The Code concerns the structure and procedure of the Danish judicial system, comprising both civil and penal jurisdiction, with administrative law being considered as part of civil law and not subject to a separate jurisdiction in Denmark.[5] As for structure, it is the Code that regulates the institutional competences of the courts, judges, prosecution, police and lawyers.[6]

The State Legal Database has registered 264 acts relating to the Procedural Code. The most important are 114 Executive Orders (*Bekendtgørelser*), to which may be added two Executive Orders in a format (*Anordninger*) that is no longer used. The Executive Orders constitute binding acts of general application that have legal basis in specific provisions of the Procedural Code, which amongst other things specify that the Executive Orders are issued by the Minister of Justice. As such, they are similar to the delegated and implementing acts of the European Commission within EU law.

In addition, both the Minister and the Ministry may issue instructions in various formats to the authorities placed below them in the administrative hierarchy. These instructions are binding upon the authorities, but do not as such grant rights to individuals. However, as in EU law, the individuals affected by administrative acts may to some extent rely on the obligation of the authorities to follow instructions.

The instructions include 38 Circulars (*Cirkulærer*), 45 Letters (*Skrivelser*), 43 Circular Letters (*Cirkulæreskrivelser*) and 6 Communications (*Meddelelser*). Some of these instructions have a specific legal basis in the Procedural Code, while other instructions are based more generally on the hierarchical relationship.

Further, the Ministry may issue Guidelines (*Vejledninger*), which are non-binding acts. As in EU law, it is assumed that the Ministry and its subject authorities will follow the guidelines, so that individuals may to some extent rely on an obligation for the Ministry and the authorities to justify any deviation from the guidelines in a specific case. A total of sixteen Guidelines have been issued for the Procedural Code.

Finally, the Procedural Code authorises and obliges the Minister and the Ministry to make decisions and undertake action in relation to specific issues of administration, which typically concern the rights and obligations of individuals under the Procedural Code, but which may also involve approval of acts of general application that are adopted by the subject authorities.

1. Judges

A. The Judicial System

While the Procedural Code has separate sections on civil and penal procedure, the court structure is unified so that the same courts will have both civil and penal jurisdiction. Although larger courts may establish separate chambers for civil and penal matters, the judges will rotate between such chambers and not in general have separate career paths.

The court system essentially has three levels, comprising the Municipal Courts, the High Courts and the Supreme Court. Outside the scope of the present chapter, separate arrangements have been made for the territories of the Faroe Islands and Greenland.

Significant reforms were undertaken in Denmark in 1919, where courts and police were institutionally separated,[7] and again in 1972, where the number of Municipal Courts was significantly reduced, and territorial jurisdiction was aligned with a new system of municipalities so as to have 102 Municipal Courts covering 277 municipalities, where there had previously been 1,090 municipalities.

A further reform was undertaken in 2007, as adopted by Parliament in 2006,[8] when the number of Municipal Courts was reduced to 24, so as to cover a reduced number of 98 municipalities.

In addition to the Municipal Courts, of which each has local jurisdiction, the Maritime and Commercial Court in Copenhagen has nationwide jurisdiction, but only in maritime and commercial matters. Previously, land registration was a task of the Municipal Courts, but this task has now been centralised nationwide in the Land Registration Court (*Tinglysningsretten*).

The two High Courts (*Landsret*), with a total of about 100 judges, have local jurisdiction in the eastern parts (*Østre Landsret*) and western parts (*Vestre Landsret*) of Denmark. They previously had first-instance competence in more serious cases, but now function essentially as courts of appeal, except that individual cases may also be referred from the Municipal Courts to the High Courts, and that certain cases of serious crime may be assigned to the High Courts.

Decisions of the Maritime and Commercial Court are not appealed to the High Court, but may instead be appealed to the Supreme Court, as may also cases that have been referred to the High Court. For cases that have already been heard on appeal at the High Courts, further appeal to the Supreme Court requires leave from the independent Appeals Permission Board.

The Special Court of Complaint (*Den Særlige Klageret*) is located in conjunction with the Supreme Court and may hear cases for dismissals of judges and revisions of judgments in criminal cases under Section 1a of the Procedural Code. It is composed of a judge of the Supreme Court, one of the High Courts, one of the Municipal Courts, a lawyer and an academic.

The Court of Impeachment, provided for in Section 59 of the Constitution, may hear cases on the responsibility of ministers, as well as cases deemed by the King to constitute crimes that are particularly dangerous to the state. In practice, the reference to the King is understood as a reference to the government.[9]

Denmark does not have a Constitutional Court, and in principle any judge may rule on the constitutionality of legislation, although in practice such claims tend to be heard mainly by the High Courts and the Supreme Court.

Finally, the Constitution in section 61 precludes *ad hoc* courts. It may be noted that the Constitution does not otherwise in general address the issue of organisation of courts, but in section 63.2 it does expressly permit the creation of administrative courts. However, no such administrative courts have been created.

B. Judicial Power

The position as a judge is regulated in section 61 of the Constitution, which provides that the Courts of Justice shall be empowered to decide any question relating to the authority of the executive, and section 64, which provides that in the performance of their duties, the judges shall be governed solely by the law. The power of the courts also to decide questions relating to the scope of the authority of the legislature is not expressly set out in the Constitution, but it follows from section 3, which imposes the classic separation of powers between the legislature, executive and judiciary.[10]

The Constitution in section 64 further guarantees judges against interference with the exercise of the judicial function, and it grants judges a special protection against dismissal as well as transfer. Judges can only be dismissed by the judgment of the Special Court of Indictment, and judges are generally not transferred against their will. Administrative leave and transfer may happen in case of a reorganisation and reduction of jurisdictions, such as was the case in the judicial reforms mentioned above.

Judges who are sixty-five may be dismissed on condition that they do not suffer any loss of income until the time when they are due for retirement on grounds of age, which for judges continues to be seventy years. This was previously a maximum age for most public service, but in some sectors, such as university positions, the maximum age has been removed so as to avoid any issue of compliance with the prohibition on age discrimination now found in the European Union Charter of Fundamental Rights.

In addition to civil cases, which as set out above are considered also to comprise administrative cases, and criminal cases, judges at the Municipal Court also have responsibility for probate and enforcement cases, including auctions as part of enforcement.

An associate judge (*Dommerfuldmægtig*) may act as a judge (*Dommer*) to the extent decided by the president of the court in which they are employed, as set out in section 19.1 of the Procedural Code. However, in the Supreme Court, associate judges may only be delegated powers to preside over the taking of evidence procedures, as set out in section 6.1 of the Procedural Code.

In practice, associate judges have to a large extent been delegated the non-judicial aspects of the work of the Municipal Courts. As set out above, land registration, which was previously performed by judges in the Municipal Courts, has been transferred to the new specialised Land Registration Court, and the educational aspect of employment as associate judge has been increased, as further addressed below.[11]

Accordingly, the position as associate judge may be regarded as a trainee position, but it is also a position in which incumbents may remain for the full period of their employment with the option of becoming senior associate judges (*Retsassessor*). It was a point of discussion in Denmark whether the granting of judicial powers to associate judges, employed on contract, complied with the requirement in section 64 of the Constitution whereby judges may be dismissed only by judgment.[12]

This issue was addressed by the insertion of sections 54 and 54a in the Procedural Code, whereby protection is established against dismissal of associate judges. Senior associate judges are employed as civil servants, for whom further protection is provided by section 34 of the Civil Service Law (*Tjenestemandsloven*),[13] which applies to both judges and other legal staff that may be employed as civil servants.

In addition to associate judges, the Procedural Code allows for the appointment of interim judges, as further addressed below. The position as interim judge is equivalent in judicial power to that of a full judge during the time of office, but the employment is contractual, which raises the same issue in relation to Section 64 of the Constitution as for associate judges, and accordingly it has been ensured that Sections 54 and 54a of the Procedural Code also apply to interim judges.

C. Citizenship of Judges

The Constitution provides in section 27.1 that a civil servant (*Tjenestemand*) must have Danish citizenship (*Indfødsret*), which as a concept in Danish law has the same scope as nationality.

Previously, most public employees were civil servants, and section 27.1 therefore presented a problem in relation to the right of free movement for workers in EU law, under which limitations may be placed only on functions that are central to the operation of the state.

At the same time, the Danish Constitution is extremely difficult to amend, requiring two referenda with a qualified majority and an intervening parliamentary election. Accordingly, the issue has been dealt with by indirect means.

One solution has been to move away from the employment of civil servants in many functions, so that public employees instead are hired under commercial contracts, which typically are subject to collective agreements entered into between the state and trade unions. This approach has been taken for the position as associate judge, whereas the position as judge requires appointment as a civil servant.

A second solution has been to adopt section 58c of the Civil Service Law,[14] which provides that persons without Danish citizenship may be employed on conditions parallel to employment as civil servants. This was originally restricted to citizens of the European Communities,[15] presently EU citizens, but later expanded to cover the Nordic Countries, which comprise Finland, Iceland, Norway and Sweden.[16] In relation to both of these developments, the legislation only empowered the Minister of Finance to adopt provisions concerning the scope of the parallel conditions. However, subsequently the provision was expanded to cover all foreigners without additional conditions to be set by the minister.[17]

Despite the wording of section 58c in the Civil Service Law, a requirement of Danish citizenship does continue to be applied in several sectors, as explained by the Minister for Refugees, Immigrants and Integration in reply of 9 May 2007 to a question from the Parliamentary Committee for Citizenship.[18]

In the reply it is mentioned that the Ministry of Justice normally, but not necessarily, will require Danish citizenship for employment as a judge. In any case, the appointment as a judge may be regarded as central to the functions of the state and thus exempt from the EU rights of free movement. However, to the extent that EU citizens are appointed as judge, they will be protected by EU law against any discrimination based on nationality in their further judicial career.

D. The Selection of Judges

The selection of judges may be seen to be covered by the requirement in section 61 of the Constitution, whereby the exercise of judicial authority shall be governed only by statute. This leaves a wide discretion for the legislator to specify selection prerequisites.

Furthermore, the Constitution provides in section 65.2 that laymen (*Domsmænd*) shall participate in criminal court procedures, and provides that the form of participation by laymen shall be regulated by statute, which may be seen to cover also the selection of laymen.

Prerequisites for selection have been established in the Procedural Code, where chapter 4, which is found in part 1 of the Code, covers the selection of judges and associate judges, whereas part 2, with chapters 6 to 9a, and part 3, with chapter 9b, covers the selection of laymen, including also jury members (*Nævninge*) and expert laymen (*Sagkyndige retsmedlemmer*).

For judges, section 42.3 in chapter 4 provides that only holders of a law degree may be appointed. The provision does not set any explicit requirements for the law degree to be held, but the reference used (*Juridisk Embedseksamen*) may be understood to refer only to the traditional law degree offered at the University of Copenhagen and a limited number of other Danish universities.

The word used for appointment (*Beskikket*) is the same as used for the issuing of Practice Certificates for lawyers (*Beskikkelse*), who are also required to hold a law degree. For lawyers, this requirement is interpreted as referring only to classic law degrees and not to cover new interdisciplinary forms, such as degrees in law and business, or law and policy, as further addressed below.

In addition to the formal requirement of a law degree, the Code provides in section 42.5 that for appointment to the Supreme Court, a candidate must first have participated in deliberation of four cases at the Supreme Court, of which at least one must have been a civil case. Effectively, this requires that the candidate must have provided four draft judgments to the satisfaction of the court, but as section 44.1 provides that interim appointment as a Supreme Court justice is not possible, the candidate will not formally be part of the bench deciding the four cases.

For other courts, section 42.4 provides that candidates must normally have been evaluated by the one of the two High Courts prior to appointment as a judge. This refers to the possibility in section 44.2 for interim appointment (*Konstitution*) as a judge, outside of the Supreme Court, where the candidate will have full judicial powers for a period of up to one year, in practice typically nine months, during which they are evaluated by their colleagues at the High Court, forming part consecutively of three different chambers of three judges. However, it should be underlined that appointment is possible under section 42.4 without a High Court evaluation.

Furthermore it should be noted that while section 52 of the Procedural Code requires that associate judges too must also hold a law degree, it is not a requirement for appointment as a judge that a candidate has experience as an associate judge, but such experience may be taken into consideration when deciding on the appointment of judges.

Concerning the use of laymen, who in criminal cases may either sit on the bench together with the judges or sit as a jury, sections 68 to 94 contained in the chapters referred to above do not set any citizenship or educational requirements for such laymen. They may not be lawyers, members of the clergy, or civil servants, as set out in section 70 of the Procedural Code, and in practice it is considered that they should not be jurists. The appointment of laymen is not further considered in this chapter.

E. Selecting and Appointing Bodies

The Court Administration Authority (*Domstolsstyrelsen*) is an independent institution, placed under the administrative responsibility of the Ministry of Justice,[19] which previously managed the courts. The Minister of Justice may not interfere with or amend the decisions of the Authority, which serves also as the secretariat of the Judicial Appointment Council (*Dommerudnævnelsesrådet*).[20] The power to appoint judges remains with the Minister of Justice, but the Council will submit proposals to the Minister.

The structure of the Judicial Appointments Council is meant to represent both the professional needs of the courts and the general interest of society. It is composed of one judge from the Supreme Court, one judge from the High Court and one judge from Municipal Courts, with the latter designated by the Association of Judges (*Dommerforeningen*), which is the trade union of judges.

In addition, it comprises one attorney designated by the Danish Bar and Law Society (*Advokatsamfundet*), as well as two representatives of civil society, designated respectively by Local Government Denmark (*Kommunernes Landsforening*), the trade association of local and regional authorities, and by the Danish Adult Education Association (*Dansk Folkeoplysnings Samråd*).

The competence of the Judicial Appointment Council is set out in sections 43a to 43c of the Procedural Code, and it comprises proposals to be submitted to the Minister of Justice for the appointment of both permanent and interim judges, as well as the appointment of court presidents, whereas the appointment of associate and senior associate judges is undertaken by the Court Administration Authority.

F. The Selection Procedure

Section 5.1 of the Civil Service Law prescribes that appointment as a civil servant may take place only after a public call, unless the appointment follows a trial period. For the Supreme Court, the trial participation in the four deliberations is seen as an integrated part of the recruitment procedure, while for other courts, the evaluation period as an interim judge at the High Court is regarded as a separate employment, so that any subsequent appointment as a judge must be based on a public call.

In practice, a public call is used for all court positions, and for judges, associate judges and senior associate judges, the call is placed both in the State Gazette and on the web page of the Court Administration Authority. In addition, advertising of the positions is undertaken in such newspapers and professional magazines as are deemed relevant.

The general approach to be taken in the appointment procedure is set out in section 43.3 of the Procedural Code, which provides that the appointment must be based on an overall assessment of qualifications of the applicant for the post. This is understood to include both the legal and personal competences of the applicant. In this connection, emphasis is placed also on the breadth of legal experience, as it has become a policy priority that the courts should have judges from different legal employment backgrounds.

However it is the normal, but not mandatory, approach that a candidate for appointment as a judge will have completed the evaluation period of nine months as interim judge at the High Court, as set out above. Accordingly, the evaluation by the High Court will have a very high level of importance.

Furthermore, in relation to the Supreme Court, the Council will only recommend to the Minister the candidate to be selected for participation in four deliberations of the Court, but it is the Court that will finally decide on whether the selected candidate has passed this practical test so as to be proposed for appointment to the position as a judge on the Supreme Court.

This has raised some concern in Denmark as to whether the procedure established with the Judicial Appointment Council is suitable for ensuring a broad representation of civil society on the bench of courts, or whether the system continues, as was previously claimed under the auspices of the Ministry of Justice, to favour selection of judges within a certain professional segment of society.

This question was also raised on the basis of a statistical analysis in 2008 in the journal *Social Economics* (*Samfundsøkonomen*),[21] but in later years some development towards a broader selection of judges has been seen, especially in the appointment of judges of the Supreme Court.

In practice, the selection of candidates to be proposed to the Minister of Justice will be based on an evaluation of written applications, which should preferably be submitted in electronic form on the webpage of the Judicial Appointment Council. The Council will draw up a list of all applicants for a given position, and the applicants will have access to the list as required by section 5.3–5 of the Civil Service Law.

For each applicant, the Council will request the president of the Court concerned to submit an opinion about the applicant. For positions in the Municipal Courts, the president of the Court concerned will first submit a draft opinion to the High Court having local jurisdiction, and subsequently the president of the High Court will submit a final opinion to the Council. This will supplement any evaluation of time spent as an interim judge.

In order to ensure the comparability of opinions, a classification scheme has been informally adopted by the High Courts and revised in 2010,[22] so as to comprise five main categories, with one subdivided in a further three categories:

- Very well qualified
- Well qualified
  - Very assuredly well qualified
  - Assuredly well qualified
  - Well qualified
- Qualified
- Not assuredly qualified
- Not qualified

The Council will evaluate the applications at its monthly meetings, and it may request further information about the applicants and also call them for personal interviews. The Council may request professional assistance for personality assessments, but has so far done so only in relation to positions as court president.

The proposal submitted by the Council to the Minister of Justice will be limited to one candidate, and were the candidate to be rejected by the Minister, the Council would need to make a new submission to the Minister. When making submissions to the Minister, the Council must include information about any dissent within the Council in relation to the submission.

G. Initial Training of Judges

The professional education of judges has been considered for many years,[23] and focus has been placed on the training of associate judges. As set out above, employment as an associate judge may be regarded as a normal, but not mandatory career path for appointment as a judge.

Likewise, peer assessment during a nine-month appointment as interim judge at the High Court may be regarded as part of the normal, but not mandatory career path.

For newly appointed judges following different career paths, training as a judge will take the form of on-the-job training, but for the normal career path, a system of initial training has been established for associate judges. The learning to be achieved was originally based on a proposal from the Court Administration Authority,[24] following a report submitted by the Vision Committee for Court Jurists (*Visionsudvalget for Domstolsjurister*).[25]

The initial training is structured to take place over a three-year period, which is also the case for lawyers, as set out below. The training comprises both on-the-job practical training and theoretical training, and it has four separate modules, which are supplemented by an introduction, internships and a continuous mentoring module. The four modules comprise:

- Enforcement (*Fogedret*)
- Succession (*Skifteret*)
- Preparation of civil cases
- Administration and management

The internships take place annually for a short duration, so as to allow the trainees to experience other courts or entities using the court system. The continuous mentoring system allows the trainee to follow the work of a judge, especially in relation to court hearings and the rendering of judicial decisions.

In the same manner as for lawyers, as set out below, the practical training supplements the mandatory theoretical training, following which an examination must be passed. Apart from an introduction, the subjects covered by the theoretical training comprise the topics of judicial procedure and enforcement procedure, as well as specific topics concerning forced sales, inheritance succession and insolvency succession, to which are added the practical topics of administration and management, accountancy and written communication.

2. Prosecutors

A. Prosecution System

The Danish system for public prosecution is regulated by the law that constitutes the Procedural Code, as set out above. In connection with the 2007 reform, where the number of Municipal Courts was reduced to twenty-four, a major reform was initiated also for the police and prosecution, so as to be gradually implemented between 2007 and 2010. For the police, this entailed a reduction in the number of local police stations and the creation of larger regional police stations, which entailed heated discussion as to whether adequate response times could be maintained.[26]

For the prosecution, the main target of the 2007 reform was organisational changes so as to achieve improvements in competence, strategy and performance measurement.[27] The legislative basis was ensured in the above-mentioned amendment of the Procedural Code, which amongst other things served to diminish the division of competence between the Municipal Courts and the High Courts.

The main structure of the prosecution authorities is provided by section 95 of the Procedural Code, which provides that public prosecutors shall comprise the Chiefs of Police, the State Prosecutors and the Prosecutor General, who all are subject to the Minister of Justice, who shall supervise them.[28] Furthermore, the number of State Prosecutors and the distribution of tasks between them are decided by the Minister of Justice under section 103 of the Procedural Code. This is deemed to comply with section 62 of the Constitution, which requires that the administration of justice is independent of executive authority, as the provision is contained in a chapter that deals only with the courts and their procedure, which may be seen not to comprise the prosecution authorities.

Accordingly, the Procedural Code provides in section 98 that the Minister of Justice may intervene in individual cases and require any of the public prosecutors to commence or desist from proceedings. However, any such direct order must be notified to the President of Parliament together with a statement of reasons. The procedural code does not provide specifically for measures that may be taken by the

President of Parliament but, as mentioned above, the Danish judicial system includes a special court for impeachment, which may be addressed in case of an abuse of powers by the Minister of Justice.

At a practical level, it is the Prosecutor General who supervises the State Prosecutors under section 99 of the Procedural Code, just as the Chiefs of Police in relation to prosecution are subject to the State Prosecutors under section 101. Accordingly, decisions may be appealed to the supervising prosecutor, but further appeal to the Minister of Justice, or in the case of Chiefs of Police, to the Prosecutor General is not possible. However, this limitation only applies to administrative appeal, as access to judicial appeal cannot be limited, especially under the principles of EU law insofar as rights under EU law are concerned. Prior to joining the EU, Denmark had several provisions precluding both administrative and judicial appeals of administrative decisions in specific fields.

In addition to supervision, it is the Prosecutor General who undertakes penal proceedings before the Supreme Court, where a second appeal under section 932 of the Procedural Code is subject to approval by the Procedural Permission Committee, as mentioned above. Such approval will be granted only in principal cases or where other special reasons so warrant. As set out above, the Danish judicial system also comprises a special court for extraordinary review of judgments, which may be addressed also in relation to penal matters.

Under the preceding division of competence, the prosecution authority in Municipal Courts had belonged to the Chief of Police of the municipal police authorities, whereas the prosecution authority in the High Courts belonged to special State Prosecutors that were each nominated with territorial jurisdictions covering regions of Denmark, and an additional State Prosecutor with jurisdiction in cases of serious economic crime and with integration of both investigative and prosecutorial authority.

In principle, this division of competence was not changed by the 2007 reform, but under section 686 of the Procedural Code all penal cases must now be initiated in the Municipal Courts. Unlike the revised provisions on civil cases, which in section 226 allow the Municipal

Court to refer a case to the High Court, no such referral is available for penal cases.

Accordingly, the State Prosecutors in general undertake only appeal cases, and their number has been reduced to two State Prosecutors, each with a territorial jurisdiction corresponding to that of one of the two High Courts, located respectively in the City of Viborg for the peninsula of Jutland, and in Copenhagen for the remaining part of mainland Denmark. In addition, the State Prosecutor for serious economic crime has been maintained.

However, under section 101 of the Procedural Code, the Prosecutor General may decide that certain penal cases are to be undertaken by the State Prosecutors, although the provision does indicate that this applies only until further notice. In practice, the General Prosecutor has issued a Circular Notice in 2012,[29] which provides that certain cases subject to jury proceedings may be taken over by the State Prosecutors.

In general, jury proceedings apply under section 686 of the Procedural Code where a penalty of more than four years of prison or confinement to a mental or other institution may be imposed, as well as cases concerning political crimes. This latter concept is not defined in the Procedural Code, but it is in practice given a narrow interpretation that does not include, for example, terrorist activities, but such activities will most often be covered by the four-year criterion.

It is important to underline that the notice does not provide that the State Prosecutor shall take over such cases, but only that the Prosecutor General may order this in specific cases. This may include cases involving international and EU law, as well as terrorist cases as well as other cases covered by chapters 12 and 13 of the Penal Code (*Straffeloven*),[30] which in practice are seen as including political cases. In general, the notice requires cooperation between the Chief of Police and the State Prosecutor in such cases, where a takeover has not been ordered by the Prosecutor General.

Although the distribution of competences refers to the persons of Chief of Police, State Prosecutor and Prosecutor General, the Procedural Code provides in section 95 that the concept of prosecutors also includes staff hired to assist these in bringing penal cases before the courts. In addition section 100 provides that the Prosecutor General is to be assisted by one or more State Prosecutors with competence to plead before the Supreme Court.

Under section 104, the Chief of Police may designate other persons to bring cases before the Municipal Courts, which is especially used to authorise police officers to act as prosecutors. Likewise, section 100 provides that the Prosecutor General may designate other persons to bring cases before the Supreme Court, while section 103 provides that it is the Prosecutor General that shall designate assistants for the State Prosecutors and may also authorise other persons to bring individual cases before the High Court.

Thus, although many interdependencies exist between the different elements of Danish public prosecution, the reform of 2007–10 has in general achieved a simplified structure that allows the different actors in the judicial system to concentrate on the respective main objectives. The overarching main object for the prosecution remains in section 96 to pursue crime in cooperation with the police, and to ensure both the rapid prosecution of every case, and also to avoid prosecution of innocent parties.

Different from other national systems of penal law, neither the Procedural Code nor the Penal Code allow prosecutors the option of settling cases by agreement, often referred to as plea bargaining. It is only the courts that may, under section 82 of the Penal Code, take into consideration, when deciding on the level of penalty, the cooperation given by a guilty party during the investigation.

However, it remains for the prosecution to decide which cases warrant being brought before the courts, based on the likelihood of achieving a conviction and also on the rational use of available resources, both by prosecution authorities and by the police authorities.

B. Efficiency in Public Prosecution

One of the objectives of the 2007–10 reform was for the prosecution authorities to achieve improvements in competence, strategy and performance measurement.

This was further defined as increasing the quality aspects of prosecution activities, specifically in relation to the development of competences and the sharing of information. Further, it was an objective to achieve an increase in efficiency by the use of modern methods for directing development based on targets and results, including the optimisation of procedures with focus on management and human resources. Within the new structure to be developed, it was also set as a priority to ensure compliance with legal standards by means of strategies to be developed with a focus on issues that reach beyond the competences of individual authorities.

As set out above, the Prosecutor General has a central task in supervising the public prosecution system, and as part of this task the Prosecutor General has also had a central role in initiating measures to be adopted during the reform period 2007–10 and in the following years, where development of the prosecution services has continued. However, an important aspect of the reform has also been decentralisation and the integration of staff members into the development of common goals and policies.

Against this background, the prosecution services now enter into a yearly agreement with the Ministry of Justice concerning targets set and results to be achieved in the coming year. For 2018 the following main targets were set:[31]

- Efficient case processing
- Increased quality
- Increased productivity
- Supervision of penal procedures
- Implementation of good behaviour

The targets, which are referred to as strategic markers, developed over the years 2007–18 for which such targets were published, with some differences between the early years 2007–9, the middle years 2011–15 and the later years 2016–18.

During the early years, the strategic markers were quality, efficiency and legality, thus reflecting the need to adjust the prosecution services to the requirements of the 2007–10 reform. These strategic markers were developed in the middle period to encompass management, IT, working methods and communication, which may be seen as a continuation from the early years, as well as the opening towards a more coherent set of strategic markers for the handling of penal cases between various authorities.

While the terms used for strategic markers in the early and middle years are no longer found in strategic markers in the later years, the issues raised continue to be relevant also for the component markers that are defined within each strategic marker for the later years, which are dealt with in more detail in the following sections.[32]

C. Cooperation between Public Prosecutors

One of the vision statements of the Ministry of Justice is that the entire justice sector is to act as one group, so as to ensure cooperation across the boundaries between the authorities in the justice sector.

Likewise, the group approach is found throughout the period of strategic markers from 2007 to 2018, where the group approach constitutes an informal heading for the first of the 2018 strategic markers, which concerns efficient case processing from the perspective of all authorities involved. As mentioned above, a group approach may also be seen in the requirement of cooperation as the standard approach to any case that could be assigned to the State Prosecutor, but which is left with the Chief of Police.

However, the legislation does not in itself provide further support for cooperation, and in section 103 only provides that the Prosecutor General may transfer a case from one State Prosecutor to another. However, in the development of strategic markers, the prosecution services have clearly granted priority to cooperation, and as a primary tool created a basis for consultation and information sharing.

At the same time, the concentration of staff in larger service units allowed for specialisation that would not have been possible in the previous decentralised model. As set out in the yearly report for 2010,[33] each Chief of Police now has five specialised prosecution services within the force, so as to achieve better quality in the processing of cases.

Although specialisation does not in itself constitute a contribution to cooperation, this was closely linked to information sharing where the use of IT services and the creation of databases were supported to ensure access for all staff to relevant practice information. The information that is added to the knowledge database is also brought proactively to the attention of prosecution staff through use of the intranet.

D. Education of Public Prosecutors

Section 105 of the Procedural Code requires that prosecutors must have a law degree, and while the term used (*Juridisk Kandidateksamen*) is not the same as for judges (*Juridisk Embedseksamen*), and while the term linguistically could be seen only to require a Master's- level degree in law, the term may be understood to refer to the same requirement as for judges. Accordingly the requirement is to have the traditional law degree offered at the University of Copenhagen and a limited number of other Danish universities.

Furthermore, section 105 indicates that prosecutors should normally fulfil the same requirements for practical experience as are imposed on lawyers. As set out below, this entails that a prosecutor should normally have worked three years with relevant legal work prior to appointment, which also applies to assistants to the State Prosecutors, but not to assistants for the Chiefs of Police.

As part of fulfilling the strategic markers, in relation to both quality enhancement and cooperation, a basic education for new prosecutors has been introduced.[34] This is provided for staff with less than three years of employment, as set out in the catalogue for 2018.[35] The education has nine modules of three days each which cover:

- The role of the prosecutor and introduction to good judicial working methods
- The methodology of the prosecutor in relation to good judicial working methods
- Penal procedure
- Court hearings
- Legality and police work
- The role of a case handler
- Communications

- Organisation
- Practice

In addition to the modular basic education for prosecutors, the prosecution services provide access to basic training for non-judicial staff, as well as continuous training for all staff members, but with emphasis on courses for prosecutors. Issues addressed include personal data protection, cybercrime and also technical subjects such as use of DNA-based evidence.

3. Lawyers

A. The Legal Profession

The legal profession is covered by the Seventh Part of the First Book of the Procedural Code. This part has six chapters with a total of forty-five sections. These sections cover all aspects of the legal profession, including the Practising Certificate (*Beskikkelse*) – also in general referred to as *Bestalling* – and both the revocation and reinstatement of the right to practise as a lawyer (*Advokat*), as well as the professional authorities, including the Bar and Law Society (*Advokatsamfundet*), the General Council (*Advokatrådet*), the District Committees and Boards (*Advokatkredse* and *Kredsbestyrelser*), and the Disciplinary Board (*Advokatnævnet*).

Several provisions of the Procedural Code authorise and oblige the Minister and the Ministry to take action in the format of binding and non-binding acts, as well as general and specific acts, as mentioned above. The required format of such acts is indicated in the Procedural Code, to which may be added the implicit powers held by the Minister and the Ministry as public authorities.

Under these provisions, found in sections 119–45, the Minister must adopt rules concerning the requirements for the theoretical basic education, examination and practical test in litigation. Furthermore, the Minister must adopt rules concerning the practice of law from a professional corporation of lawyers in a company format, including ones concerning tests in relation to rules of importance for the legal profession, which must be passed by persons owning shares in a professional corporation of lawyers without being lawyers.

Furthermore, the Minister must approve the statutes of the Bar and Law Society, which concern the organisation and activities of the Bar and Law Society. In addition to this general approval, the Minister must adopt rules concerning the functioning of the Disciplinary Board of the Bar and Law Society, as well as rules concerning the handling of cases by the District Boards of the Bar and Law Society, where these are to assist the Disciplinary Board.

Specifically, the Minister must approve rules adopted by the Bar and Law Society for the legal profession concerning fiduciary funds, security for liabilities, and reporting to the Bar and Law Society of accounting and financial information, as well as necessary control measures.

In addition to this obligation to adopt rules, the Minister may decide to adopt further rules that designate types of activity in the legal field that may count towards obtaining a Practising Certificate for lawyers, as well as rules concerning implementation of the obligation to follow ongoing continuing education.

In relation to EU obligations, the Minister may adopt rules concerning the Practising Certificate, so as to comply with EU requirements, including rules on the handling of disputes concerning the Practising Certificate, and also rules concerning the use of lawyer titles, as covered by EU law, including fines for violation of these rules.

Based on these provisions, the Minister has adopted several executive orders that cover various aspects of the legal profession, including an order on mandatory basic education as a condition for admission to practise law[36] and an order on ongoing mandatory continuing education for lawyers and assistant attorneys.[37]

B. The Bar and Law Society

The Bar and Law Society is covered by chapter 15 of the Seventh Part of the First Book of the Procedural Code. Membership of the Bar and Law Society is mandatory for a lawyer, and use of the title lawyer is reserved for persons with a Practising Certificate, for whom the right to practise as a lawyer is not subject to temporary exclusion and has not been revoked, and who has not voluntarily deposited the Practising Certificate.[38]

The regulatory and administrative powers of the Bar and Law Society, under sections 124–44 of the Procedural Code, include responsibility for the basic theoretical education, examination and practical test in litigation, subject to approval by the courts of whether a case is suitable as the practical test, and subject to the powers of the Minister as set out above.

Furthermore, the Bar and Law Society must establish a Disciplinary Board, and appoint nine of the twenty members of the board from amongst lawyers, with the president and the vice-president of the Board being appointed by the President of the Supreme Court, and the remaining nine members being appointed by the Minister. Likewise, the Society must establish District Committees, and the Boards of the District Committees must support the General Council, and may be called upon to support the Disciplinary Board.

In order to fulfil these obligations, the Bar and Law Society has adopted its by-laws, most recently at the General Meeting of Lawyers on 25 October 2008, as amended in 2009,[39] as well as a Procedural Code of Conduct, which has been adopted by the General Council.[40]

C. Rights and Duties of Lawyers

The Bar and Law Society was established in 1919 and originally served as the sole professional organisation for lawyers in Denmark, ensuring both the supervision and regulation of the profession, as well as representation of the interests of the profession and the provision of professional services.

However, it was found that the mandatory membership of the Bar and Law Society, as a precondition for holding a Practising Certificate and practising law, made it necessary to separate the representation of the profession and the provision of professional services from the tasks imposed on the Bar and Law Society in relation to supervision and regulation.

As a first step, the provision of professional services was placed in a limited liability company, entitled the Service Company for Lawyers

(*Advokaternes Serviceselskab*), of which the Bar and Law Society was the sole shareholder. Subsequently, separate trade associations were established for the legal profession, and one of these, entitled Danish Lawyers (*Danske Advokater*) has purchased the Service Company from the Bar and Law Society. Membership of trade associations, as well as use of the professional services from the Service Company, is entirely voluntary.

However, the Bar and Law Society continues to hold representative functions of the legal profession insofar as these do not concern financial, political or marketing issues. Accordingly, the Society continues to undertake the representative functions connected to the title *Advokat* as well as representative functions vis-à-vis the judiciary, the executive and the legislator.

The objectives of the Danish Bar and Law Society may be summarised in the following manner:

- To safeguard the independence and integrity of lawyers
- To ensure and enforce the discharge of the duties and obligations of lawyers
- To ensure the professional competence of lawyers
- To work for the benefit of rule of law in Denmark

The duties of lawyers to the Bar and Law Society are mainly to respect the norms of professional conduct as defined in the Procedural Code and in the supporting acts adopted by the Minister, the Ministry and the Bar and Law Society, which serve to define the understanding of appropriate professional conduct.

Concerning the rights of lawyers, holding a Practice Certificate, this previously included a monopoly on professional party representation before the courts. However, since 2007 the monopoly has been modified, as set out in sections 260 and 730 of the Procedural Code. Today, any person may act as legal adviser and may appear before the district court in cases heard in the small claims procedure, which are cases with a value of up to 6,700 Euros (50,000 DKK), as well as enforcement cases heard before the bailiff court. In other cases, the parties may appear for themselves, but insofar as they wish to be represented by counsel, this must be a lawyer with a Practice Certificate as set out in section 131 of the Procedural Code, although associate lawyers (*Advokatfuldmægtige*) may to some extent appear on behalf of their principals, as set out in section 136 of the Procedural Code.

All lawyers are entitled to appear before the Municipal Courts under section 132 of the Procedural Code, but to appear before the High Court and the Maritime and Commercial Court requires the passing of a practical test in litigation, as set out in section 133, in the same manner as for obtaining the Practice Certificate. To appear before the Supreme Court requires having practised law for a minimum of five years as a lawyer entitled to appear before the High Court, as set out in section 134 of the Procedural Code, but there is no formal test to be passed in order to be able to appear before the Supreme Court.

Lawyers may practise law acting as sole practitioners or in a grouping of lawyers, as set out in section 124 of the Procedural Code. The only permitted object of a professional corporation of lawyers is to practise law. It is therefore not possible under Danish law to establish multidisciplinary partnerships. If practising in a partnership with others, such a law firm may only be in the form of public limited, private limited or limited partnership companies.

D. Requirements for Licensing

The requirements for receiving the Practising Certificate are set out in section 119.2 of the Procedural Code, which provides as a basic requirement that a candidate must hold a Danish bachelor and master's degree in law. This wording is different from that used for judges and prosecutors, but it effectively refers to the same law degree, which although technically divided into bachelor and master's components, continues to constitute a consolidated programme in law, with a duration of five years.

New interdisciplinary law degrees have been developed in Denmark, such as the law and business programme offered by the Copenhagen Business School, but as mentioned above, such interdisciplinary degrees are deemed not to fulfil the requirements for licensing, although debate on this issue continues.

However, section 135a.1 provides that the Minister for Justice may fix a trial period, where a candidate holds a master's degree in law from another EU member state or any other state with which an agreement has been made. The trial period will constitute a condition for commencing practical training as an associate lawyer. Furthermore, section 135a.2 provides that the Minister may more generally dispense from the requirement for a Danish law degree and the imposition of a trial period, if this should be required by EU obligations.

The candidate must also be legally competent and not under guardianship, not subject to suspension of payments or bankruptcy. As a matter of practical training, legal work must have been carried out for a duration of three years, and additionally the candidate must have followed a theoretical basic education and passed an examination in matters of special importance to the profession of lawyer as well as a practical test in litigation.

Originally, Denmark had no Bar examination, and qualification was obtained on the basis of only the requirement of three years of practical legal work and the holding of a Danish law degree. However, with mutual recognition obligations for legal education, this could have obliged Denmark to grant Practising Certificates to foreign lawyers from EU member states without checking their actual knowledge.

Accordingly, the Bar examination was introduced, and because of the non-discrimination clause in EU law it had to be made applicable also to Danish applicants. This was a departure from the old system, where the lawyer employing an assistant attorney also took responsibility for their obtaining the qualifications to become a lawyer. However, the new system was seen as an improvement in relation to quality control.

For the practice period of three years, section 119.3 provides that the legal work shall consist in participation in general legal practice, including acquiring experience in hearing cases, as an authorised associate lawyer working for a practising lawyer, or in work in a legal capacity in the courts, the prosecution service or the police, in which the hearing of cases forms a substantial part.

According to section 119.4, the Minister for Justice may decide or lay down rules whereby other types of work may be considered.

However, the Minister has not adopted any such rules, and the approval of other types of work in the legal field will therefore be subject to a decision by the Minister in the individual case. In practice, the Minister accepts employment in legal positions in public authorities or private firms as qualifying, though merit may in general only be given with a maximum of two years, and experience gained in such positions is only credited with 50 per cent of the time actually spent in employment.

It may be argued that it would have been preferable to have general rules adopted by the Minister concerning the acceptance of education from other EU member states, but the current provisions in the Procedural Code, granting the Minister a margin of discretion in matters of mutual recognitions, may be assumed to comply with the requirements of EU law.

As for the right of lawyers with Practice Certificates from other EU member states to establish themselves and provide services in Denmark, section 130 of the Procedural Code provides that the Minister may lay down rules on both the right to practise and the use of titles. Such rules have been adopted separately for the provision of services in Denmark by EU lawyers and the establishment in Denmark by EU lawyers.[41]

Rules have also been adopted on mandatory basic education as a condition for admission to practise law.[42] In relation to the question of payment for theoretical basic education, section 8.2 of the Order sets out that payment is made to the Bar and Law Society, while section 8.1 refers to section 126 of the Procedural Code, which provides that a lawyer shall guide an associate lawyer, who is authorised to practise with the lawyer, and that the lawyer shall pay the expenses for the theoretical basic education, examination and practical test in litigation.

E. Theoretical Basic Education, Examination and Practical Test in Litigation

The rules on basic education provide in section 3.1 that the theoretical basic education programme shall consist of twenty course days spread over one year and shall conclude with a written examination as well as that examinations shall be held at least twice a year.

Concerning the content of the theoretical basic education, section 9 of the rules provides that the Ministry of Justice shall set up a course committee, to be supported by the Bar and Law Society, which is to be tasked with laying down guidelines for the content and organisation of the basic education programme, for appointment and dismissal of teachers, and for the theoretical examination. The course committee shall also lay down detailed guidelines for the litigation test, including the possible use of a moot course, following negotiation with the presidents of the High Courts, the Maritime and Commercial Court and the district courts.

The current theoretical basic education includes the following eight courses, each of which has a duration of two to thee days. The issues addressed include:

- Written pleadings
- Relations between the lawyer and the client
- Negotiations, fiduciary funds and money laundering
- Communication
- Understanding accounting
- Professional conduct
- Oral hearings
- Advanced professional conduct

As set out above, the format of the examination is decided by the Course Committee. Concerning the actual examination, section 3.3 of the Executive Order provides that candidates can only enter the examination three times, unless special reasons exist, which is to be evaluated on application by the course committee.

The practical test in litigation takes place in relation to a real case, as provided by section 4.1 of the Order, which specifies that the case may be conducted before a Municipal Court, the High Court or the Maritime and Commercial Court. As set out above, the court shall assess whether the case is suitable for forming the basis of the litigation test, which shall be based on whether the case is of such nature as to enable the assessment of the ability of the candidate to participate in litigation.

However, it may in practice be difficult to find suitable cases for the practical test in litigation, and section 6 of the rules therefore provides for substitution by a moot court, for which the candidate may submit a request to the course committee within the last year of working as an associate lawyer.

The Bar and Law Society is obliged to arrange moot courts at least twice a year, and such moot courts must have participation by one judge and one censor, both appointed by the Bar and Law Society. As for the judge to be appointed, the Bar and Law Society is to base itself on joint recommendation from the presidents of the High Courts, the Maritime and Commercial Court and the district courts.

F. Continuing Education

The obligation to follow ongoing continuing education is set out in section 126.5 of the Procedural Code, which provides that any lawyer or associate lawyer shall participate in ongoing continuing education relevant to the profession of lawyer.

To this legal basis should be added section 130.1 of the Procedural Code, which, as referred to above, entitles the Minister to set conditions for the practice of law in Denmark by lawyers from other EU member states. On this joint legal basis, the Minister has adopted rules on ongoing mandatory continuing education for lawyers and associate lawyers.[43]

Concerning the required scope of education, section 4.1 of the rules provides that the lawyer or associate lawyer shall within a period of three years have participated in at least 54 lessons of continuing education relevant to the profession of lawyer, with each lesson having lasted 45 minutes.

However, certain exemptions apply, including an exemption for a lawyer from another EU member state being subject to similar requirements for ongoing continuing training in the home country. To this may be added that, according to section 5 of the rules, teaching on courses that would have been eligible under section 3.1 may qualify for up to a maximum of 27 of the required 54 hours. Likewise, legal writing at an academic level may under section 6 qualify for up to a maximum of 18 of the required 54 hours.

According to section 13, the lawyer is only required to make a statement concerning fulfilment of the 54-hour requirement for each three-year period, and according to section 7, the lawyer may request that excess hours are carried forward to the next reporting period. However, the lawyer is required to maintain full documentation for the ongoing continuing training, as under section 14 the Bar and Law Society will be entitled to review the documentation on demand.

Conclusion

Judges may be regarded as central to the functioning of a member state, and accordingly the requirements of EU law have little force to create an internal market for free movement of judges. The same may be seen to apply for prosecutors, whereas the market for lawyers is largely subject to the right of free movement. However, interaction with the courts may still be argued to require specific knowledge of the local legal system, and therefore mutual recognition continues to have limited impact on the licensing of practising lawyers.

In Denmark, the education of judges, prosecutors and lawyers has traditionally been on-the-job training, following a classical law degree. Previously, this was formalised only for lawyers, for whom the on-the-job-training was required for the duration of three years. On this background, two developments have taken place.

Firstly, the notion of the three-year programme has spread to judges, where associate judges are subject to the three-year initial training, and to prosecutors, where initial training is offered for staff with less than three years of employment. Secondly, theoretical training and examination has been added as a mandatory element for lawyers, judges and prosecutors.

As for continuing education, this is imposed as an obligation on lawyers, and it may be argued that further development of continuous training for judges and prosecutors should be regarded as an important policy objective.

There is little doubt about the independence of the Danish judiciary, both from a legislative and a practical point of view, and judicial corruption is not in any manner a current topic in Denmark.[44] For the prosecution, the legislative basis is different, as the prosecution is seen as part of the executive, but traditionally Denmark has not seen political intervention in matters of police and prosecution, although recent events in relation to a Chinese state visit caused concern.

For lawyers, rights and obligations are covered by both the legislation and the professional rules of the Bar and Law Society. However, as in other EU jurisdictions, the wish to promote effective prosecution of financial fraud and terrorism entails reporting obligations that may be questioned in relation to the protection of client confidentiality. Although falling outside the scope of the present chapter, this constitutes a topic of priority for future consideration.

Notes

1. Published in English by the Danish Parliament.
2. Restatement Law 1101/2017.
3. Amended by Law 1679/2017, Law 1680/2017, Law 130/2018, Law 503, Law 708, Law 709/2018, Law 710/2018, Law 713/2018, Law 714/2018 and Law 715/2018.
4. The Karnov Group, which issues a compilation of Danish legislation with explanatory footnotes.
5. One of the early authorities on judicial procedure in Denmark was Anders Sandøe, *Ørsted: Om en almindelig frie Retspleje* (Eunomia, Part 3, 1819), published as part of *Processuelle Skrifter i Udvalg* (Copenhagen: Gyldendalske Boghandel & Nordisk Forlag, 1932).
6. The English language does not have a generic term for a practising and licensed lawyer, and although the Scottish term Advocate and the American term Attorney are frequently used, they both have implicit national references. Accordingly, the term Lawyer is used as the generic term in this chapter.
7. Ditlev Tamm, *Retshistorie*, Bind 1: *Dansk Retshistorie* (Copenhagen: Jurist- og Økonomforbundets Forlag 1990), p. 271.
8. Amendment Law 538/2006.
9. See Henrik Palmer Olesen, 'Noget nyt og noget gammelt', p. 22, published in Jens Ole Rytter, *Grundrettigheder* (Copenhagen: Jurist- og Økonomforbundet, 2000), as well as Peter Gjørtler, 'Deux approches de

l'intégration européenne – le Danemark et la Lettonie', in Carine Berbéri and Alexis Chommeloux, *L'Europe en pièces* (Paris: Éditions Le Manuscrit Savoirs, 2017), p. 256.

10. See Henning Koch, 'Grundretlige værdiers prøvelse', in Jens Ole Rytter, *Grundrettigheder* (Copenhagen: Jurist- og Økonomforbundet, 2000), p. 141.
11. See also Merete Schlüther, 'Et rigtigt job', in Rikke Plesner Skovby, Nina Palesa Bonde and Dennis Pagh Asanovski, *Jubilæumsskrift for Dommerfuldmægtigforeningen* (Copenhagen: Jurist- og Økonomforbundets Forlag, 2014), p. 61.
12. See also: *Domstolsudvalgets* Betænkning 1319 (Copenhagen, 1992, p. 283.
13. Consolidation Law 488/2010, as amended most recently by Law 628/2016.
14. Restatement Law 511/2017.
15. Law 384/1990.
16. Law 382/1991.
17. Law 346/1999.
18. Available at the website of the Danish Parliament.
19. Årsberetning 2017, Domstolsstyrelsen (Copenhagen, 2018).
20. Årsberetning 2017, Domerudnævnelsesrådet (Copenhagen, 2018).
21. Samfundsøkonomennr 6 (December) (Copenhagen, 2008), p. 14. See also Michael Gøtze, 'Danske domstole mellem tradition og fornyelse', *Tidsskriftet Politik* (Copenhagen, 2010), 66.
22. Årsberetning 2015, Dommerudnævnelsesrådet (Copenhagen, 2016), p. 19.
23. Betænkning Vedrørende Dommeres Uddannelse, Justitsministeriet (Copenhagen, 1951).
24. Domstolsstyrelsen, J.nr. 2009-3302-0117 (Copenhagen, 2010).
25. Rapport afgivet af Visionsudvalget for Domstolsjurister, Version nr. 1.0 (Copenhagen, 2008).
26. See also *Politikommissionen*, '*Betænkning om politiets struktur*, Betænkning' 1409 (Copenhagen, 2002), as well as Retsplejerådet, 'Betænkning om *anklagemyndighedens struktur, Betænkning*' 1194 (Copenhagen, 1990), and Justitsministeriet. '*Betænkning om en fremtidig statsadvokatordning, Betænkning*' 1523 (Copenhagen, 2010).
27. See also: Virksomhedsstrategi, Anklagemyndigheden, 2017.
28. The Police and Prosecution services issue joint yearly reports, see: '*Politiets og Anklagemyndighedens Årsrapport* 2017' (Copenhagen, 2018).
29. Communication 9755/2012, No. 3/2012.
30. Restatement Law 977/2017.
31. '*Mål- og resultatplan for anklagemyndigheden*', *Justitsministeriet* (Copenhagen, 2018), p. 5.

32. See also, '*Anklagerfaglige fokusområder i retspraksis* I' 2018, Rigsadvokaten (Copenhagen, 2018), which provides the priorities drawn up by the Prosecutor General for the year 2018.
33. Resultater 10, *Anklagemyndigheden* (Copenhagen, 2010), p. 60.
34. *Grunduddannelse som Anklager, Anklagemyndigheden*, p. 6.
35. *Uddannelse, Anklagemyndigheden* (Copenhagen, 2018), p. 10.
36. Executive Order 1473/2007.
37. Executive Order 1474/2007.
38. See sections 120.1 and 140.1, where exclusion refers to a temporary exclusion applicable during the hearing of a case involving revocation of the right to practise as a lawyer.
39. Executive Order 907/2009 approving the amendment.
40. *De Advokatetiske Regler*, revised with effect from 1 October 2018.
41. Executive Order 1429/2007 on the provision of services in Denmark by EU lawyers, and Executive Order 1431(2007 on the establishment in Denmark by EU lawyers.
42. Executive Order 1473/2007.
43. Executive Order 1474/2007.
44. See Årsberetning 2017, *Domstolsstyrelsen*, J.nr. 2009-3302-0117 (Copenhagen, 2010), p. 4

6

Diversity and Judicial Independence in Quebec and Canada

Michel Morin[1]

In this chapter, Professor Morin addresses the issue of judicial diversity in terms of minorities' rights, starting with the cultural-ethnic group of indigenous people in Canada then moving to linguistic diversity in Quebec, a small nation with a strong sense of its distinct identity. He thus paves the way for the case of Wales later developed in the book by Welsh legal experts.

As is well known, Quebec has been a mixed jurisdiction ever since 1774, when the Royal Proclamation of 1763, which had imposed English law upon the colony, was superseded by the Quebec Act.[2] Indeed, in 1774 the British Parliament restored the law pertaining to 'property and civil rights' that had been in force until the conquest of this formerly French colony by the British in 1760.[3] Exceptions were quickly made to the restoration of French law: although the Quebec Act provided for complete testamentary freedom, an ordinance enacted in 1777 introduced English rules of evidence in commercial matters, followed in 1785 by the introduction of optional trial by jury for disputes between merchants or for personal injury.[4] In general, the fields of civil procedure, evidence and commercial law were heavily influenced by the common law tradition. As for Quebec judges, compared to what occurred in other colonies, there was no distinctive pattern for their appointment, apart from the fact that Catholics were eligible.[5] This made it possible for jurists trained before the British conquest to hold judicial positions, although until the middle of the nineteenth century, a majority of judges were anglophones. As in other colonies, security of tenure was only granted by specific legislation, in 1843.[6]

By the 1850s, the confusing mix of eighteenth-century French sources, common law rules and local legislation led to the decision to codify the law. Codifiers were to follow the style and outline of the Napoleonic Code (1804), but a fourth book would include commercial laws. Two codes were adopted: the *Civil Code of Lower Canada* (1865, in force in 1866) and the *Code of Civil Procedure* (1866, in force in 1867). Though the Civil Code retained a large number of local rules (for example, divorce was not allowed), it definitely bore a family resemblance to its French model.[7]

Confederation gave the provincial legislature of Quebec control over property and civil rights and the two Codes that had recently been adopted, with some exceptions such as marriage and divorce, which fell under federal jurisdiction. For about fifty years, the courts often referred to common law precedents when interpreting the Code, but later this became quite rare.[8] Quebec legislation was often based on common law models. It either remained separate from the Code or introduced new articles into the Code that were very ill suited to its overall design.

Finally, in the 1960s, it was deemed that the economic liberalism and the discriminatory family law rules that infused the Code required a wholesale recodification, in order to modernise the law and to protect vulnerable persons.[9] The reform was finally completed in 1991 and the new *Civil Code of Quebec* came into force on 1 January 1994.[10] In 2016, the fourth *Code of Civil Procedure* was adopted.[11] Is has been influenced by a concern for access to justice; however, this chapter will not address this issue. Although the civil law and the rules of civil procedure have been codified, when Quebec judges preside over trials and write their judgments, they behave like other common law judges. These distinctive features are sometimes criticised for adulterating the civil law tradition, although they are generally well accepted by practitioners.[12]

As for the appointment, remuneration, removal and continuing education of judges, it has remained firmly grounded in the common law tradition. The Constitution Act 1867 grants jurisdiction over such matters either to the Federal or to the provincial government, depending on the court involved.[13] This immensely complicates attempts to reform the court system, another issue that will not be addressed here. Instead, we will focus on the requirement of judicial independence; to a lesser extent, we will mention the current importance of diversity in the appointment process and in continuing education programmes. To do this, it is important to distinguish between federally appointed judges, whose status will be discussed in section 1, and judges appointed by the Quebec government, who will be examined in section 2. In both cases, the relevant rules are contained in a few constitutional provisions that are supplemented by legislation, regulations and official webpages.

1. Judges Appointed by the Federal Government

Under the Constitution of Canada, superior courts are the cornerstone of the judicial system. Their eminent position, which is well illustrated by the high level of remuneration afforded to their judges, will be described in subsection (A). Subsection (B) will explain the rules governing their appointment, while subsection (C) will analyse those that pertain to their removal. Subsection (D) will discuss the special cases of the federal courts and of the Supreme Court of Canada. Finally, subsection (E) will briefly present the support provided by Canadian institutions of government for the continuing legal education of judges.

A. The Constitution and the Judicial Independence of Superior Court Judges

In Canada, superior courts enjoy a privileged status under the Constitution Act 1867. Their judges are appointed by the Governor General, who exercises the powers of the Queen in Canada at the federal level, but who acts only on the advice of the cabinet.[14] They must be selected from the Bar of the province in which they will perform their duties.[15] Judges hold office 'during good behaviour', but may be removed by the Governor General on address of the Senate and House of Commons. However, they are required to retire at the age of seventy-five.[16] Their salaries, allowances and pensions must be determined by Acts of Parliament.[17] For their part, provincial legislatures can legislate 'for the Constitution, Maintenance, and Organization of Provincial Courts, both of Civil and of Criminal Jurisdiction'; this power extends to superior courts.[18] It includes the name and jurisdiction of each court, the number of positions, judicial districts and courthouses, and administrative resources.

Currently, all federally appointed judges earn the same yearly salary ($314,100), which is a very substantial sum; the various chief justices earn more ($344,400), while the salaries of the justices of the Supreme Court of Canada ($373,900) and of the Chief Justice of Canada ($403,800) are markedly higher.[19] However, the difference between the salaries of a chief justice and the salary of his or her puisne judges is relatively small, while there is no salary discrepancy between a trial court and an appeal court judge. Furthermore, a generous pension is part of the compensation scheme.[20] In this regard, judges who are eligible for an annuity may elect to become supernumerary judges; this will allow them to receive their full salary until they reach the age of seventy-five while performing significantly reduced duties, for instance, one half of the regular caseload.[21]

The remuneration of federally appointed judges must be revised periodically by an independent advisory committee called the Judicial Compensation and Benefits Commission; however, its recommendations are non-binding.[22] This system was put in place in 1981, but the recommendations of various commissions were either ignored or unimplemented, while the provision for the automatic indexation of judges' salaries were suspended in the early nineties.[23] As a result, in real value, the salaries of judges fell below the mid-point of the salary scale for the most senior federal Deputy Ministers, which was considered a 'benchmark' in 1975; judges expected their remuneration to remain at this level, but the government did not agree.[24] In 1997, the Supreme Court of Canada held that the principle of judicial independence demanded that provincial governments provide rational answers to the recommendations of provincial judicial compensation commissions.[25] As a result, the federal government modified its approach. From 1990 to

2010, but mostly after 1998, the salary of federally appointed judges rose from $140,400 to $271,400, an increase of 93.3 per cent; meanwhile, the Consumer Price Index increased by only 49,7 per cent and average weekly earnings by 62,1 per cent.[26]

Since their creation during the colonial era, Canadian superior courts have enjoyed the special attributes of their British counterparts.[27] Perhaps ironically, these features are well summarised by Quebec's *Code of Civil Procedure*. In that province, the '[...] Superior Court is the court of original general jurisdiction'; therefore, it shall '[...] hear and determine any application not formally and exclusively assigned by law to another court or to an adjudicative body.'[28] In so doing it can apply either federal or provincial law; furthermore, provincial private law may be referred to in order to resolve issues that are not dealt with by the wording of a federal statute or its stated objectives.[29] This Court is also 'vested with a general power of judicial review over all courts in Quebec other than the Court of Appeal, over public bodies, over legal persons established in the public interest or for a private interest, and over partnerships and associations and other groups not endowed with juridical personality'.[30] This power cannot be removed for cases in which '[...] there is lack or excess of jurisdiction'.[31]

Similarly, the jurisdiction to review the constitutionality of federal or provincial laws cannot be removed by legislation, because it forms part of the 'core or inherent jurisdiction' of superior courts.[32] Finally, powers that were exercised exclusively by superior courts in 1867 cannot be exercised by another court, unless this '[...] judicial power [...] is either subsidiary or ancillary to a predominantly administrative function or necessarily incidental to such a function', provided that this does not detract from the core or inherent jurisdiction of superior courts.[33] Judges of a court of appeal are also considered superior court judges within the meaning of section 96 of the Constitution Act 1867.

Judicial independence is also ensured through unwritten constitutional conventions. As late as the 1970s, at least four federal ministers and one provincial minister did not hesitate to call judges to discuss a pending case over the phone. In 1976, the Prime Minister of Canada declared before the House of Commons that this practice would stop.

Following this, both federal and provincial ministers had to resign after it was disclosed that they had attempted to influence a judge.[34]

B. The Appointment of Superior Court Judges and the Recent Concern for Diversity

A federal statute, the Judges Act, provides that a person who is appointed to a superior court must have accumulated at least ten years' standing at the Bar or have 'exercised powers and performed duties and functions of a judicial nature on a full-time basis in respect of a position held pursuant to a law of Canada or a province'.[35] This provision covers appointments both to the trial or the appellate level, such as the Quebec Superior Court or the Quebec Court of Appeal. A Commissioner for Federal Judicial Affairs assists the Minister of Justice in the selection process.[36] To this end, beginning in 1988, independent advisory committees have been put in place in each province. Their composition is currently as follows: one nominee of the provincial or territorial law society; one nominee of the provincial or territorial branch of the Canadian Bar Association; one judge nominated by the Chief Justice of the province or by the senior judge of the territory; one nominee of the provincial Attorney General or territorial Minister of Justice; three nominees of the federal government representing the 'general public'; and finally, one *ex officio* non-voting member, namely the Commissioner for Federal Judicial Affairs or the Executive Director, Judicial Appointments. Each nominating body must submit a list of three persons, from which the federal Minister of Justice may select a member to serve on the relevant committee.[37]

A detailed questionnaire must be filled in by each judicial candidate, who must provide the names of six referees, examples of publications or legal writings, and answers to a long list of questions, including their level of bilingualism. For an appellate court appointment, a provincial court judge or a member of the Bar must follow the same procedure that applies for superior courts; however, the files of federally appointed judges are reviewed by the Minister of Justice and are not assessed by the advisory committee. The role of this committee can be summarised in the following manner:

- Extensive consultations in both the legal and non-legal community are undertaken by the committee in respect of each applicant.
- Professional competence and overall merit are the primary qualifications for judicial appointment. In this respect, Committee members are provided with Assessment Criteria [...] for evaluating fitness for the bench. These relate to professional competence and experience, personal characteristics, and potential impediments to appointment.
- Jointly with this assessment of professional competence and overall merit, Committees must strive to create a pool of candidates that is gender-balanced and reflective of the diversity of each jurisdiction, including Indigenous peoples, persons with disabilities, and members of linguistic, ethnic and other minority communities, including those whose members' gender identity or sexual orientation differs from that of the majority. In doing so, Committees should give due consideration to all legal experience, including that outside of mainstream legal practice. Broad consultations by the committees, and community involvement through these consultations, are essential elements of the process.

The committee can make three types of recommendations: 'highly recommended', 'recommended', or 'unable to recommend' for appointment. The assessment is valid for a period of two years, following which the candidate must submit a new application. The decision of the committee is subsequently forwarded to the Minister. The candidate is only apprised of the date on which the decision was made and is not made aware of its contents. The final decision rests with the Minister, who recommends to the cabinet an applicant whose candidacy has been retained by the committee. The Minister's recommendation is always followed by the cabinet. However, 'the Minister may at his or her discretion seek further information from the committee on any candidate.' Furthermore, if a committee's advice appears to be 'contrary to the information received from other sources by the Minister', he or she 'may ask the committee for a reassessment of the candidate'. This implies that a candidate will not be appointed unless he or she has been highly recommended by the committee. However, it is not known whether some candidates who were not highly recommended have been appointed in the past.[38]

From 21 October 2016 to 27 October 2017, after the process had been revised and all previous applications were discarded, 441 candidates were assessed; 129 were highly recommended, 82 were simply recommended and 230 were not recommended. Only 74 appointments were made during this period, excluding appointments made to a higher court.[39] The following year, 629 candidates were assessed. 125 were highly recommended, 132 were recommended and 372 were not recommended, while 79 appointments were made. The current Liberal government has emphasised the need to appoint more judges who are women, Indigenous, LGBTQ2, members of visible minority or cultural/ethnic communities, or who have a disability. It has also encouraged candidates to self-identify. Therefore, we know that from November 2015 to August 2019, out of 252 judicial appointees, 56 per cent were women; furthermore, 8 appointees were Indigenous, 22 were members of visible minority communities, 12 self-identified as LGBTQ2 and 3 self-identified has having a disability.[40] Still, women represent only 43 per cent of federally appointed judges; for other groups, the gap seems to be larger.[41]

Surprisingly perhaps, candidates are not legally required to be bilingual, even in provinces in which litigants and lawyers can use either the French or the English language; the same rule applies to the Federal Courts.[42] Specific legislation also grants the right to bilingual trials, for instance in criminal cases,[43] or for civil matters in Ontario.[44] In other cases, provincial law provides that judicial proceedings shall be held in English.[45] Therefore, the Minister of Justice must make sure that in each province, there is a sufficient number of bilingual judges to preside over bilingual criminal trials, as well as over the other types of bilingual trials to which litigants may be constitutionally or legally entitled. There does not seem to be any precise rule pertaining to the fulfilment of this obligation.

In general, only candidates with many years of experience (far more than ten) have been appointed. However, for each appointment, there will normally be a large number of candidates who have been highly recommended, at least in well-populated districts. The final say belongs to the Minister of Justice, who enjoys a considerable discretion in this regard. A recent newspaper report shows that in the relatively small province of New Brunswick, many recent appointees were related to, or well known by, a Minister of the Liberal Government.[46] In other provinces, nothing of the kind has surfaced. The Minister of Justice has also acknowledged that information about a candidate's political activities or donations to the Liberal Party were taken into consideration, arguing that this was necessary if there were a need to justify the final decision later.

According to a newspaper report, 25 per cent of appointees had financially supported the Liberal Party in the past, as opposed to a total of 6 per cent who supported either the Conservatives, the New Democratic Party or the Green Party of Canada.[47] This tends to show that Liberal supporters enjoy an advantage when the Liberals are in power. Similar allegations have been made for the period when the Conservative Party was in power.[48] This being said, there is widespread agreement in Canada that after their appointment, judges are truly independent; for instance, they regularly reject government arguments, whether or not the political party that appointed them is in power.

C. Judicial Independence and the Removal of Superior Court Judges

We have seen that superior court judges cannot be removed from office without a motion to this effect from the House of Commons and the Senate.[49] The importance of judicial independence in Canada is well illustrated by the role played by the Canadian Judicial Council (hereafter the CJC). The CJC is composed of all chief justices and associate chief justices of Canadian superior courts. It is charged with conducting inquiries or investigations concerning superior court judges.[50] At the 'request of the Minister or the Attorney General of a province', it must 'commence an inquiry as to whether a judge of a superior court should be removed from office' for being unable to perform his duties due to age or infirmity, misconduct, failure in the execution of his or her office, or being placed in a position incompatible with the due execution of that office.[51] It may also 'investigate any complaint or allegation made in respect of a judge of a superior court' by ordinary citizens.[52]

The CJC has established a particularly rigorous screening process of complaints. For this purpose, it appoints some of its members to a Judicial Conduct Committee.[53] Under the relevant by-laws, the Chair of this committee must determine if a complaint or allegation might be serious enough to warrant the removal of the judge. If such is the case, a Judicial Conduct Review Panel must be established. Its members are designated by the senior member of the Judicial Conduct Committee, who cannot be the Chair. Three of the members must also be members of the Canadian Judicial Council; a fourth member must be a puisne judge, and the fifth must be a lay person (i.e., neither a judge nor a member of a Bar). The panel must 'determine if the matter might be serious enough to warrant the removal of the judge'; if this is the case, an Inquiry Committee will be constituted. Written reasons and a statement of the issues are then sent to the judge, his or her chief justice, the federal Minister of Justice, and the Inquiry Committee. If no inquiry is to be held, the Chair of the Judicial Conduct Committee will decide 'on the most appropriate way' to resolve the matter.

The Council has also adopted 'Procedures' that supplement the by-laws. They confer an important role on the Executive Director of the CJC, who must review any correspondence that 'appears intended to make a complaint' and determine 'whether it warrants consideration', in which case it is referred to the Chair of the Judicial Conduct Committee. The Executive Director must reject complaints that are trivial or vexatious, complaints that are made for an improper consideration or that are manifestly without substance, complaints that constitute an abuse of the complaint process or that do not involve conduct, and complaints that it would not be in furtherance of the public interest and the due administration of justice to consider. This very wide discretion is exercised by an official who is not a member of the CJC; it is not specifically recognised by the relevant legislation and by-laws.

Similarly, the Chair may consider that a matter forwarded by the Executive Director does not warrant further consideration. He or she may also seek additional comments from the complainant, from the judge and from his or her chief justice. If need be, an investigator may be retained to obtain further information. Following this, the matter may be dismissed, held in abeyance pending the pursuit of remedial measures or referred to a Judicial Conduct Review Panel. If the matter is dismissed, the Chair may provide a 'written assessment' of the judge's conduct and express 'any concern' that he or she may have. This is, in effect, a power to reprimand or at the very least to criticise a judge, although the legislation and by-laws are silent about this. This goes hand in hand with the Canadian judiciary's conception of judicial ethics. This is considered a subject fit for discussion among judges, perhaps an opportunity to provide support between peers, but not a basis for the determination of judicial misconduct.

A matter may be held in abeyance, with the consent of the judge and his or her chief justice, to ensure that 'any problems identified as a result of the complaint be addressed by way of counselling or other remedial measures', until such time as the issue has been appropriately dealt with. If the matter is referred to a panel, the Chair must provide written reasons, on which the judge is then invited to comment; these documents are forwarded to the Panel. Alternatively, the judge may be asked to comment on the report of an investigator before the Chair makes a decision on the matter. The Executive Director must notify a complainant of the decision to close the file; in other cases, the Executive Director 'may' do so. The judge and his or her chief justice must receive a copy of a complaint and of the letter dismissing it. However, communications with a judge who remains seized of the matter that is the subject of the complaint may be deferred.

As we have seen, a Judicial Conduct Review Panel may determine that an Inquiry Committee should be constituted. An Inquiry Committee is composed of CJC members; the Minister of Justice may also appoint one or more lawyers having at least ten years of experience. The Minister may require that the proceedings be public. In other cases, the Committee can order that the hearing, or a part of the hearing, be held in private, if this is required by 'the public interest and the due administration of justice'. The committee is not limited to the reasons provided by the Judicial Conduct Review Panel; it may consider any 'complaint or allegation brought to its attention'. It may engage a legal counsel to provide advice and assistance in the conduct of the inquiry.[54]

The judge whose conduct is being examined must be 'afforded an opportunity, in person or by counsel, of being heard at the hearing, of cross-examining witnesses and of adducing evidence on his or her own behalf".[55] The judge must also be given the opportunity to make written submissions to the CJC regarding the report.[56] The CJC may recommend the removal of a judge who, in its opinion, 'has become incapacitated or disabled from the due execution of the office of judge' due to age or infirmity, misconduct, failure in the execution of his or her office, or being placed in a position incompatible with the due execution of that office; it must also forward the record of the inquiry or investigation to the Minister.[57]

The CJC is perfectly free to reject the recommendations of the Inquiry Committee. Furthermore, the decisions of a committee of inquiry can be reviewed by the Federal Court. During the last decade, protracted proceedings have led to the resignation of all the members of an Inquiry Committee, to a request by the federal and provincial ministers of justice that an inquiry be held following the refusal of the CJC to recommend a removal, and to a legal counsel challenging the decisions of a Committee.[58] Whether a court can review the decisions of the Canadian Judicial Council is currently being debated before the courts.[59]

After receiving the report of the CJC, the Minister of Justice must decide if both Houses of Parliament should be asked to approve the removal of the judge. In practice, judges whose removal has been recommended by the Council have resigned before this stage or, in one case, after a joint committee of the Senate and House of Commons recommended the removal.[60] It can be seen that these important procedural safeguards ensure a robust security of tenure for judges. On the other hand, they may very well discourage complainants or shield judges from well-deserved criticism. As well, it should be mentioned that in Canada, judges cannot be held liable for acts performed in their official capacity.[61]

D. Judges of the Federal Courts and of the Supreme Court of Canada

Section 101 of the Constitution Act, 1867 grants Parliament power to constitute 'any additional Courts for the better Administration of the Laws of Canada'. The Federal Court and the Federal Court of Appeal perform this function, but for a limited number of issues. In many cases, the Federal Court has concurrent jurisdiction with the superior courts of each province.[62] It has an exclusive original jurisdiction for administrative law relief 'against any federal board, commission or other tribunal', as well as for some specific issues pertaining to patents of invention or to the Integrated Circuit Topography Act.[63] The Federal Courts Acts protects the status and independence of the judges of these courts, who are generally assimilated to superior court judges; the same holds true for judges of the Tax Court of Canada.[64] The importance of the civil law tradition of Quebec is also acknowledged: prior to their appointment, at least five judges of the Federal Court of Appeal and at least ten judges of the Federal Court must have been judges of the Court of Appeal or of the Superior Court of Quebec, or members of the Bar of that Province.[65]

Section 101 of the Constitution Act, 1867 also provides for the constitution of a 'General Court of Appeal for Canada'. This was done in 1875 with the creation of the Supreme Court of Canada, whose jurisdiction extends to both federal and provincial law. To assuage the concerns of the legal community of Quebec, the Court's constitutive statute specifically provided that two of the six justices were to be appointed from the Quebec Bar, the Superior Court or the court of appeal of Quebec (called the Queen's Bench at the time).[66] Currently, for the six positions (out of nine) that come from common law provinces, a person 'may be appointed a judge who is or has been a judge of a superior court of a province or a barrister or advocate of at least ten years standing at the bar of a province'.[67] This includes justices of the Federal Courts, because they had been members of a provincial Bar for at least ten years prior to their appointment to the Bench. However, at least three Supreme Court judges 'shall be appointed from among the judges of the Court of

Appeal or of the Superior Court of the Province of Quebec or from among the advocates of that Province'.[68] This excludes judges who are no longer members of the Quebec Bar because they have been appointed to a Federal Court.[69]

Furthermore, section 41(d) of the Constitution Act, 1982, requires the unanimous consent of both Houses of Parliament and of all provincial legislatures for constitutional amendments relating to the 'composition of the Supreme Court'; this protects the seats reserved for judges trained in the civil law tradition.[70] Rightly or wrongly, this rule has been considered an obstacle to the adoption of legislation requiring the justices of the court to be bilingual.[71] As for security of tenure, the Supreme Court Act provides that the judges of this court 'hold office during good behaviour, but are removable by the Governor General on address of the Senate and House of Commons'; they must retire at the age of seventy-five.[72] Finally, the court hears only a limited number of cases per year (approximately seventy) for which leave appeal must be obtained from the Court itself, with a few exceptions where a statute grants a right of appeal to one party.[73]

Over the last fifteen years or so, the Canadian government has established a special procedure for the selection of Supreme Court Justices that it is free to modify or even ignore.[74] Currently, an independent, non-partisan Advisory Board seeks out applications and develops a shortlist of three to five names. Following this, the Minister of Justice will consult with the Chief Justice of Canada, relevant provincial and territorial attorneys general, relevant cabinet ministers, opposition justice critics, as well as members of both the House of Commons Standing Committee on Justice and Human Rights and the Standing Senate Committee on Legal and Constitutional Affairs. The Prime Minister will then choose the nominee and publicly announce his or her name. Next, the Minister of Justice and the Chair of the Advisory Board will appear before the House of Commons Standing Committee on Justice and Human Rights to explain why the nominee was selected. The nominee also appears before Members of Parliament to answer questions, but no vote is taken. Following this, the appointment is made.

E. Continuing Legal Education for Judges and the Turn to Diversity

Legal scholars from various countries have taken a wide array of views with respect to how the scope, content and methods of continuing judicial education of judges should be defined. For instance, Benton and Sheldon-Sherman have argued that '[p]rogramming and recommendations for programming should be founded on judges' preferences and needs'.[75] Meanwhile, S. I. Strong has raised objections over the control exerted by the judiciary over continuing judicial education, and has likened it to regulatory capture – that is, the vindication of an organised interest group's goals through government policy at the expense of the public interest.[76] Indeed, 'there is concern that judges may not be the best evaluators of what they do not know.'[77]

Some authors have argued that mandatory continuing judicial education should be implemented in areas that are not necessarily legal in nature but which impinge on the law or affect the administration of justice, such as science, drug abuse, family violence, human rights, and access to justice,[78] as well as in new and emerging areas of law, such as sustainability.[79] Compulsory continuing education in targeted areas where deficiencies have been identified may be preferable to optional instruction, since

> judges who do not believe that they are prone to implicit bias or who do not find such biases problematic may not choose to receive training in this particular subject matter area, even though social scientists and judicial education experts all agree that '[e]veryone, judges … included, harbors attitudes and stereotypes that influence how he or she perceives and interacts with the social world.[80]

This being said, the need for continuing education programmes is widely acknowledged, if not the topics that should be prioritised in this context. It should be said that, in the 1990s, some Canadian judges opposed the very idea of continuing legal education, or the relevance of more specific programmes on 'social context', although this is no longer seems to be the case.[81] Parliament has authorised the Canadian Judicial Council to 'establish seminars for the continuing education of judges'.[82] To this end, the CJC has entered into partnerships with independent, not-for-profit organisations such as the National Judicial Institute and the Canadian Institute for the Administration of Justice[83]. The National Judicial Institute is controlled by judges, who are involved in the planning and delivery of its programmes.[84] As well, during the first five years following a judge's appointment to the Bench, he or she is expected to attend special seminars organised by a local court, although there is no sanction for failing to do so. Travel funds are provided to participate in these activities, often with the prior authorisation of the Chief Justice, but 'each judge is responsible for their [sic] own training.'[85] Important resources are therefore devoted to these activities.

Judicial ethics have also been an important topic for continuing education. The CJC has adopted an ethical framework entitled 'Ethical Principles for Judges'; it provides useful guidance to judges, but it does not have the force of law.[86] Put differently, judicial ethics in Canada 'is premised on the notion that there are not right or wrong answers, but rather preferred choices'.[87] As well, a consultative committee provides confidential advice to judges; however, its members cannot be members of the CJC or sit on committees that examine the conduct of judges.[88]

Finally, attention should be drawn to Bill C-337, which was not adopted prior to the dissolution of Parliament in September 2019, but was reintroduced in December.[89] This bill had three central purposes:[90]

- A new eligibility requirement for lawyers to qualify to become a judge of a superior court in any province – namely, that they must have completed recent and comprehensive education in sexual assault law, as well as social context education, to the satisfaction of the Commissioner for Federal Judicial Affairs.
- Requiring the Canadian Judicial Council (CJC) to submit an annual report to Parliament through the Minister of Justice on the delivery and uptake of sexual assault law seminars established by the CJC.
- Requiring reasons for decisions in sexual assault cases to be recorded or provided in writing.

In this section, we have seen that superior courts enjoy a pre-eminent position in Canadian constitutional law, because they are courts of original general jurisdiction having supervisory powers over governmental agencies, tribunals and inferior courts. They have the power to declare enactments unconstitutional, and can apply both federal and provincial law. The provisions of the Constitution pertaining to superior courts are rather laconic, but they provide for appointments to be made by the federal government, security of tenure, and salaries guaranteed by federal legislation. In practice, salaries are quite generous and do not vary from court to court or between judges, except for chief justices and the justices of the Supreme Court of Canada. Appointees must have at least ten years of experience at the Bar prior to their appointment. They cannot be removed without a resolution of the Senate and House of Commons approving this measure, and they can be fully represented during an investigation following a complaint or request from a Minister of Justice or Attorney General. As for complaints from the public, the Canadian Judicial Council has put in place an extremely rigorous screening process before a public inquiry can be launched.

Judges of the Tax Court of Canada, the Federal Court and the Federal Court of Appeal, who have a limited jurisdiction to apply some, but by no means all, federal laws, enjoy a similar protection under the Federal Courts Act. As for the Supreme Court of Canada, judges of the superior courts, the Federal Courts, and members of the Bar having at least a ten-year experience at the Bar can be appointed to this court; however, to provide expertise in the civil law tradition, three positions are reserved for members appointed from the Superior Court, from the Court of Appeal or from the Bar of Quebec. The Supreme Court of Canada Act provides them with security of tenure. The composition of the Court cannot be modified without a constitutional amendment requiring the approval of the Houses of Parliament and of all provincial legislative assemblies. Finally, the Canadian Judicial Council is responsible for the continuing legal education of judges. Financial resources are provided to this end, including the reimbursement of judges' travelling expenses.

2. Provincially Appointed Judges in Quebec

Provincially appointed judges are not specifically mentioned in the Canadian Constitution, except for the inconsequential Courts of Probate of Nova Scotia and New Brunswick.[91] They owe their existence to provincial legislation. However, the important role that they play has been recognised by the Supreme Court of Canada. Subsection A will therefore analyse the constitutional position of provincially appointed judges. Next, subsection B will consider the Court of Quebec and the appointment of its judges. Subsection C will deal with the issue of remuneration and subsection D will examine the removal procedure. Subsection E will discuss continuing legal education.

A. The Constitutional Protection for Provincially Appointed Judges

We have seen that section 92.14 of the Constitution Act 1867 grants to provincial legislatures the power to legislate for the 'Constitution, Maintenance, and Organization of Provincial Courts, both of Civil and of Criminal Jurisdiction'; this is confirmed by section 91.27, which excludes the 'Constitution of Criminal Courts' from the federal jurisdiction over criminal law and criminal procedure. Despite the somewhat unclear wording of sections 96 to 100, it is now well established that provinces may constitute courts, appoint their judges, and provide for their remuneration and removal.[92] Federal legislation may grant a limited jurisdiction to these courts, for instance over specific indictable offences.[93] Similarly, '[…] provinces may confer to their inferior courts general jurisdiction including actions arising out of federal matters […] in the absence of federal legislation specifying a particular forum.'[94] As mentioned above, the jurisdiction of provincial courts cannot usurp the exclusive jurisdiction conferred upon superior courts by virtue of the Constitution Act 1867 or its core elements.[95]

In 1982, the adoption of the Canadian Charter of Rights and Freedoms transformed the legal landscape.[96] Section 11(d) guarantees to every person charged with an offence the right 'to be presumed innocent until proven guilty according to law in a fair and public hearing by an independent and impartial tribunal'. Therefore, provincial courts hearing criminal trials are constitutionally required to be independent and impartial. In 1985, the Supreme Court of Canada ruled that judicial independence entailed security of tenure, security of remuneration and administrative independence for matters bearing directly on the exercise of judicial functions.[97] However, the court made a point of noting that various provincial schemes could meet these requirements without replicating the relevant provisions of the Constitution Act 1867.[98] In the aftermath of this Supreme Court decision, this new constitutional requirement was limited to provincial courts with criminal jurisdiction.

All this changed in 1997, when the Supreme Court of Canada declared that judicial independence was an unwritten constitutional principle.[99] Focusing on the important responsibilities assigned to provincial courts since Confederation, especially with the advent of the Charter, Chief Justice Lamer noted that 'these statutory courts play a critical role in enforcing the provisions and protecting the values of the Constitution'; it followed that 'they must be granted some institutional independence'.[100] He summarised his lengthy reasons in the following way:[101]

1. It is obvious to us that governments are free to reduce, increase, or freeze the salaries of provincial court judges, either as part of an overall economic measure which affects the salaries of all or some persons who are remunerated from public funds, or as part of a measure which is directed at provincial court judges as a class.
2. Provinces are under a constitutional obligation to establish bodies which are independent, effective, and objective, according to the criteria that I have laid down in these reasons. Any changes to or freezes in judicial remuneration require prior recourse to the independent body, which will review the proposed reduction or increase to, or freeze in, judicial remuneration. Any changes to or freezes in judicial remuneration made without prior recourse to the independent body are unconstitutional.
3. As well, in order to guard against the possibility that government inaction could be used as a means of economic manipulation, by allowing judges' real wages to fall because of inflation, and in order

to protect against the possibility that judicial salaries will fall below the adequate minimum guaranteed by judicial independence, the commission must convene if a fixed period of time (e.g. three to five years) has elapsed since its last report, in order to consider the adequacy of judges' salaries in light of the cost of living and other relevant factors.

4. The recommendations of the independent body are non-binding. However, if the executive or legislature chooses to depart from those recommendations, it has to justify its decision according to a standard of simple rationality – if need be, in a court of law.
5. Under no circumstances is it permissible for the judiciary to engage in negotiations over remuneration with the executive or representatives of the legislature. However, that does not preclude chief justices or judges, or bodies representing judges, from expressing concerns or making representations to governments regarding judicial remuneration.

This innovation (to put it mildly) has been roundly criticised, not least because judges are ruling on the process used to set their own remuneration.[102] This 'measure to protect and enhance judicial salaries' has been described as a 'ridiculously time-consuming and cumbersome solution to a non-problem'[103] for judicial independence, and as a principle 'that appears to operate in large measure for the benefits of the judges'.[104] Furthermore, meeting the 'standard of simple rationality' has not been difficult for provincial governments.[105] Nonetheless, following this judgment, the remuneration of judges increased substantially at the beginning of the twenty-first century. In Quebec, from 1990 to 2010, the salaries of judges rose from $102,380 to $225,737, an increase of 120,5 per cent; meanwhile, the Quebec Consumer Price Index rose by 47 per cent and the average weekly earnings in Quebec increased by 51,3 per cent.[106] Finally, it is worth mentioning that provincially appointed justices of the peace, who perform 'numerous judicial functions – most notably presiding at bail hearings and issuing search warrants – that significantly affect the rights and liberties of individuals', are also protected by the principle of judicial independence.[107]

B. The Court of Quebec and its Judges

In Quebec, the Court of Appeal, the Superior Court, the Court of Quebec and the Municipal Courts are recognised as courts of justice.[108] For the Court of Appeal and the Superior Court, the number of judges, the districts, the jurisdiction and various other matters are regulated by the Courts of Justice Act.[109] This legislation is silent with respect to the appointment, remuneration and removal of the judges of these two courts, because the relevant rules are found in the Constitution Act 1867 or in federal legislation. As for the Court of Quebec, it 'is a court of original jurisdiction in civil, criminal and penal matters and in youth matters'; it also hears administrative law cases or appeals from tribunals or agencies.[110] This last power is subject to the supervisory power of the superior court on questions of jurisdiction.[111]

The Court of Quebec has three divisions: the Civil Division, the Criminal and Penal Division, and the Youth Division.[112] However, with few exceptions, each of its judges 'has jurisdiction throughout Quebec over all matters under the jurisdiction of the Court, whatever the division to which he is assigned'.[113] This is typical of the common law tradition, in which judges are considered qualified to hear any type of case, whatever the area of the law. The Courts of Justice Act also provides for the appointment during good behaviour of 'Presiding Justices of the Peace' who have important but strictly defined adjudicatory power, essentially in criminal matters.[114] We will not discuss the legislative framework pertaining to these justices, which is similar to the one that applies to Court of Quebec judges.

The jurisdiction of the Criminal and Penal division is defined both by the Canadian Criminal Code and by the Code of Penal Procedure of Quebec, which deals with provincial regulatory offences.[115] Similarly, the jurisdiction of the Youth Division is exercised within the limits provided for by the Canadian Young Offenders Act, as well as by the Youth Protection Act and the Code of Penal Procedure (for defendants who are minors) of Quebec.[116] This Division also has an exclusive jurisdiction in respect of adoption.[117]

Only 'advocates having at least ten years' practice' in Quebec may be appointed to the Court.[118] The selection procedure is determined by regulation.[119] It is administered by the 'Secretariat for the selection of candidates for judicial office [...] within the *Ministère de la Justice*'.[120] A competition is held each time one or more positions must be filled, after taking into consideration the needs expressed by the chief judge, or, for a municipal court judge, by the associate chief judge responsible for municipal courts and the relevant municipality. A notice must be published containing the relevant information for candidates, such as the final date for submitting an application in the approved form; the notice may specify the division in which an office is vacant, but this is not mandatory. Compared to the federal procedure for appointing judges, this is not an ongoing process, but a competition targeting one or more positions for a given judicial district.

The members of the selection committee are appointed by the Minister of Justice. The chief judge or the person that he or she designates acts as Chair; two members are designated by the *Barreau du Québec*, one of whom is a lawyer, the other being a 'person who works in law', but whose 'professional activities do not include representation before the courts, promoting the presence of representatives of Québec universities where possible'; two members designated by the *Office des professions* are neither judges, lawyers nor notaries. For a municipal court judge, the Chair of the committee is 'the associate chief judge of the Court of Québec who is responsible for municipal courts or a judge designated by the associate chief judge from among municipal court judges'; as for other members, the rules for the members of the Court of Quebec selection committee apply.

Importantly, for the members that they designate, 'the *Barreau du Québec* and the *Office des professions du Québec* must, on a yearly basis and where possible to do so, tend towards gender parity and promote the representation of cultural communities and that of the population of the region covered by the position of judge to be filled'. Members must undergo the training organised by the secretariat mentioned above. Of course, they are disqualified if there is reasonable cause to believe they will not be impartial towards a candidate. The committee must interview the candidate (whereas the federal committees will do not do this).

To assess the application, the committee must consider a list of criteria, which consist mainly of the candidate's personal qualities, such as integrity, knowledge and experience (both generally and in the legal field), capacity for judgement, insight, level-headedness, ability to set priorities and to render a decision within a reasonable time, and quality of expression. The committee must also consider the candidate's conception of the judicial office and his or her motivation and awareness with respect to social realities, as well as the recognition by the legal community of his or her qualities and competences. Bilingualism is not officially required, but the committee and the Minister of Justice may take this factor into consideration, as the candidates must provide information on this subject when they complete the application form.

The committee, or at least a majority of its members, must recommend to the Minister of Justice three candidates for each office that must be filled, unless it cannot do so, in which case it must explain why this is so. The report must give a 'personalised appreciation of the proposed candidates'. The Minister of Justice then makes a recommendation to the cabinet, which is always accepted. Neither the committee nor the Minister may consider 'political affiliation'.[121] The proposal of a candidate is valid only for the office for which the competition was organised. For each proposed candidate, the head of the secretariat must make the necessary verification with disciplinary bodies, professional orders, police authorities and credit agencies. After the position has been filled, each candidate is informed of the fact that he or she was recommended by the committee, or that a negative decision was made.

If the Minister is of the opinion that, in the best interests of justice, he or she cannot recommend to the cabinet any of the three candidates proposed, he or she may request that the committee propose other candidates who are considered qualified in accordance with the regulation. Where the committee is unable to do so, a new competition is launched. However, candidates who submitted their application as part of the first competition may not submit it again. This reduces the likelihood that a Minister will reject some candidates in the hope that another application that he or she has become aware of will be selected.

However, the regulation requires that everyone involved in the process, including the candidates, must strictly preserve the confidentiality of all applications.

Overall, this regulation significantly reduces the discretion of the Minister, who has no say in the composition of the selection committee; as long as a candidate keeps his or her application strictly confidential, political affiliations or personal connections with the government will not weigh in the process, except perhaps at the final stage, when the Minister must choose between the three candidates that have been recommended by the committee. This is not surprising, since the reform of 2012 took place following a commission of inquiry that rejected specific allegations of partisan interference in the appointment of judges in Quebec; nonetheless, the report emphasised that the 'process is vulnerable to all manner of interventions and influence' and that the 'candidates' political affiliation or acquaintance with representatives of the political party in power may play a role'.[122] As for gender parity, under the revamped appointment procedure, 48 per cent of judges were women in 2019. However, one study found that in the Montreal area, taken together, racialised, Aboriginal and LGBTQ persons represented only 3.53 per cent of judges, much lower than the percentage of these groups in the local population.[123]

C. Remuneration of Court of Quebec Judges

The Quebec government sets the salary of Court of Quebec judges, as well as the additional remuneration of the chief judge, senior associate chief judge, associate chief judge, coordinating judge, associate coordinating judge and judge responsible for the professional development of judges of the Court of Quebec. The other judges receive the same salary, whatever their experience or the judicial districts in which they perform their duties.[124] Pension benefits for judges and their spouses or family are regulated in detail by specific provisions.[125] In addition, a 'Committee on the remuneration of Judges and Justices of the Peace must be established to ascertain, every four years, whether the salary, pension plan and other benefits of judges are adequate'.[126] It consists of three 'panels' of three members: one for the judges of the Court of

Quebec, one for presiding justices of the peace and one for the judges to whom the Act respecting Municipal Courts applies.[127] We will focus on the first of these panels.

The five members of the committee are appointed by mutual agreement between the chief judge of the Court of Quebec, the government and various associations of judges (called 'conferences').[128] If no agreement can be reached, one member is designated by the chief judge and the *Conférence des juges de la Cour du Québec*, one by the chief judge and the *Conférence des juges municipaux à titre exclusif* and the *Conférence des juges municipaux*, one by the chief judge and the association representing presiding justices of the peace, one by the government, and one by all the parties involved or, if no agreement is possible, by the government after consultation with all the parties.[129] A member designated by one or more *conférences* or associations will review the remuneration of the members of those *conférences* or associations with the chief judge. Members are appointed for a term of four years, but they remain in office until replaced or reappointed.[130]

The committee may ask for reports from experts and receive 'observations' from the *conférences* mentioned above or from another person or body.[131] It must consider the following factors: the judges' functions, the need for an adequate remuneration of judges and for attracting outstanding candidates, the cost of living index, the economic situation in Quebec and trends in real *per capita* income, the state of public finances, the level of remuneration of judges and of other persons paid out of public funds, the remuneration of judges exercising similar functions in Canada, and any other factor considered relevant.[132]

The Minister of Justice must table a report of the committee before the National Assembly within ten days of receiving it, or within ten days of the date where the Assembly resumes its activities.[133] The Assembly may approve, amend or reject the committee's recommendations in a resolution that the government must take steps to implement 'with diligence'.[134] If the Assembly fails to act within the thirtieth day of sitting following the tabling of the report, the government must take, with diligence, the necessary steps to implement the committee's recommendations.[135]

Rejecting a report can trigger a court challenge that will censure the government. This happened in 2005 when the Supreme Court of Canada considered that the response of the Quebec government to the recommendations of the committee did not meet the standard of rationality, because the government's position was 'tainted by a refusal to consider the issues relating to judicial compensation on their merits and a desire to keep them within the general parameters of its public sector labour relations policy'. Furthermore, the government 'did not seek to consider what should be the appropriate level of compensation for judges, as its primary concerns were to avoid raising expectations in other parts of the public sector and to safeguard the traditional structure of its pay scales'; as a result, the matter was remitted to the National Assembly for reconsideration.[136] Over the years, the salaries of provincially appointed judges have increased substantially in Quebec.[137]

D. Removal of Court of Quebec Judges

In Quebec, the *Conseil de la magistrature* (hereafter referred to as 'Council') is composed of the chief judge of the Court of Quebec, the senior associate chief judge, the four associate chief judges, a president judge of a municipal court, one of the 'persons exercising the functions of president of the Human Rights Tribunal', two judges of the court appointed upon the recommendation of the *Conférence des juges de la Cour du Québec*, one judge chosen among the judges of the Municipal Courts and appointed upon the recommendation of the *Conférence des juges municipaux du Québec*, one judge chosen among the presiding justices of the peace and appointed upon the recommendation of the *Conférence des juges de paix magistrats du Québec*, and two advocates appointed upon the recommendation of the *Barreau du Québec*.[138] Except for the chief judge and the associate chief judges, the appointments are made by the government.[139]

Power is conferred upon the Council to organise refresher programmes for judges, to adopt a judicial code of ethics, to receive and examine any complaint lodged against a judge, and to hear and decide appeals pertaining to the assignment by the chief judge of a judge to a division or a place of residence that is different from the one mentioned in his or her notice of appointment.[140] The Council may make recommendations to the Minister of Justice pertaining to the administration of justice and cooperate with any body pursuing similar purposes outside Quebec.[141]

The code of ethics is adopted after a meeting has been called to consult the judges to whom it shall apply.[142] It 'determines the rules of conduct and the duties of the judges towards the public, the parties to an action and the advocates, and it indicates in particular which acts or omissions are derogatory to the honour, dignity or integrity of the judiciary and the functions or activities that a judge may exercise without remuneration'.[143] Incidentally, Quebec is the only province that has adopted a binding code of ethics.[144] This may facilitate the task of the Council, which must examine a 'complaint lodged by any person against a judge alleging that he has failed to comply with the code of ethics'.[145] The judge shall receive a copy of the complaint and the Council may ask for an explanation.[146] The Council can decide that the complaint is not justified or 'that its nature or importance does not justify an inquiry'.[147] Conversely, it may decide to make an inquiry; it is obligated to do so if the complaint was lodged by the Minister of Justice or if the Minister requests an inquiry to ascertain whether a judge is suffering from a permanent physical or mental disability that prevents the effective performance of his or her duties.[148] The Council may suspend the judge concerned for the duration of an inquiry.[149]

The inquiry is conducted by a committee of five persons chosen by the Council from among its members; however, up to two ex-members can be selected instead of current members.[150] The committee communicates to the judge a copy of the complaint or of the request made by the Minister of Justice, and calls the complainant and the judge to a hearing where attorneys and witnesses may be heard.[151] If it comes to the conclusion that the complaint is not justified, the Council will notify the judge, the Minister and the plaintiff of the grounds for this decision.[152] If the report of the inquiry establishes that the complaint is justified, the Council may reprimand the judge or recommend that the Minister of Justice file an application with the Court of Appeal.[153]

If this recommendation is followed, the judge is suspended from office until the report of the Court.[154] The government 'may remove a judge only upon a report of the Court of Appeal'.[155]

This procedure has been held to be compatible with the principle of judicial independence, because the grounds for removal are established by a body independent from the government.[156] Furthermore, the Supreme Court of Canada has observed that the Judicial Council of New Brunswick, whose composition and role are similar to those of the *Conseil de la magistrature*, is particularly well positioned to decide such issues, because it is 'a large collegial body composed primarily of judges of all levels of jurisdiction in the province, but also of non-judges whose input is important in formulating' a decision.[157] Its decisions are therefore entitled to deference.

Moreover, a judge who has reached the age of retirement (seventy years) may be authorised by the government, for the period it determines, to continue to hold office. Upon the request of the chief judge, the government may also, for the time it determines, authorise a retired judge to exercise specific judicial functions assigned to him or her by the chief judge.[158] Therefore, a renewal of the authorisation does not depend solely on the will of the government; this removes the threat to judicial independence.[159]

E. Continuing Education

As mentioned above, the Council can establish 'refresher programs for judges'.[160] To this end, the government sets an amount above which expenditures must be approved by the Minister of Justice.[161] Therefore, the Council has a budget at its disposal, part of which is discretionary. Furthermore, the chief judge must designate, with the approval of the government, a 'judge responsible for the professional development of the judges of the Court' and determine his or her functions.[162] In its latest report, the Council mentions the sixteen topics of the various seminars it organised. Most of these pertain to the role of the judge or to specific areas of the law, but one is specifically devoted to 'social realities'.[163]

To summarise: prior to 1982, provincially appointed judges enjoyed only the protection afforded to them by legislation. That year, the

Canadian Charter of Rights and Freedoms guaranteed to each person charged with an offence the right to be tried by an independent and impartial tribunal. Therefore, a provincial court judge who exercises a criminal jurisdiction must enjoy security of tenure, security of remuneration and the administrative independence of his or her court, albeit in a form that is potentially less robust than the guarantees of the Constitution Act 1867. Since 1997, all provincial judges have been constitutionally entitled to have their salaries reviewed periodically by an independent commission that would make non-binding recommendations which the government could then accept or reject on a rational basis. Following this, the remuneration of Canadian judges increased substantially, much faster than inflation, as did those of the Court of Quebec.

Judges of the Court of Quebec are appointed by a committee composed of the chief judge or the person he or she designates, two members designated by the *Barreau du Québec* and two members designated by the *Office des professions*. Therefore, it is truly independent from the government. A competition is held for each position that must be filled, and only three candidates are recommended by the committee. The Minister of Justice may ask that other names be submitted, but the committee may refuse to do so. In such a case, a new competition is launched, and the candidates who took part in the previous competition are ineligible. In this way, the possibility of political influence is greatly reduced, more so than in the federal selection procedure.

An independent committee periodically examines the remuneration of Court of Quebec judges. Its report is tabled before the National Assembly. The Assembly may approve, amend or reject the committee's recommendations in a resolution that the government must take steps to implement 'with diligence'. If the Assembly fails to do so within a thirty-day period, the government must take, with diligence, the necessary steps to implement the committee's recommendations. Furthermore, the response of the government to the committee's report may be deemed insufficient by the courts.

The removal of judges is the subject of detailed regulation. The *Conseil de la Magistrature du Québec*, which is composed almost exclusively of judges, decides if a complaint should form the basis of an inquiry, or if it should be rejected, except when it was lodged by the Minister of Justice. An independent committee of inquiry, composed of members or ex-members of the *Conseil de la Magistrature*, must summon the complainant, the judge, their lawyers and witnesses, and recommend either the rejection of the complaint, a reprimand or the removal of the judge. The Minister of Justice may then ask the Court of Appeal to make a report, following which the judge may be removed by the government. Finally, programmes for continuing education are put in place by the *Conseil de la Magistrature*, which has a budget set aside for these activities. Furthermore, a judge is specifically responsible for the professional development of his or her colleagues. Overall, Court of Quebec judges enjoy guarantees that are practically indistinguishable from those of superior court judges, except for the fact that their salaries are much lower.

Conclusion

The appointment, training, remuneration and removal of Canadian and Quebec judges are firmly anchored in the common law tradition. Appointees must have at least ten years of experience at the Bar, but in practice, they have generally accumulated much more experience. The final selection is made by the executive, although a selection committee vets the candidates at the federal level. In Quebec, the selection committee produces a list of three candidates only. In both jurisdictions, in recent years, larger numbers of women and members of underrepresented groups have been appointed, but the gap remains important, except for the achievement of gender parity in the Court of Quebec.

Remuneration of federally appointed judges is set by legislation; it varies for chief justices or justices of the Supreme Court of Canada, but not for ordinary judges. In Quebec, remuneration is set by the government, but it does not vary for ordinary judges. The relevant legislation provides for the periodic revision of remuneration by a committee whose recommendations are non-binding. Surprisingly, the establishment of such committees has been considered a requirement flowing from an implicit constitutional principle of judicial independence for provincially appointed judges. As a result, the salaries of all judges have increased at a much faster pace than salaries or the Consumer Price Index.

The removal of judges necessitates an independent inquiry by committees established by judicial councils composed exclusively or almost exclusively (in Quebec) of judges. The final decision belongs to the Houses of Parliament and the government for superior judges, and to the Quebec government for Court of Quebec judges, following a report by the Court of Appeal. Judicial independence is strongly protected here. Finally, continuing education is well developed and funded by the government, both at the federal level and in Quebec. Although controversial, diversity has been more and more important in these programmes. Overall, the independence and political neutrality of the judiciary is guaranteed by a number of important constitutional and legal provisions, but also by an ethos acknowledging the important role played by judges in Canada and in Quebec.

Notes

1. Full Professor, University of Montreal; the author would like to express his gratitude to Mr Bradley Wiseman, JD candidate, Faculty of Law, University of Montreal, for his outstanding assistance in the preparation of this paper.
2. *Royal Proclamation (UK)*, 3 Geo III (1763), reprinted in RSC 1985, Appendix II, No. 1.
3. An Act for making more effectual Provision for the Government of the Province of Quebec in North America (UK), 14 Geo III, c 83, reprinted in RSC 1985, Appendix II, No. 2 (1774).
4. This paragraph draws on the following piece, where additional references can be found: Michel Morin: 'Dualism, mixedness and cross-breeding in legal systems: Quebec and Canadian law', in Jean-Paul Saucier Calderón and Herber Joel Campos Bernal (eds), *Viajes y fronteras de la enseñanza del derecho comparado* (Lima: Pontificia Universidad Católica del Perú, Departamento Académico de Derecho y Centro de Investigación, Capacitación y Asesoría Jurídica, 2019), pp. 151–4.
5. Quebec Act, above note 3, s. VII.

6. Philip Girard, Jim Phillips and R Blake Brown, *A History of Law in Canada*, Osgoode Society for Canadian Legal History (Toronto: Published for The Osgoode Society for Canadian Legal History by University of Toronto Press, 2018), pp. 387–8; Jim Phillips, 'Judicial Independence in British North America, 1825–67: Constitutional Principles, Colonial Finances, and the Perils of Democracy', *Law and History Review*, 54/3 (August 2016), 689–742.
7. John E. C. Brierley, 'Quebec's Civil Law Codification: Viewed and Reviewed', (1968)14 McGill LJ 521; Brian Young, *The Politics of Codification, The Lower Canadian Civil Code of 1866* (Montreal: McGill-Queen's University Press, 1994); Sylvio Normand, 'An introduction to Quebec Civil Law', in Louise Bélanger-Hardy and Aline Grenon (eds), *Elements of Quebec Civil Law: A Comparison with the Common Law of Canada* (Toronto: Thomson/Carswell, 2008), p. 25; Michel Morin, 'Blackstone et le bijuridisme québécois de la Proclamation royale de 1763 au Code civil du Bas Canada', in Stéphane Rousseau (ed.), *Un juriste sans frontières. Mélanges Ejan Mackaay* (Montréal: Thémis, 2015), p. 585.
8. Michel Morin, 'Des juristes sédentaires? L'influence du droit français et du droit anglais sur l'interprétation du Code civil du Bas Canada', (2000) 60 R du B, 247–386.
9. John E. C. Brierley, 'The Renewal of Quebec's Distinct Legal Culture: The New Civil Code of Quebec', (1992) 42 UTLJ 484.
10. Jean-Louis Baudouin, 'Quo Vadis?', (2005) 46/1–2; C de D 613–24; Normand, above note 7; Jean-Louis Baudouin, 'What does the future hold for the Civil Code of Quebec?' (2009) 88/1 Can Bar Rev 506–14; Jean Pineau, 'A very brief history of a recodification and its problems' (2009), 88/1 Can Bar Rev 223–9; Rosalie Jukier, 'Canada's Legal Traditions: Sources of Unification, Diversification, or Inspiration?' (2018) 11 J of Civ L Stud, online: <*https://digitalcommons.law.lsu.edu/jcls/vol11/iss1/3*>.
11. *Code of civil procedure*, CQLR, c. C-25.0; Sèdjro Axel-Luc Hountohotegbè, 'De l'ombre à la lumière: l'hypothèse de la renaissance de la filiation romano-germanique de la procédure civile québécoise' (2015) 60/2 RD McGill.
12. See the discussion in Morin, above note 4 at 154–7; Jukier, 'Impact', above note 11; Jukier, 'Canada's Legal Traditions', above note 10.
13. Constitution Act 1867, c. 3 (UK).
14. Constitution Act 1867, c. 3 (UK), s. 96.
15. Constitution Act 1867, c. 3 (UK), ss. 97–8.
16. Constitution Act 1867, c. 3 (UK).
17. Constitution Act 1867, c. 3 (UK), s. 100.

18. Constitution Act, 1867, c. 3 (U.K.), s. 92.14.
19. Judges Act, RSC (1985) c.j-1, ss. 9–22.
20. Judges Act, RSC (1985) c.j-1, s. 42 and fol.
21. Judges Act, RSC (1985) c.j-1, s. 29; in New Brunswick this privilege has been held to be constitutionally protected by the principle of security of remuneration: *Mackin v. New Brunswick (Minister of Finance)*; *Rice v. New Brunswick, 2002 SCC 13*, [2001] 1 SCR 403.
22. Judges Act, above note 19, ss. 26–26.4.
23. Graeme Bowbrick, *Judicial Compensation in Canada: An Examination of the Judicial Compensation Experience in Selected Canadian Jurisdictions 1990–2010* (submitted in partial fulfilment of the requirements of the degree of Master of Law, University of British Columbia, 2013) (unpublished), pp. 90–1; Peter H Russell, *The Judiciary in Canada: The Third Branch of Government* (Toronto: McGraw-Hill Ryerson, 1987), pp. 152–3.
24. Bowbrick, *Judicial Compensation in Canada*, p. 91.
25. *Reference re Remuneration of Judges of the Provincial Court (PEI)*, [1997] 3 SCR 3.
26. Bowbrick, *Judicial Compensation in Canada*, pp. 97–106.
27. Mark Walters, 'The British Legal Tradition in Canadian Constitutional Law', in *The Oxford Handbook of the Canadian Constitution* (New York: Oxford University Press, 2018), pp. 115–16.
28. Code of civil procedure, above note 11, s. 33.
29. Interpretation Act, RCS (1985), c. I-21, s. 8.1–2.
30. Code of civil procedure, above note 11, s. 34.
31. Code of civil procedure, above note 11, s. 34; this restriction has been considered an implicit constitutional requirement: *Crevier v. AG (Québec)*, [1981] 2 SCR 220.
32. *R v. Ahmad, 2011 SCC 6*, [2011] 1 SCR 110 at paras 61–2.
33. *R v. Ahmad, 2011 SCC 6*, [2011] 1 SCR 110 at paras 57–9; *Trial Lawyers Association of British Columbia v. British Columbia (Attorney General), 2014 SCC 59*, [2014] 3 SCR 31.
34. See Russell, *The Judiciary in Canada*, pp. 78–81; Adam Dodek and Richard Devlin, 'Fighting words: regulating judges in Canada', in *Regulating Judges: Beyond Independence and Accountability* (Cheltenham: Edward Elgar, 2016), 76 at 84; for Professor Valois, judicial independence contributes to a differentiation of social roles and insulates the legal system from extra-legal influences: Martine Valois, *Judicial Independence: Keeping Law at a Distance from Politics* (Markham, ON: LexisNexis, 2013), pp. 220–45.
35. Judges Act, s. 3.

36. Judges Act, ss. 73–4; on the importance of political patronage until 1987, see Russell, *The Judiciary in Canada*, pp. 112–24.
37. Office of the Commissioner for Federal Judicial Affairs Canada, 'Guide for Candidates', online: *<https://www.fja.gc.ca/appointments-nominations/guideCandidates-eng.html#Judicial>*.
38. Sean Fine, 'Four of six judges appointed to New Brunswick courts have links to Liberal cabinet minister Dominic LeBlanc', *Globe and Mail* (2 July 2019), online: *<https://www.theglobeandmail.com/canada/article-four-of-six-judges-appointed-to-new-brunswick-federal-branch-have/>*.
39. Office of the Commissioner for Federal Judicial Affairs Canada, 'Statistics regarding Judicial Applicants and Appointees, October 21, 2016–October 27, 2017', online: *<https://www.fja.gc.ca/appointments-nominations/StatisticsCandidate-StatistiquesCandidat-2017-eng.html>*.
40. Department of Justice Canada Minister's Transition Book (Pocket version).
41. Sean Fine, 'Federal judiciary edges closer to gender parity, but numbers of minorities drop', *Globe and Mail* (11 November 2019).
42. Constitution Act, 1867, ss. 133 (Quebec and Federal Courts, Canadian Charter of Rights and Freedoms, Part I of the Constitution Act, 1982), being Schedule B to the Canada Act 1982 (UK) 1982, s. 19(2) (New Brunswick); Manitoba Act, 1870, S.C. 1870, c. 3, s. 23.
43. Criminal Code, RSC (1985), c. C-46, s. 530.
44. Courts of Justice Act, RSO 1990, c. C.4, s3, s. 126.
45. *Conseil scolaire francophone de la Colombie-Britannique v. British Columbia, 2013 SCC 42*, [2013] 2 SCR 744; *Bessette v. British Columbia (Attorney General), 2019 SCC 31*.
46. Fine, 'Federal judiciary edges closer'.
47. Daniel Leblanc, 'Justice minister says he will keep looking at partisan past of prospective judges', *Globe and Mail* (30 April 2019).
48. Sean Fine, 'Stephen Harper's courts: How the judiciary has been remade', *Globe and Mail* (24 July 2015).
49. Constitution Act 1867, s. 99(1).
50. Judges Act, ss. 59(1) and 60(2).
51. Judges Act, ss. 63(1) and 65(2).
52. Judges Act, s. 63(2).
53. Canadian Judicial Council Inquiries and Investigations By-laws, 2015, SOR/2015-203, s. 2.
54. Canadian Judicial Council Inquiries and Investigations By-laws, 2015, s. 4.
55. Judges Act, s. 64.
56. Canadian Judicial Council Inquiries and Investigations By-laws, 2015, s. 9(1).

57. Judges Act, ss. 65(1) and (2).
58. Luc Huppé, *Histoire des institutions judiciaires du Canada* (Montreal: Wilson and Lafleur, 2007), pp. 215–17, 242–3, 262–3, 275–9 and 520–1; see also Dodek and Devlin, 'Fighting words', 90–1.
59. The Federal Court of Appeal has decided that the Federal Court can review the decisions of the Council, which has announced its intention to seek leave to appeal from the Supreme Court of Canada: *Canada (Judicial Council) v. Girouard, 2019 FCA 148.*
60. William A Kaplan, *Bad Judgment: The Case of Mr. Justice Leo A. Landreville* (Toronto: University of Toronto Press, 1996).
61. Dodek and Devlin, 'Fighting words', 93; *Morier and Boily v. Rivard,* [1985] 2 SCR 716; see also *Ernst v. Alberta Energy Regulator, 2017 SCC 1,* [2017] 1 SCR 3.
62. Federal Courts Act, RSC (1985), c. F-7, ss. 17, 20(2), 22 and 23.
63. Federal Courts Act, RSC (1985), c. F-7, ss. 18 and 20(1).
64. Federal Courts Act, RSC (1985), c. F-7, ss. 5.3 and 8; *Tax Court of Canada Act*, RSC (1985), c. T-2 2019, ss. 4(3) and 7.
65. Federal Courts Act, note 89, s. 5.4.
66. *Reference re Supreme Court Act*, ss. 5 and 6, [2014] SCC 21, [2014] 1 SCR 433 at para. 21.
67. Supreme Court Act, RSC (1985), c. S-26, s. 5.
68. Supreme Court Act, RSC (1985), c. S-26, s. 6.
69. *Reference re Supreme Court Act*, ss. 5 and 6, 2014 SCC 21, note 93; on the other hand, section 98 of the Constitution Act 1867 does not prevent the appointment to a superior court in Quebec of a justice of a Federal Court: *Quebec (Attorney General) v. Canada (Attorney General), 2015 SCC 22,* [2015] 1 SCR 179.
70. Constitution Act, 1982, c. 11 (UK), Schedule B, s. 41(d); however, six months after the resolution of the House of Commons, an amendment may be proclaimed without the consent of the Senate, if the Commons renew their resolution (s. 47); *Reference re Supreme Court Act, ss. 5 and 6, 2014 SCC 21,* note 93 at para. 91.
71. A constitutional amendment is also required to change the essential features of the Court: Constitution Act, 1982, note 97, s. 42(1)(d); *Reference re Supreme Court Act*, ss. 5 and 6, 2014 SCC 21, note 93 at para. 94.
72. Supreme Court Act, note 94, s. 9; this provision is probably protected by section 42(1)(d) of the Constitution Act, 1982, whose extent is unclear.
73. Supreme Court Act, note 94, ss. 35–43.
74. Dodek and Devlin, 'Fighting words', 85.

75. Duane Benton and Jennifer A. L. Sheldon-Sherman, 'What Judges Want and Need: User-Friendly Foundations for Effective Judicial Education' (2015) 1 J Disp Resol 23 at 32.
76. S. I. Strong, 'Judicial Education and Regulatory Capture : Does the Current System of Educating Judges Promote a Well-Functioning Judiciary and Adequately Serve the Public Interest?' (2015) 1 J Disp Resol 1.
77. Laurel Besco, 'Judicial Education for Sustainability' (2018) 14/1 MJSDL 1.
78. Patricia H. Murrell, 'Judging: A Role with Soul' (2006) 451; Judges' Journal 1 at 5.
79. Besco, 'Judicial Education'.
80. Strong, 'Judicial Education', 20; National Center for State Courts, 'Helping Courts Address Implicit Bias: Resources for Education', online: <*http://www.ncsc.org/ibeducation*>; Dodek and Devlin, 'Fighting words', 88.
81. Dodek and Devlin, 'Fighting words', 87–8; Rosemary Cairns Way, 'Contradictory or complementary? Reconciling judicial independence with judicial social context education', in *Judicial Independence in Context* (Toronto: Irwin Law, 2010) 220 at 223.
82. Judges Act, s. 60(2)(b).
83. On the creation of these institutes, see Russell, *The Judiciary in Canada*, pp. 186–7.
84. Richard Devlin, C. Adèle Kent and Susan Lightstone, 'The Past, Present … and Future(?) of Judicial Ethics Education in Canada' (2013) 16/1 Legal Ethics 1–35 at 7–8.
85. Judges Act, s. 41; Canadian Judicial Council, 'Professional Development', online: <*https://cjc-ccm.ca/en/what-we-do/professional-development*>.
86. Canadian Judicial Council, *Ethical Principles for Judges* (Ottawa: Canadian Judicial Council, 2004).
87. Devlin, Kent and Lightstone, 'The Past, Present … and Future(?)', 9.
88. Devlin, Kent and Lightstone, 'The Past, Present … and Future(?)', 8–9; Dodek and Devlin, 'Fighting words', 88–9; Huppé, *Histoire des institutions judiciaires*, pp. 32–3.
89. An Act to amend the Judges Act and the Criminal Code, Bill C-5 (second reading), 43rd Parliament, 1st sess., 19 February 2020.
90. Library of Parliament, 'Legislative Summary of Bill C-337: An Act to amend the Judges Act and the Criminal Code (sexual assault)'.
91. Constitution Act 1867, s. 100.
92. Re BC Family Relations Act, [1982] 1 SCR 62 at 106–7 and 112–13.
93. Criminal Code, above note 43, ss. 2 (definition of 'provincial court judge'), 553 and following.

94. *Ontario (Attorney General) v. Pembina Exploration Canada Ltd*, [1989] 1 SCR 206 at para. 28.
95. See, most recently, *In the matter: Reference to the Court of Appeal of Quebec pertaining to the constitutional validity of the provisions of article 35 of the Code of Civil Procedure which set at less than $85,000 the exclusive monetary jurisdiction of the Court of Québec and to the appellate jurisdiction assigned to the Court of Québec*, 2019 QCCA 1492.
96. Canadian charter of rights and freedoms, c. 11 (UK), Schedule B, Part I.
97. *Valente v. The Queen*, [1985] 2 SCR 673.
98. *Valente v. The Queen*, [1985] 2 SCR 673 at para 26.
99. *Reference re Remuneration of Judges of the Provincial Court (P.E.I.)*, at para. 83.
100. *Reference re Remuneration of Judges of the Provincial Court (P.E.I.)*, at para. 126.
101. *Reference re Remuneration of Judges of the Provincial Court (P.E.I.)*, at para. 287.
102. See the dissenting opinion of La Forest J, *Reference re Remuneration of Judges of the Provincial Court (P.E.I.)*, at paras 296–352; Jean Leclair and Yves-Marie Morissette, 'L'Indépendance Judiciaire et la Cour Suprême: Reconstruction Historique Douteuse et Théorie Constitutionnelle de Complaisance' (1998) 36/3 Osgoode Hall Law Journal 485–514; Harry W. Arthurs, 'Constitutional Courage' (2003) 49: RD McGill 1–19 at 18; for an early warning, see Russell, *The Judiciary in Canada*, p. 97.
103. Peter W. Hogg, 'The Bad Idea of Unwritten Constitutional Principles: Protecting Judicial Salaries', in *Judicial Independence in Context* (Toronto: Irwin Law, 2010), 25 at 26.
104. Brian W. Lennox, 'Judicial independence in Canada : the evolution continues', in *Judicial Independence in Context* (Toronto: Irwin Law, 2010), 623 at 629.
105. *Provincial Court Judges' Assn of New Brunswick v. New Brunswick (Minister of Justice)*; *Ontario Judges' Assn v. Ontario (Management Board)*; *Bodner v. Alberta; Conférence des juges du Québec v. Quebec (Attorney General)*; *Minc v. Quebec (Attorney General), 2005 SCC 44*, [2005] 2 SCR 286.
106. Bowbrick, *Judicial Compensation in Canada*, pp. 200–2.
107. *Conférence des juges de paix magistrats du Québec v. Quebec (Attorney General), 2016 SCC 39*, [2016] 2 SCR 116 at para. 32; see also *Ell v. Alberta, 2003 SCC 35*, [2003] 1 SCR 857.
108. Courts of Justice Act, CQLR, c. T-16, s. 1.
109. Courts of Justice Act, CQLR, c. T-16, ss. 2–78.
110. Courts of Justice Act, CQLR, c. T-16, s. 79.

111. *In the matter: Reference to the Court of Appeal of Quebec pertaining to the constitutional validity of the provisions of article 35 of the Code of Civil Procedure which set at less than $85,000 the exclusive monetary jurisdiction of the Court of Québec and to the appellate jurisdiction assigned to the Court of Québec, 2019 QCCA 1492.*
112. Courts of Justice Act, CQLR, c. T-16, s. 80.
113. Courts of Justice Act, CQLR, c. T-16, s. 106.
114. Courts of Justice Act, CQLR, c. T-16, ss. 161–82 and Schedule V.
115. Courts of Justice Act, CQLR, c. T-16, s. 82.
116. Courts of Justice Act, CQLR, c. T-16, s. 83.
117. Code of civil procedure, above note 11, s. 37; Courts of Justice Act, CQLR, c. T-16, s. 83(4).
118. Courts of Justice Act, CQLR, c. T-16, s. 87.
119. Courts of Justice Act, CQLR, c. T-16, s. 88.
120. Regulation respecting the selection procedure of candidates for the office of judge of the Court of Québec, municipal court judge and presiding justice of the peace, CQLR, c. T-16, r. 4.1, s. 3.
121. Regulation respecting the selection procedure of candidates for the office of judge of the Court of Québec, municipal court judge and presiding justice of the peace, CQLR, c. T-16, r. 4.1, s. 26.
122. Marc Seguin, 'Jean Charest cleared in Bastarache influence-peddling probe', *The Globe and Mail* (19 January 2011).
123. Avner Levin and Asher Alkoby, 'Shouldn't the Bench be a Mirror? The Diversity of the Canadian Judiciary' (2017).
124. Courts of Justice Act, CQLR, c. T-16, s. 115.
125. Courts of Justice Act, CQLR, c. T-16, ss. 224.1–246.28.
126. Courts of Justice Act, CQLR, c. T-16, s. 246.29.
127. Courts of Justice Act, CQLR, c. T-16, s. 246.30.
128. Courts of Justice Act, CQLR, c. T-16, s. 246.31.
129. Courts of Justice Act, CQLR, c. T-16.
130. Courts of Justice Act, CQLR, c. T-16, s. 246.33.
131. Courts of Justice Act, CQLR, c. T-16, ss. 246.36 and 246.41.
132. Courts of Justice Act, CQLR, c. T-16, s. 246.42.
133. Courts of Justice Act, CQLR, c. T-16, s. 246.43.
134. Courts of Justice Act, CQLR, c. T-16, s. 246.44.
135. Courts of Justice Act, CQLR, c. T-16, s. 246.44.
136. *Provincial Court Judges' Assn. of New Brunswick v. New Brunswick (Minister of Justice)*; *Ontario Judges' Assn. v. Ontario (Management Board)*; *Bodner v. Alberta; Conférence des juges du Québec v. Quebec (Attorney General)*; *Minc v. Quebec (Attorney General), 2005 SCC 44*, at para. 120.

137. See above, text corresponding to note 88, and Bowbrick, *Judicial Compensation in Canada*, pp. 200–1.
138. Courts of Justice Act, CQLR, c. T-16, s. 248.
139. Courts of Justice Act, CQLR, c. T-16, s. 249.
140. Courts of Justice Act, CQLR, c. T-16, ss. 256(a–c and g); for the assignment of a judge to a different division or place of residence, see ss. 108 and 112.
141. Courts of Justice Act, CQLR, c. T-16, s. 256(d) (f).
142. Courts of Justice Act, CQLR, c. T-16, s. 261.
143. Courts of Justice Act, CQLR, c. T-16, s. 262.
144. Huppé, *Histoire des institutions judiciaires*, p. 624.
145. Courts of Justice Act, CQLR, c. T-16, s. 263.
146. Courts of Justice Act, CQLR, c. T-16, s. 266.
147. Courts of Justice Act, CQLR, c. T-16, s. 267.
148. Courts of Justice Act, CQLR, c. T-16, s. 268.
149. Courts of Justice Act, CQLR, c. T-16, s. 276.
150. Courts of Justice Act, CQLR, c. T-16, ss. 269–269.1.
151. Courts of Justice Act, CQLR, c. T-16, ss. 271–2.
152. Courts of Justice Act, CQLR, c. T-16, s. 279.
153. Courts of Justice Act, CQLR, c. T-16, s. 279.
154. Courts of Justice Act, CQLR, c. T-16, s. 280.
155. Courts of Justice Act, CQLR, c. T-16, s. 95.
156. *Valente v. The Queen*, [1985] 2 SCR 673, at paras 27–31; *Therrien (Re), 2001 SCC 35*, [2001] 2 SCR 3 at paras 63–78.
157. *Moreau-Bérubé v. New Brunswick (Judicial Council), 2002 SCC 11*, [202AD] 1 SCR 249 at para. 72.
158. Courts of Justice Act, above note 108, ss. 92.1–93.
159. *Valente v. The Queen*, [1985] 2 SCR 673, at paras 32–9.
160. Courts of Justice Act, CQLR, c. T-16, ss. 257–8.
161. Courts of Justice Act, CQLR, c. T-16, s. 259.
162. Courts of Justice Act, CQLR, c. T-16, s. 105.6–7.
163. Conseil de la magistrature du Québec, *Activity Report 2016–2018* (Québec: Conseil de la magistrature du Québec, 2019) at 18.

PART III

Access to Justice

7

Judging Access to Justice: The Case of the United Kingdom and France

Géraldine Gadbin-George[1]

After having seen in the previous chapter that linguistic and cultural barriers can limit access to the law, Géraldine Gadbin-George discusses the denial of access to justice based on financial considerations in the wake of the Legal Aid, Sentencing and Punishment of Offenders Act 2012 which drastically reduced legal aid to the detriment of the most vulnerable especially in Wales.

The status of judges, of the law professions – like solicitors/barristers (in the United Kingdom) or *avocats* (in France) – and of litigants who wish to access justice is never set in stone. In September 2017, Sir Henry Brooke[2] – a former member of the British Bach Commission on Access to Justice chaired by Labour peer (and barrister) Lord Bach – said, 'Justice is too precious for political football.'[3] However, there is no doubt that on both sides of the Channel, the protection of the status of judges, of the legal professions and, beyond that, of access to justice, is closely related to the national and European political environment in place.

The keyword for the British and French judiciary has always been, and remains, 'independence'. However, recent events show that the judiciary's willingness to assert its independence may sometimes backfire against it. On 13 October 2016, the French judiciary was accused by former socialist President François Hollande of being an 'institution of cowards'[4] on the grounds that they 'don't like politicians. Justice does not like politicians.'[5] A few days later, on 4 November 2016, and further to the United Kingdom Supreme Court's ruling that Conservative Prime Minister Theresa May could not trigger Article 50 of the Lisbon Treaty – the formal two-year process for leaving the European Union – without a vote by Parliament, the political editor of the British newspaper *Daily Mail*, James Slack, accused the British judiciary of being 'enemies of the people'.[6] In both cases these criticisms, unsupported by evidence, show a shift which the executive power in both countries, helped in that respect by the media, is hoping to provoke in the apportionment of responsibilities at the highest level.

It seems that times are not easy for the judiciary in France and the United Kingdom. Are times also hard for litigants? The purpose of this chapter is to explore the recent and forthcoming legal and mostly judicial reforms in both countries in order to see to what extent they are meant to improve access to justice for litigants and how they have affected or are likely to affect the judiciary in France and the United Kingdom. We will focus on civil law, as opposed to criminal law, which will be mentioned only when relevant.

1. Judicial Agendas in the United Kingdom and in France: Is the Grass Always Greener?

On 9 March 2018, the former French Justice Minister Nicole Belloubet officially announced the future French justice reform. Her presentation followed the publication, on 15 January 2018, of a report entitled *Chantiers de la Justice* ('construction sites of French justice'), which covered five core issues: digital transformation, improvement and simplification of criminal litigation, improvement and simplification of civil litigation, adaptation of the court network and the meaning and efficiency of criminal sentences. Already praised as innovative by the media and criticised (at least in part) by the French judiciary and the law professions, the proposed reform gives a sense of *déjà vu* to those who are familiar with the British judicial system, and in particular the now defunct 2017 Prisons and Courts Bill (the White paper of which was called 'Transforming our Justice System').

Despite reaching committee stage in the House of Commons, the Prisons and Courts Bill could not be passed before Parliament was dissolved on 3 May 2017, after Prime Minister Theresa May announced the June 2017 general election. The bill covered four main topics: the need for a court reform (the emphasis being placed on the greater protection of victims and generally on the most vulnerable, as well as the improvement, through digitisation, of access to justice), a reform of the judiciary (to provide judges with modern facilities, and thus give them a better work environment leading to better justice), a reform of whiplash compensation and a reform of prisons safety. Since the 2017 Prisons and Courts Bill was scrapped, HM Courts and Tribunals Service published a 'Reform Update' report in May 2018, setting out an 'ambitious' programme 'to make the courts and tribunals system more straightforward, accessible and efficient', whilst stressing that 'effectiveness for the individual citizen and efficiency for the taxpayer go hand-in-hand'.[7]

Whether we look at the proposed reforms in France or the United Kingdom, the underlying message seems to be the modernisation of access to justice whilst saving public money. The similar aims currently shared by both countries, at a time of political and cultural turmoil with Brexit, is both reassuring and worrying: it is worrying in that both proposed reforms show that the two judicial systems are no longer able to respond to the needs of litigants (whether because they have become out of date or are too costly); and it is reassuring as it is evidence that the Brexit turmoil – which is, and will be felt on both sides of the Channel – is not sufficient to lead to the divorce of countries which, throughout history, have had a lot in common.

Charles Caleb Colton said: 'Imitation is the sincerest form of flattery.' Just by looking back over the last thirty years, we see that France and the United Kingdom have developed a tradition of imitating each other – whether that can be attributed or not to the United Kingdom joining the European Union in 1973. For example, the Civil Procedure Rules which came into force in 1999 resemble the French *Code de Procédure Civile*. Their drafter, Lord Woolf, a keen Francophile, described his approach to civil procedure as being a 'mid-Channel' one.[8] Litigants were given the option to seek the appointment of a single joint expert,[9] as opposed to the prior system consisting of each party instructing its own expert. Having one expert report instead of various potentially conflicting ones is an obvious advantage for the judiciary. Because it makes litigation less costly, it is an advantage to litigants. Another example from the Woolf civil reform was the introduction of the case management system,[10] which transformed, to some extent, a formerly exclusively accusatorial civil procedure into a more inquisitorial one, as in France.

The French reciprocated by copying the British in a number of areas, for instance, the *Rapport de la Commission de Réflexion sur la Réforme de la Cour de Cassation* – a report setting out the various ways to reform the French equivalent of the Supreme Court – which was published in April 2017. The report proposed to 'make *Cour de cassation* decisions clearer and more widely available'.[11] This was rendered necessary by a 'changed environment'[12] revolving around the increased use of modern technologies and big data[13] in general.[14] The French concept of having an 'enriched legal reasoning'[15] (currently tested) brings *Cour de cassation* decisions closer to their British counterparts, in which the detailed opinions of all the judges, including concurring or dissenting ones, are set out.[16] If the French report gives credit to the procedural codes,[17] article 6(1) of the European Convention on Human Rights,[18] article 47 of the Charter of Fundamental Rights and 'evolutions imposed by European case law'[19] for this reform, the need for the judges to set out their detailed legal reasoning derives directly from the common law.

Another example of the French imitating the British is the creation by statute no. 2016-1547 of 18 November 2016 relating to the modernisation of justice in the twenty-first century, nicknamed '*loi J21*', of the position of 'assistant jurists'[20] at the *Cour de cassation* to work with the President of each chamber/division to assist him with his work.[21] The scope of their work is not yet defined precisely but in an era focused on big data, we can imagine that, like their British counterparts, they may eventually be required to carry out legal research, help with the writing of decisions or draft *Cour de cassation* press summaries, which is an ideal way to summarise a court decision and make it understandable by most lay people. The various aspects of the reform of the French *Cour de cassation* move in the right direction to improve access to justice or at least, to judicial decisions.

As another example of the French imitating the United Kingdom, we can mention statute no. 2015-990 of 6 August 2015 for the development, activity and equality of economic opportunities[22] (aka *loi Macron*). This French law deregulated a number of professions, like those of *avocat* and *notaire*, by allowing the creation of the *Sociétés Pluri-professionnelles d'Exercice* (SPE), in the same way as the Legal Services Act 2007 had allowed the creation of Alternative Business Structures.[23] On both sides of the Channel, the reforms are too recent to be possible to assert with certainty that they serve the best interests of people. If having access in one place to a solicitor, an accountant and an estate agent can be seen as a way to simplify access to various services, it can also be argued that the close proximity between various professions who do not share the same code of ethics may lead to conflicts of interests.

Strictly speaking, the deregulation of the legal professions in France and the United Kingdom derives from the incorporation into national law of Directive 2006/123/EC of the European Parliament and of the Council of 12 December 2006 on services in the internal market (aka as the Services Directive or Bolkenstein Directive). However, the wording of the Bolkenstein Directive closely follows the Review of the Regulatory Framework for Legal Services in England and Wales (aka the Clementi report) published in 2004. David Clementi had been appointed by Lord Falconer, Lord Chancellor and first Secretary of State for Constitutional Affairs under former New Labour Prime Minister Tony Blair. The deregulation of the legal professions in France by President Macron is therefore an indirect consequence of Tony Blair's policy when he was Prime Minister of the United Kingdom.[24]

It is the same Tony Blair who, at the Knowledge 2000 conference, said, 'The e-generation is with us.'[25] This view was then shared by the European Council, who met in Lisbon in March 2000 and expressed the general wish for '[t]he shift to a digital, knowledge-based economy, prompted by new goods and services'.[26] Amusingly, the present French President Emmanuel Macron and founder of the all-encompassing political movement *La République en Marche*, who served as *Ministre de l'Économie, de l'Industrie et du Numérique* in socialist Manuel Valls's government under François Hollande's presidency, was *co-rapporteur* in the Darrois Commission[27] set up by former conservative President (and *avocat*) Nicolas Sarkozy, which published a governmental report in March 2009 advocating, amongst other things, a modernisation of the legal professions and access to justice.[28]

This background information illustrates two things: through the membership of the European Union, there has been a harmonisation of reforms in member states; this harmonisation (which could be said to be the cause or the consequence of the globalisation of the economy, including the legal market) is meant to happen irrespective of the political colour of the government in place, thus leading to a cross-European political consensus to reform the economy in general, and justice in particular. Of course, political agendas and cultural backgrounds may influence, at least in part, the ways these reforms will be thought of, designed, voted and later implemented in each member state. But whether we talk about France or the United Kingdom, the underlying message of the forthcoming reforms is to make justice more accessible and cheaper.

Whether this is achievable remains to be seen, but there is no doubt that, one way or another, these reforms will have an impact on the judiciary, on the legal professions in general and on litigants. After trying to define the contours of the concept of access to justice both in France and in the United Kingdom, we will consider the proposed plan to digitise justice and the possible dehumanisation of the judicial process.

2. What is Access to Justice?

The question of the nature and scope of access to justice is not straightforward. The British tend to talk about access to justice when the French refer to *accès à la justice* or *accès au droit*, meaning access to justice or to the law. From a language point of view, the French access to the law seems to have a wider scope, at least in theory, but not necessarily in practice. Various constructions of these expressions are possible at any given time, and indeed are likely to evolve depending on the countries' respective political, historical, social, cultural and of course legal backgrounds.

In the United Kingdom, *Magna Carta* and in particular clause 29 of the 1297 Great Charter of Liberties (which retained the gist of clauses 39 and 40 of the 1215 Charter) seems to be the first document expressly protecting access to justice by providing: 'We will sell to no man, we will not deny or defer to any man either justice or right.' In France, the spirit of the right to access to justice – the word justice not being used once – is contained in articles 8–10 of the 1789 *Déclaration des Droits de l'Homme et du Citoyen*. They recognise the right for everyone to have 'an actual recourse against acts in breach of the fundamental rights which are recognised by the Constitution or the law before the national courts having jurisdiction' and the right 'to have one's case heard equitably and publicly by an independent and impartial court'.[29]

Today, of course, both France and the United Kingdom are bound by the principles laid out in article 6(1) of the European Convention on Human Rights according to which 'everyone is entitled to a fair and public hearing within a reasonable time by an independent and impartial tribunal established by law.'[30] The meaning of the expressions 'fair and public hearing' and 'independent and impartial tribunal' has been subject to construction by the European Court of Human Rights itself. In *Golder v. UK*,[31] the European Court of Human Rights ruled that there was a right of access to a 'tribunal' – the word 'court' being more appropriate in the English language[32] – whilst admitting that this did not expressly appear in the Convention itself.[33] According to the Court's ruling

> It would be inconceivable, in the opinion of the Court, that Article 6 para.1 (art. 6-1) should describe in detail the procedural guarantees afforded to parties in a pending lawsuit and should not first protect that which alone makes it in fact possible to benefit from such guarantees, that is, access to a court.[34]

This did not meet with the approval of Sir Gerald Fitzmaurice, a judge from the United Kingdom, who filed a dissenting opinion:

> It is an understandable, reasonable and legitimate point of view that access to the courts of law is, or should be, regarded as an important human right. Yet it is an equally justifiable view to say that the very importance of the right requires (more especially in a convention based on inter-State agreement, not sovereign legislative power) that it should be given explicit expression, not left to be deduced as a matter of inference.[35]

Forty years after the *Golder* case, the right of people to have access to justice through access to a court still raises two major issues: the financing of access to the courts, and alternatives to the judicial resolution of a dispute.

The financing of access to justice is a sore subject in the United Kingdom. The Legal Aid, Sentencing and Punishment of Offenders Act 2012 (LASPO) reform was passed under the coalition government of former Conservative Prime Minister David Cameron and Liberal Democrat Deputy Prime Minister Nick Clegg. By removing the benefit of legal aid from various legal fields (such as family law, except in case of domestic violence or child abuse, most employment law, most debt recovery work, housing matters, except where there is an immediate risk to the home, for example),[36] LASPO was a major blow to one of the pillars of the welfare state, created after the Second World War by the Legal Aid and Assistance Act 1949. In March 2014, the day before she was due in court to cross-examine the man who had allegedly raped her, Caroline Alexander, a lady litigant who could not afford to instruct a solicitor or Counsel, posted a request on Twitter which read: 'I need a law degree by 9am.'[37] In a report commissioned by the Law Society – the solicitors' professional body – Donald Hirsch wrote|:

> [a]t the maximum level of disposable income at which legal aid is allowed, households have too little income to reach a minimum standard of living even before footing any legal bills. Typically, they have disposable incomes 10 per cent to 30 per cent too low to afford a minimum budget. Even those below the disposable income limit, while eligible for legal aid, are required to make a

> contribution to legal costs, unless their income is extremely low. Some households who can afford less than half of a minimum budget must still contribute to legal expenses.[38]

At today's date, few people are eligible for civil legal aid. A review of LASPO is currently under way, but the law professions are not optimistic as to its future outcome. Concern over the future of legal aid – and hence, of the court resolution of disputes – led to the publication of a report from a commission set up by former Justice Minister and Labour peer, Lord Bach. That report was presented to the Labour Party conference in Brighton in September 2017. Entitled 'The Right to Justice', it proposed to pass a Right to Justice Act which would '[c]odify our existing rights to justice and establish a new right for individuals to receive reasonable legal assistance without costs they cannot afford'.[39] Whether this can be implemented remains to be seen.

Unlike the United Kingdom, French legal aid has not been adversely affected over the last few years.[40] The civil court system in France is less accusatorial than in the United Kingdom, thus substantially reducing the cost of justice. The lower cost of French civil justice probably explains why, unlike the British system, French legal aid is a gift of public money as opposed to a loan subject to clawback.[41] However, three years ago, the French criminal legal aid system (and beyond it, the provisions of article 6 of the European Convention on Human Rights) was criticised for the unfair advantage it confers on defendants in criminal proceedings. The mother of deceased Chloé Boissinot, a victim of the Bataclan terrorist attacks of 13 November 2015, expressed her discontent that she had to pay tax so that her daughter's alleged killer, Salah Abdeslam, would be granted legal aid to defend himself.[42]

Whenever legal aid is not available either in France or in the United Kingdom, whether because the legal field concerned is excluded from the benefit of legal aid or the litigant does not comply with the financial criteria applicable, how is access to justice protected? There are three options: the first is for the litigant to act in person – without being assisted or represented by a professional lawyer. This is always open to litigants in the United Kingdom, as opposed to France when it may be mandatory to instruct an *avocat*. The *ministère d'avocat obligatoire* usually applies before the Court of Appeal and of course, before the equivalents of the Supreme Court, i.e. the *Cour de cassation* and the *Conseil d'État*. Therefore, in France, someone may be deprived of access to justice when he is not financially eligible for legal aid but does not want to spend money on lawyers' fees, for instance to defend a claim before the Court of Appeal. And in the United Kingdom, a litigant in person may be at a disadvantage – because he is a lay person – compared to someone represented by a solicitor and/or counsel.

A second option is available for small claims in the United Kingdom, with the small claims court where representation by a law professional is discouraged through the absence of costs orders against the losing party. The same comment as above – on the lack of balance between represented and non-represented parties – can be made, even if simplified procedural rules apply before the small claims court. In France, there used to be a quasi-equivalent of the small claims court with the *juges de proximité* – who used to work within the *Tribunaux d'instance* whilst having a separate jurisdiction from that of the *Tribunaux d'instance* – but they were scrapped in July 2017 for financial reasons. Of course, this does not plead in favour of an improvement of access to justice.

The third option consists in alternatives to the judicial resolution of disputes, with British Alternative Dispute Resolution (ADR) and French *Modes amiables de règlement des différends* (MARD). Both countries encourage the non-representation of the parties by a law professional for ADR and MARD.

In the United Kingdom, just before Conservative Prime Minister Margaret Thatcher's election in 1979, the Benson commission warned the then Labour government of the dangers of allowing the representation of the parties by a solicitor/barrister in an ADR, the law professions being 'exposed to strong temptation to settle the claim before incurring the heavy expense of preparing for trial and of trial itself, although it may not be in [their] client's interests to do so'.[43] The Benson commission implied that solicitors and barristers were not above breaching their code of conduct to place the payment of their fees above their clients' best interests. This shocking comment was one of the first signs of the willingness of politicians to see justice being rendered without lawyers and, beyond that, possibly without judges. In his 1995 interim report which led to the Civil Procedure Rules, Lord Woolf strongly encouraged ADR,[44] and in his final report,he insisted again on the need to 'explore the scope of ADR or settlement'[45] as '[l]itigation [should] be avoided wherever possible'.[46] In 2005, the Legal Services Commission (then in charge of the administration of legal aid) said that: 'all forms of ADR are accepted to have at least equal validity to court proceedings'.[47] This tendency to try to avoid the court resolution of disputes. and this comment – made by an institution close to the government – as well as the implication that ADR could be of greater value than court litigation, are dangerous. Indeed, there are some downsides to ADR. Most of the time, there is no appeal against an ADR decision. And the harmonious development of case law is not possible through ADR, as stressed by Lord Thomas of Cwmgiedd, a former Lord Chief Justice, who argued that 'the increase of arbitration in England, with its proceedings in private and limited rights of appeal, is impeding the development of the common law'.[48] For the litigant in person, ADR can make justice more opaque.

Comments similar to those of Lord Thomas could be made about the French MARD which, for Philip Milburn, developed 'in France in the mid-1980s, an era when alternatives to judicial action are encouraged by public policies, who see in it a modernisation in terms of the civil society's powers and a softening of institutions'.[49] MARD, as an alternative to the court resolution of legal disputes, was developed to avoid slow and fairly expensive court proceedings. By decree no. 2015-282 of 11 March 2015 relating to the simplification of civil procedure, electronic communication and the amicable settlement of disputes, 'recourse to alternative ways of resolving disputes [was] favoured, in particular by forcing the parties to indicate, in the claim filed with the court, the steps of amicable resolution previously taken.'[50]

As well as alternatives to the court resolution of legal disputes, another aspect of ADR and MARD has emerged, which is their introduction into the court resolution of legal disputes by way of judicial mediation. In France, it was mainly introduced by statute no. 95-125 of 8 February 1995 relating to the organisation of the courts and civil, criminal and public procedure.[51] Both in France and in the United Kingdom, judicial mediation has become an essential part of, and a quasi-obligation for, family and employment disputes. The use of the prefix 'quasi' is important, as failure to resort to the forms of judicial mediation which are made available to litigants may result in the defaulting litigant being penalised by way of a costs order against him.

The general question has arisen as to whether ADR (in the United Kingdom) and MARD (in France) are a mandatory prior stage of the judicial process. This is an important issue, not only for litigants but also for the judiciary.

In the United Kingdom, in *Halsey v. Milton Keynes* (2004), Lord Justice Dyson held

> It is one thing to encourage the parties to agree to mediation, even to encourage them in the strongest terms. It is another to order them to do so. It seems to us that to oblige truly unwilling parties to refer their disputes to mediation would be to impose an unacceptable obstruction on their right of access to the court'[52]

In an interim report published in October 2017, a working group of the Civil Justice Council wondered once more whether promoting the use of ADR should be made a 'compulsion or persuasion'.[53] It said: 'The fact is that in England and Wales there are a number of ADR processes that are effectively or actually compulsory. The obvious examples are the RTA portal, ACAS conciliation, family MIAMs [...]'[54]

No definite answer has been given yet and the situation is similar in France. For the executive power or the legislator on both sides of the Channel, making judicial mediation compulsory (bearing in mind that in France, for example, it is not carried out by a professional judge before the equivalent of the employment tribunal, the *Conseil des Prud'hommes*) would amount to giving a no-confidence vote against the judiciary, opening the floodgates of ADR/MARD and, in the long run, potentially closing the doors to standard court litigation.

3. From the Digitisation to the Dehumanisation of Traditional Justice?

If ADR and MARD are given increasing importance in the United Kingdom and France, traditional court resolution of disputes is quickly changing.

Between 1978 and 1981, the BBC broadcast Terry Nation's science fiction TV series *Blake's 7*. The plot took place in a totalitarian Terran Federation set 700 years in the future. Two episodes, called *The Way Back* and *Trial*, showed computers playing a major role in the judicial process. One was a non-speaking computer called the *Judgment Machine*, able to convict and sentence people. The other computer, using software called *One Oblique Three*, expressed itself verbally and fulfilled the role of a judge. The potential use of computers to render justice is no longer science fiction but close to reality. In June 2016 in the United Kingdom the Law Society organised a conference entitled 'Robots and Lawyers' where Katie Atkinson, an IT professor from Liverpool University, demonstrated a software she designed which reproduced the legal reasoning of human judges. The experience was carried out on thirty-two already decided cases, and the computer 'only' differed once.[55] However, for the party who would have won before the human judge and lost through the computer's order, the digitisation and dehumanisation of justice is an obvious problem.

Digitisation of the courts is a recent but fast-developing phenomenon. In France, decree no. 2015-282 of 11 March 2015, which relates to the simplification of civil procedure, to electronic communication and to the amicable resolution of disputes,[56] simplified the administrative work of the courts by making emails the norm and registered post (for sending court documents) the exception. The January 2018 governmental *Chantiers de la Justice* report provides that there will be an 'adaptation of the court network' including '[g]uaranteeing a meshing of justice irrigating the whole territory, a more readable geographical organisation and a better access to the law and the judge'.[57] This will not lead to an increase in the number of courts available but to a merger of existing first-instance courts: 'Instauration, in lieu of the *Tribunaux d'instance* and *Tribunaux de grande instance*, of proximity courts and judicial courts depending on the characteristics of the territories and the volumes and types of litigation'.[58] The report further provides: 'Digitisation must be inclusive and mostly ensure that poorer people will not be led further away from the judicial offer [...] Digitisation offers possibilities of an amicable settlement of disputes, prior to the judge's stage.' There could be

> an initial mediation phase, with no intervention from the judge but with accredited operators [...] Then the litigation stages will be made speedier and more interactive [...] In criminal as well as civil litigation, the aim is that of the native digitisation of procedures, leading to the creation of unique digital files, accessible by all the actors.[59]

A digital platform for the amicable settlement of small claims up to 5,000 euros, as well as for consumer litigation, should be set up, and 'the parties might have to justify having attempted to settle their dispute amicably, before potentially lodging a court claim', and for civil matters there would be a unique way of lodging a digital court claim with a unique *Tribunal judiciaire*.[60]

In the United Kingdom and in his final report, 'Civil Courts Structure Review', published in July 2016,[61] Lord Justice Briggs proposed setting up an online civil court (HMOC) which would have jurisdiction over all cases involving up to £25,000. He suggested there should be three stages in this online court judicial process: an interactive triage; a conciliation phase; and finally, if everything else had failed, resolution by a judge. The judge would therefore be used as a last resort, a new category of legal workers playing an important role during the conciliation phase, called 'case officers' in the interim report[62] and 'case lawyers' in the final report. The status of these 'case officers' or 'case lawyers' has until now not been clearly defined, and it seems that the prospect of setting up the HMOC has been delayed, no doubt due to the current Conservative government's other priorities with Brexit. At the Bar conference held in November 2017, HM Courts and Tribunals Service's chief executive, Susan Acland-Hood,[63] played down the possible future role of the online court, which had caused the fury of the judiciary and the legal professions, who were concerned about the possible lesser quality of services which would be rendered to litigants.

Further to the 2017 Prisons and Courts Bill being scrapped, HM Courts and Tribunals Service published a reform update in May 2018. Fifty projects are considered, which should all be implemented in the near future. Regarding civil law, family law and tribunals, some of the proposed projects include: 'Online Civil Money Claims', described as '[a] new online process will be used for the management of relatively simple and lower value civil disputes. The project will also automate and streamline the procedure for other civil money claims'; an 'Upper Tribunal' with '[n]ew digital ways of working across Upper Tribunal and the RCJ'; for 'Civil Enforcement', '[r]eviewing the structure of civil enforcement to deliver better information and increase the likelihood of successful enforcement. This includes increased guidance, a simplified process, and a digital system to increase efficiencies'; and for 'divorce',

> delivering a transformed divorce service for people who want to end their marriage or civil partnership. This project will also reduce the HMCTS resource required to administer those cases. A digital service for applications for: divorce, nullity or judicial separation of marriage or civil partnerships, and online payment of fees.[64]

Other plans include the development of 'Video hearings' to '[i]mplement [...] hearings in a digital environment outside traditional courts or tribunals'; and a feasibility study across a series of sites in different locations and jurisdictions to examine the feasibility of flexible, extended operating hours for hearings.[65]

Both France and the United Kingdom appear keen on developing a form of e-justice as soon as possible, aiming to make access to justice more modern and cheaper, and bringing justice closer to the litigants. Is that feasible? Is it in the best interests of litigants and their purse, or is it merely a way for the French and British governments to cut down on costs by eventually replacing the judiciary with less qualified people and/or machines? It is difficult to say at this stage.

What we notice is the similarity of the proposed reforms in both countries. Despite their different legal cultures, the fact that the United Kingdom and France are European member states – up to Brexit in January 2020 – partly explains this resemblance, as well as the general evolution towards an increasingly global and digital market which applies to legal services.

In France, between 2007 and 2011, and under former conservative President Nicolas Sarkozy, a reform of the judicial map (*carte judiciaire*) led to the suppression of 401 courts including 21 *Tribunaux de grande instance* (the French equivalent of the High court), 178 *Tribunaux d'instance* (similar to the British County Court), 62 *conseils de prud'hommes* (which can be compared to the British employment tribunals) and 55 commercial courts.[66] In the United Kingdom, over two years, 86 courts and tribunals were closed.[67] The morale of the French and British judiciary is low. In France, a report entitled *Souffrance au travail des magistrats* (work- related suffering) was published in February 2015 by the main trade union of the French judiciary, the *Union Syndicale des Magistrats* (USM),[68] denouncing their difficult work conditions. Likewise, in the United Kingdom, in his 2017 (and last) report as Lord Chief Justice, Lord Thomas referred to a 2014 Judicial Attitude Survey (the results of which were confirmed in 2016) showing a 'serious loss of morale across the judiciary and continuing dissatisfaction over (1) working conditions, (2) the volume of work [...]'[69]

Having fewer courts means that judges, law professionals and litigants will need to travel more when they need to go to court. The elderly and the poor will not necessarily be able to travel, either because of their age or their lack of resources. The judiciary may not be keen on using computers. For some litigants – here again, the elderly or the poor – access to a computer may not be easy. There is a risk that additional pressure will be exerted on the already busy Citizens Advice Bureaux (CAB) in the United Kingdom or their twenty-year old quasi-equivalent in France, the *Points Information Médiation Multi-Services* (PIMMs).[70] If the French and British reforms purport to harmonise judicial services throughout the country, this may not be the case as the risk of a two-tier judicial system – between those who are computer literate and the others – remains.

If both the French and British reforms wish to give a more important place to mediation, including judicial mediation, it is not clear what role will be left to the judiciary if 'case officers' or 'case lawyers' (in the United Kingdom) or accredited operators (*opérateurs homologués*) (in France) are introduced into the court system and are in charge of a conciliation stage. Neither reform is clear as to what legal qualifications these people would have and to what extent they might encroach on the work of the judiciary.

Digitisation can be a way to improve access to justice for all. It may bring justice closer to the people by making it possible for them to lodge their claims online and follow the online evolution of their case. Unlike digitisation, which may be a positive step, the dehumanisation of the courts, the slow replacement of judges by 'case officers' or accredited operators placed behind a court computer, as well as the increased part played by ADR and MARD to the detriment of the judiciary and the natural evolution of its case law, is a possible danger. In 2017, it was announced in the United Kingdom that Lavender Hill Magistrates' court in London had used a paperless procedure to inform 3,000 fare dodgers of the sentence passed against them.[71] Where is the deterrent element of criminal law if sentences are sent by email? The same comment could be made about civil court orders, the social link provided by the judicial court process with contact between litigants and with the judiciary being important. Terry Nation's *Blake 7* was interesting to watch on television but should remain fiction.

Notes

1. Unless indicated otherwise, translation of French text into English is the author's own.
2. Sir Henry Brooke, former Lord Justice of Appeal, died on 30 January 2018.
3. Sir Henry Brooke, 'Justice is too precious for political football', *Law Society Gazette* (22 September 2017), accessed online on 6 August 2018.
4. In the text: '*institution de lâcheté*'.
5. In the text: '*[On] n'aime pas le politique. La justice n'aime pas le politique …*' Extracts from Gérard Davet and Fabrice Lhomme, *Un président ne devrait*

pas dire ça … (Paris: Stock, 2016), quoted in '*"Lâcheté" des juges: la magistrature vent debout contre Hollande*', *L'Obs* (12 October 2016). Accessed online on 31 August 2018.

6. *R (Miller) v. Secretary of State for Exiting the European Union* [2017] UKSC 5.
7. HM Courts and Tribunals Services, Reform Update, May 2018, p. 4. Available online at *https://assets.publishing.service.gov.uk/government/uploads/system/uploads/attachment_data/file/711535/HMCTS_Reform_Update_May_2018.pdf*
8. The words he used were '*à mi-Manche*'. See Bernard Stirn, Duncan Fairgrieve and Mattias Guyomar, *Droits et libertés en France et au Royaume-Uni* (Paris, Odile Jacob, 2006), p. 53, note 53.
9. Which, together with Part 36 payments, Michael Zander QC described as being 'some improvements' as opposed to the rest of the reform, which he foresaw would 'do more harm than good'. See Michael Zander QC, 'Zander on Woolf', *New Law Journal* (13 March 2009). Accessed online on 8 August 2018.
10. In French: '*procédure de mise en état*'.
11. In the text: '*rendre plus compréhensibles et mieux diffuser les arrêts de la Cour de cassation*', *Rapport de la Commission de Réflexion sur la Réforme de la Cour de Cassation* (April 2017), p. 129.
12. In the text: '*environnement modifié*'.
13. Regarding big data and court decisions, and parallel to the *Cour de cassation* reform, a report by Loïc Cadiet was published by the French Justice Minister in January 2018. See Arnaud Dumourier, 'Rapport Cadiet: 20 recommandations sur l'open data des décisions de justice', *Le Monde du droit* (10 January 2018). Accessed on line on 20 July 2018.
14. The text provides: '*La diffusion de la jurisprudence n'est plus cantonnée aux professionnels du droit. Le développement des technologies de l'information rend possible l'accès quasiment en temps réel à l'ensemble des décisions de la Cour de cassation. Demain, celui du big data permettra un re-traitement de l'ensemble de leur contenu* […]'; Arnaud Dumourier, 'Rapport Cadiet' (2018), p. 137.
15. In the text: '*motivation enrichie*', defined as '*style libre, explications plus complètes, citation de précédents ou de décisions de cours européennes, etc*', 'Rapport Cadiet' (2018), p. 149.
16. The UKSC and its predecessor, the appellate committee of the House of Lords, have been admired for their ability in using literature to explain or justify their legal reasoning. For example, see Géraldine Gadbin-George, 'Literary references in United Kingdom common law judgments', *GRAAT Anglophone Studies*, 14 (2013), 79–95. Accessible online at *http://www.graat.fr/4gadbin.pdf*

17. Article 455 of the *Code de procédure civile* and article 485 of the *Code de procédure pénale.*
18. ECHR, 19 April 1994, *Van de Hurk c. Pays-Bas*, no 16034/90.
19. In the text: '*évolutions imposées par la jurisprudence européenne*'. Rapport de la Commission de Réflexion sur la Réforme de la Cour de cassation, 'Rapport Cadiet' (2018), p. 145.
20. In the text: '*juristes assistants*'.
21. The position was created by article 24 of the loi *n° 2016-1547 du 18 novembre 2016 de modernisation de la justice du XXIe siècle*, and created article L. 123-4 of the *Code de l'Organisation Judiciaire.*
22. In French: *loi n° 2015-990 du 6 août 2015 pour la croissance, l'activité et l'égalité des chances économiques.*
23. It went one step further than the *loi n° 2011-331 du 28 mars 2011 de modernisation des professions judiciaires ou juridiques et certaines professions réglementées* (which can be found at the *Journal Officiel* of 29 March 2011, p. 5447, which had authorised the creation of the ancestor of ABS, the '*société de participations financières de professions libérales* (SPFPL)'.
24. For more information on the background of the Clementi report and deregulation of the legal professions in the United Kingdom, see Géraldine Gadbin-George, *Déréglementation et Professions du Droit Outre-Manche* (Paris, Dalloz, 2016), paras 22–91ff.
25. 'Tony Blair's full speech', *The Guardian* (7 March 2000). Accessed online on 13 July 2018.
26. Lisbon European Council, 23 and 24 March 2000, Presidency conclusions, para. 8. Available online at *http://www.europarl.europa.eu/summits/lis1_en.htm*
27. Commission Darrois, *Rapport sur les professions du droit* (March 2009), annex 2, p. 131.
28. The letter by which then President Sarkozy instructed the Commission Darrois stated: '*l'attractivité du droit et de l'organisation juridique est devenue un enjeu fondamental de nos économies. [L]e recours aux modes alternatifs de règlement des différends, en matière commerciale ou familiale, s'impose peu à peu comme un mode pacifié de règlement des litiges dans lequel l'assistance d'un conseil conduit à redéfinir ses missions*'. See Commission Darrois, *Rapport sur les professions du droit*, annex 1, p. 127.
29. In French, articles 8 to 10 of the *Déclaration des Droits de l'Homme et du Citoyen* provide respectively: '*La Loi ne doit établir que des peines strictement et évidemment nécessaires, et nul ne peut être puni qu'en vertu d'une Loi établie et promulguée antérieurement au délit, et légalement appliquée. Tout homme étant présumé innocent jusqu'à ce qu'il ait été déclaré coupable, s'il est jugé indispensable*

de l'arrêter, toute rigueur qui ne serait pas nécessaire pour s'assurer de sa personne doit être sévèrement réprimée par la loi.' 'Nul ne doit être inquiété pour ses opinions, même religieuses, pourvu que leur manifestation ne trouble pas l'ordre public établi par la Loi.'

30. In French: '*Toute personne a droit à ce que sa cause soit entendue équitablement, publiquement et dans un délai raisonnable, par un tribunal indépendant et impartial, établi par la loi [...]*'
31. ECHR, *Golder v. the UK*, 21 February 1975.
32. In English law, the word 'tribunal' conveys the idea of a specialist jurisdiction, where the law is rendered by professionals in a specific field, as opposed to legally trained judges.
33. ECHR, *Golder v. the UK*, para. 28 of the ruling.
34. ECHR, *Golder v. the UK*, para. 35 of the ruling.
35. ECHR, *Golder v. the UK*, para. 32 of Sir Gerald Fitzmaurice's dissenting opinion.
36. Part One, Schedule One of LASPO gives a list of the matters still within the scope of the statute.
37. Emma Howard, 'Legal aid cuts: The forgotten pillar of the welfare state – a special report', *The Guardian* (25 September 2014). Accessed online on 17 July 2018.
38. Donald Hirsch, *Priced out of Justice? Means Testing Legal Aid and Making Ends Meet* (Loughborough University, March 2018), p. 3.
39. The Right to Justice, The final report of the Bach Commission, Fabian Policy Report, September 2017, p. 6. Accessible online at *http://www.fabians.org.uk/wp-content/uploads/2017/09/Bach-Commission_Right-to-Justice-Report-WEB.pdf*
40. Unlike litigants, *avocats*, on the other hand, feel that the evolution of legal aid through various changes is detrimental to their profession, as it makes it more difficult for them to be paid for the services they render. But this is outside the scope of the present study.
41. For more information, see Géraldine Gadbin-George, *Déréglementation*, para. 11.55, p. 44.
42. Ludovic Galtier, 'Salah Abdeslam: la mère d'une victime des attentats de Paris menace François Hollande de ne pas payer ses impôts', *RTL* (3 May 2016). Accessed online on 8 August 2018.
43. Royal Commission on Legal Services (Benson commission), Final Report, Cmnd 7648 and 7648-1 (1979), para. 16.4, p. 177.
44. Harry Woolf, *Access to Justice*, p. 137.
45. Harry Woolf, *Access to Justice*, p. 62.
46. Harry Woolf, *Access to Justice*, p. 4.

47. Legal Services Commission, Funding Code Guidance Amendments: 'A New Focus for Civil Legal Aid', Non-Family Guidance, Part 7, Alternative Dispute Resolution, 2005.
48. Zachary Segal, 'Arbitration and the Common Law', *Law Society Gazette* (6 June 2016). Accessed online on 18 July 2018.
49. In French: '*en France au cours des années 1980, période durant laquelle des alternatives à l'action judiciaire sont encouragées par les politiques publiques, qui y voient une modernisation en termes de valorisation des pouvoirs de la société civile et d'assouplissement des institutions*'. Philip Milburn, 'Panorama des formes et des pratiques de médiation en France', *Informations sociales*, 2012/2 (no. 170), p. 51.
50. In French: '*le recours aux modes alternatifs de résolution des litiges [a été] favorisé, en particulier en obligeant les parties à indiquer, dans l'acte de saisine de la juridiction, les démarches de résolution amiable précédemment effectuées.*' *Décret n° 2015-282 du 11 mars 2015 relatif à la simplification de la procédure civile à la communication électronique et à la résolution amiable des différends*,
51. In French: *Loi n° 95-125 du 8 février 1995 relative à l'organisation des juridictions et à la procédure civile, pénale et administrative*. Article 21-3 applies to civil courts.
52. *Halsey v. Milton Keynes General NHS Trust* [2004] EWCA Civ 576 (11 May 2004).
53. Civil Justice Council, *ADR and Civil Justice, CJC ADR Working Group, Interim Report*, October 2017, Section 8, p. 45. Accessible online at *https://www.judiciary.gov.uk/wp-content/uploads/2017/10/interim-report-future-role-of-adr-in-civil-justice-20171017.pdf*
54. Civil Justice Council, *ADR and Civil Justice, CJC ADR Working Group, Interim Report*, October 2017, para. 8.5.8, p. 46.
55. Fouzder Monidipa, 'Artificial intelligence mimics judicial reasoning', *Law Society Gazette* (22 June 2016). Accessed online on 27 June 2018.
56. In French: *Décret n° 2015-282 du 11 mars 2015 relatif à la simplification de la procédure civile à la communication électronique et à la résolution amiable des différends.*
57. In French: '*garantir un maillage de la justice irriguant l'ensemble des territoires, une organisation géographique plus lisible et un meilleur accès au droit et au juge*'. Ministère de la Justice, *Chantiers de la Justice: L'essentiel des propositions des référents*, January 2018, p. 10. Accessible online at *http://www.justice.gouv.fr/publication/chantiers_justice/Chantiers_justice_DP.pdf*
58. In French: '*Instauration, aux lieu et place des TI et TGI, de tribunaux de proximité et de tribunaux judiciaires en fonction des caractéristiques des territoires et des volumes et types de contentieux*'. Ministère de la Justice, *Chantiers de la Justice*, p. 11.

59. In French: '*La transformation numérique doit être inclusive et surtout veiller à ne pas éloigner davantage les plus démunis de l'offre de justice […] Le numérique ouvre des possibilités de résolution amiable des litiges, préalablement à toute saisine du juge.*' There could be '*une phase initiale de médiation, sans intervention du juge mais avec des opérateurs homologués. Ensuite, les phases contentieuses seraient rendues plus interactives et rapides […] En matière pénale comme civile, l'objectif poursuivi est celui d'une dématérialisation native des procédures, aboutissant à la création de dossiers numériques uniques, accessibles à tous les acteurs.*' Ministère de la Justice, *Chantiers de la Justice*, p. 3.
60. In French: '*les parties pourraient avoir à justifier d'une tentative de résolution amiable, avant d'éventuellement saisir la juridiction.*' Ministère de la Justice, *Chantiers de la Justice*, p. 8.
61. Michael Briggs (Lord Justice), Judiciary of England and Wales: Civil Courts Structure Review; Final Report, July 2016.
62. Michael Briggs (Lord Justice), Judiciary of England and Wales: Civil Courts Structure Review; Interim Report, paras 12.6, 12.7 and 12.9, p. 122.
63. Michael Cross, 'News focus: Don't blow a fuse over online civil court', *Law Society Gazette* (13 November 2017). Accessed online on 29 July 2018.
64. HM Courts and Tribunals Service, Reform Update, May 2018, pp. 22, 23. Accessible online at *https://assets.publishing.service.gov.uk/government/uploads/system/uploads/attachment_data/file/711535/HMCTS_Reform_Update_May_2018.pdf*
65. HM Courts and Tribunals Service, Reform Update, May 2018, p. 24.
66. Portail du Gouvernement, 'Tribunaux: la nouvelle carte judiciaire est en place', 7 January 2011. Accessible online at *http://archives.gouvernement.fr/fillon_version2/gouvernement/tribunaux-la-nouvelle-carte-judiciaire-est-en-place.html*
67. John Hyde, 'More court closures coming, lord chief justice tells MPs', *Law Society Gazette* (14 September 2017). Accessed online on 5 August 2018.
68. Union Syndicale des Magistrats, *Souffrance au travail des magistrats, état des lieux, état d'alerte*, February 2015. Accessible online at *http://www.union-syndicale-magistrats.org/web/upload_fich/publication/livre_blanc_2015/livre_blanc_soufffance.pdf*
69. The Lord Chief Justice's Report 2017, p. 12. Accessible online at *https://www.judiciary.gov.uk/wp-content/uploads/2017/09/lcj-report-2017-final.pdf*
70. For a comparative study of the CAB and the PIMMs, see Géraldine Gadbin-George, 'Le troisième secteur et l'accès aux droits en France et au Royaume-Uni: l'exemple des CABx et des PIMMs', *Revue de Droit Sanitaire et Social* (September–October 2018).
71. Monidipa Fouzder, 'Magistrates decide 3,000 fare dodgers' fates on a laptop', *Law Society Gazette* (9 December 2017), accessed online on 17 August 2018.

8

Demystifying the Laws and the Work of Judges in Wales

Milwyn Jarman

In chapter 8 a new perspective on the theme of access to justice is provided. If Wales contributes to the diversity of the law and the judiciary, it is faced with its own challenges in terms of access to justice due to growing divergences between Welsh and English law. While the codification of Welsh law may improve its accessibility, Wales is still looking for its judicial independence from England through a distinct Welsh jurisdiction extending the process of devolution to the realm of justice.

1. The Origins of Welsh Law

It is now over twenty years since the UK Parliament, following a referendum in favour of devolution, passed the Government of Wales Act 1998, which devolved law-making powers to the National Assembly for Wales. Since then, law-making powers have been increasing, and there is now beginning to be a real divergence between laws applicable in Wales and those applicable in England, particularly at present in the areas of social care, renting homes and planning.

Whilst many aspects of social justice have been devolved, the administration of justice at present is not. However, in the wake of devolution there have been changes in relation to such administration in Wales. For the first time in centuries, judges who hear cases in

Wales now receive training in the laws applicable only in Wales and in the Welsh language. Not since the autonomous Welsh Princes of the Middle Ages has there been this difference. In order to understand these changes, and what further changes there may be in the future, some historical context is necessary, although for present purposes, such context must be briefly set out.

The system of governance and law making which the Romans brought with their invasion extended to that part of the British Isles now known as Wales. By the early fifth century, Roman occupation had come to an end, and dynasties slowly emerged by which that part was ruled. Land rights were inherited by the owner's sons, although the owner would in his lifetime nominate one of his sons to become the principal ruler of his dynasty, and hence, Prince.

It was not until the time of Hywel ap Cadell that most of present-day Wales came under the control of one prince. It was during his time (910–49) that it is thought that most of the laws applicable under his rule were reduced to writing, influenced as they were by other systems such as Roman civil law and the Church. These became known as the Laws of Hywel Dda (Hywel the Good).[1] At about the same time the invading Angles and Saxons were establishing their own laws in what was to become England.

The Laws of Hywel Dda were written in manuscripts of pocket size, so that judges travelling throughout Wales to hear cases could take a copy of the manuscripts with them.[2] An example of what judges were advised by the manuscripts may be seen as pertinent today as a thousand years ago, which is, as roughly translated: 'A judge should listen thoroughly, remember well, learn earnestly, pronounce courteously, and judge mercifully.'[3]

The Laws of Hywel Dda largely survived the Norman conquest of England. However, gradually Norman lords encroached into south and east parts of Wales, which became known as the Marches. In the courts of the Marcher Lords, the Welsh laws were applied but often using common law procedures. By 1267 Llywellyn ap Gruffud was granted the title and precedence of Prince of Wales by Henry III. Llywellyn refused to pay homage to Henry's successor, Edward I, and in the ensuing war between the two countries, was killed in battle. By the Statute of Rhuddlan in 1284, Edward brought the two systems of law closer together, but they remained distinct, and the judiciary who heard cases in Wales remained largely based in Wales.

2. Unification

It was not until Henry VIII enacted the Acts relating to the Administration of Justice in Wales between 1535 and 1543 (now usually referred to collectively as the Acts of Union) that a unified system of law became applicable to Wales and to England. The Marches were amalgamated into the shires of Wales with new courts in each shire. Justices of the peace were appointed to hear the less serious criminal cases and administrative and licensing matters. The more serious cases were heard in courts known as the Court of Great Sessions of Wales.[4]

However, some cases, such as chancery cases could not be litigated in Wales and had to be litigated in London, where the legislative and executive power was centralised. Moreover, the language of all courts was prescribed as English, despite the fact that a significant minority of the Welsh population at the time could not speak English. A witness who could not do so would have to give evidence in the Welsh language, but the deposition would be written in English.

Over the next 200 years, the Great Sessions were gradually eroded, principally by the King's Bench Court in London removing cases from the Great Sessions to be heard in England. In removing a murder case from the Great Sessions to Hereford Assizes in England in 1723, the King's Bench judge commented adversely on the standard of justice in Wales.[5] Eventually, the Great Sessions were abolished by the UK Parliament in 1830. Thus, although justices of the peace continued to hear the less serious cases, judges based in London travelled around Wales as well as England to hear the more serious cases, in courts known as assizes.

In 1846 county courts were established in the major towns of England and Wales to hear civil claims under a modest financial limit. The Lord Chancellor, who then had the power of judicial appointment, indicated that he would give preference in the appointment of county court judges in Wales to those who spoke Welsh.

Furthermore, laws were now made only in London, and with exceptions that were very few and far between (such as liquor licencing and education) were made to apply to both countries without distinction.

In 1857, further centralisation of litigation into London was brought about. Previously, disputes concerning probate, matrimony and defamation, as well as Church matters, were heard in ecclesiastical courts in Wales as well as in England. The courts applied canon laws of Europe rather than the common law, and often the clerics had little or no legal education. For example, the General Report of the Ecclesiastical Courts 1831–2 reveals that the clerical judge in Bangor and his deputy had no regular legal education.[6] The Probate Act 1857 transferred such disputes to a new Court of Probate based in London.

By the Supreme Court of Judicature Acts 1873–5, the divisions of the High Court (including the Queen's Bench Division, as the King's Bench had become known after the accession of Queen Victoria) were streamlined into three, the others being the Chancery Division and the Probate, Divorce and Admiralty Division. Various other courts were abolished, and the jurisdiction transferred to the High Court.

All judges of the High Court, as well as the appellate courts, the Court of Appeal and the House of Lords, continued to be based in London. High Court Judges occasionally heard commercial cases in the courts of assize, including in Wales, but most commercial cases from Wales and from the English regions continued to be heard in London.

This, in outline, was the legislative and judicial landscape of Wales at the turn of the century.

3. Difficulties with a Unified System in Post-industrial Wales

At that time, Wales was at the height of commercial activity, driven largely by what could be extracted from the ground. Coal, metals and slate were exported to many countries around the world. Inevitably the increase in trade led to an increased demand for dispute resolution. There continued to be dissatisfaction particularly in south Wales, and in commercial centres outside London, over the speed and costs of conducting litigation, especially commercial litigation. In Wales, there also continued to be difficulties experienced in cases where a witness could not speak English and the judge could not speak Welsh.

In 1919 a Parliamentary conference was established to consider the creation of legislatures for each of the four nations of the UK. Evidence from some Welsh judges suggested that Wales should have the judicial independence which ended in 1830 and should have a Court of Appeal and High Court of its own. Others were opposed, principally on the grounds of cost and the fear that such a change would result in talented Welsh lawyers moving their practices to England. However, there was little political motivation for change at this time and the proposals went nowhere.[7]

The dissatisfaction did not abate, however, and in 1934 a Royal Commission (the Peel Commission) was appointed to examine how court cases might be heard more expeditiously. The evidence heard included that from Welsh county court judges, who pointed out that regard had to be paid to national identity in Wales and the Welsh language. Although its recommendations included improvements to the administration of judges in Wales and the Welsh language, they did not go very far.[8]

It was not until the passing of the Welsh Courts Act 1942 that there was some, albeit limited, relaxation of the principle introduced by the Acts of Union that English was the language of the court. The 1942 Act enabled oaths to be taken in the Welsh language and for witnesses to give evidence in Welsh if the witnesses would be disadvantaged by having to give evidence in English. The principle of equality of both languages in the courtroom was not recognised until the Welsh Language Act 1967.

Administrative changes were also slow in coming. The Beeching Commission[9] was set up in 1966 to consider reforming the courts of assizes. It recommended that the courts in Wales should be administered as a single circuit from Cardiff. It also recommended the abolition of the assize system and the transfer of civil cases to the High Court and criminal cases to a newly formed Crown Court.

The Lord Chancellor accepted the main recommendations in respect of administration, although Chester was also included in the circuit, which accordingly was known as the Wales and Chester Circuit. He also decided that leading barristers, known as Queen's Counsel, no longer had to practise from London. The recommendations as to the abolition of the courts of assizes and the creation of a new Crown Court were put into effect by the Courts Act 1971. Crown Courts were established in each of the main towns of Wales.

The High Court and the appellate courts, the Court of Appeal and the House of Lords, continued to be based in London. Judges of the Queen's Bench Division travelled to courts in Wales, and to the regions of England, to hear the most serious civil and criminal cases. Judges of the Family Division, as the Probate, Family and Admiralty Division had become, also travelled to hear cases in Wales.

However, specialist litigation from Wales, such as High Court chancery and commercial cases, continued to be heard in London. It was not until 1989 that a judge was appointed to hear chancery cases in Cardiff, Birmingham and Bristol. The judge was a circuit judge, appointed to sit as a judge of the High Court under section 9 of the Senior Court Act 1981, known as section 9 judges.

4. The Growth of Tribunals

Tribunals in the UK have their origins in ministerial nominations to deal with disputes between the state and its citizens, for example as to Customs and Excise. The introduction of the welfare state in the early part of the twentieth century followed by the First World War saw a huge increase in the number of state benefits to which citizens became entitled, such as pensions, unemployment benefit and disablement benefit. Statutory tribunals were set up to deal with disputes in relation to such entitlements in an informal and accessible way.

The trend extended to other disputes such as those relating to employment, asylum, land registration, planning and mental health, so that by the end of the century tribunals dealt with disputes in over sixty jurisdictions.

From time to time, concern was voiced about judicial or quasi-judicial powers being exercised by ministerial tribunals. Concerns also grew as to the lack of cohesion and uncertainty of procedure, until in 1957 the Lord Chancellor appointed the Franks Committee to report on such matters.

The committee's report[10] set out the main advantages of tribunals as cheapness, accessibility, freedom from technicality, expedition and expert knowledge. It adopted three guiding principles: openness, fairness and impartiality. It also concluded that tribunals should properly be seen as machinery provided by Parliament for adjudication of disputes rather than part of the machinery of administration.

It made recommendations aimed at ensuring that tribunals should be independent of the Ministry concerned. These included that there should be a Council on Tribunals, that Chairs of tribunals should be appointed by the Lord Chancellor and should be legally qualified, that they should give reasons for their decision, should sit in public and that there should be a right of appeal to the High Court.

The recommendation as to legally qualified Chairs was implemented in some categories of tribunals, such as Employment Tribunals and Mental Health Tribunals. These appointments were made by the Lord Chancellor, who was a minister in the UK government.

Such tribunals, of necessity, held their public hearings locally and usually the Chairs were appointed from local lawyers. This was as true of Wales as it was of England, but the administration remained generally centralised in London. There were a few exceptions, such as the Agricultural Land Tribunal, and the Mental Health Review Tribunals, each of which was administered with a Welsh dimension.

As in the case of the courts, devolution was to have a significant effect on the tribunals system as it existed in Wales, but in the case of tribunals, that effect was more direct.

5. Devolution

There had been attempts in the late nineteenth and early twentieth centuries to introduce Home Rule for Wales bills in the UK Parliament and campaigns for a Welsh jurisdiction, but these had not progressed very far.[11] Attention then focused on a ministerial office for Wales. This was achieved in 1964 with the creation of the office of Secretary of State for Wales. Executive functions and subordinate law-making powers were transferred to the new Minister in such fields as housing, public health and agriculture so far as they concerned Wales. Subsequently, individual statutes which granted such powers in other fields to other Ministers, now granted such powers, insofar as it was thought necessary, to the Welsh Secretary in respect of Wales.

This led to a rather piecemeal growth of powers. Moreover, the Welsh Secretary was directly accountable to the UK Parliament rather than to the people of Wales. It was primarily this lack of accountability which led to a referendum in Wales as to whether the nation should have its own assembly. The result in 1997 was in favour, albeit by a narrow margin.

The subsequent Government of Wales Act 1998 created the National Assembly for Wales as a body corporate with legislative and executive functions. The former functions were limited to subordinate legislation. At the same time, the Scottish Parliament was created, but in contrast to the position in Wales, with primary law-making powers and an executive which was separate from the legislature.

The legislative and executive functions transferred to the Assembly were mainly those which had previously been exercised by the Secretary of State for Wales but were now being exercised by a body directly accountable to the people of Wales.

However, this model was seen as unsatisfactory compared to the Parliaments of UK and Scotland. The Government of Wales Act 2006 created a separate executive called the Welsh Assembly Government and paved the way for the Assembly to be given primary law-making powers on a gradual basis (which proved cumbersome) or with approval in a second referendum. Such approval was obtained in 2011. The result was that the Assembly could pass primary legislation on listed subjects which generally followed those in respect of which subordinate law-making powers had been devolved. However, such a conferred powers model differed from that in Scotland, where the reserved powers model allowed the Scottish Parliament to legislate on any subject not expressly reserved to the UK Parliament.

After the Silk Commission[12] recommended a move to a reserved powers model in Wales, the Wales Act 2017 was passed to implement that recommendation. The list of reserved powers in Schedule 7A is a long one, and debate continues as to whether that Act gives more or fewer powers to the Assembly. However, the 2017 Act conferred, for the first time, executive ministerial functions on Welsh ministers. This means that like their counterparts elsewhere in the UK, they can bring or be defendants in common law actions.

The precise nature of Acts passed by the National Assembly for Wales is debatable. This legislative competence is derived from an Act of the UK Parliament, and in that sense may be seen as subordinate. On the other hand, unless a reserved matter, Assembly Acts may contain any provision which could be made by the UK Parliament. Moreover, the law makers in Wales are accountable not to the UK Parliament but to the people of Wales. Their Acts are generally regarded as a form of primary legislation.[13]

6. Courts in Wales after Devolution

Although the administration of justice as such in Wales was not and is not devolved, it was recognised by senior judiciary in London that devolution brought with it an expectation of change in the way that justice is administered in Wales. In 1998 and 1999, practice directions implemented provisions for the use of the Welsh language in proceedings in the Crown Court and in civil proceedings.[14] In 1999, Lord Bingham, the then Lord Chief Justice of England and Wales, and Presidents of the divisions of the High Court, gave directions for the hearing of devolution issues in Wales, and for proceedings for judicial review involving Welsh public bodies to be issued in Cardiff, and not just in London as had previously been the case.[15]

In 1999, the Administrative Court in Wales was set up, with an office in Cardiff.[16] However, at this time, claims could be lodged in Cardiff but would be sent to the Administrative Court Office in

London to process. The public interest in challenges to the decisions of public authorities is such that it is desirable that such challenges are heard locally. This was recognised, and some judicial review cases and other challenges to the decisions of public authorities, such as local planning authorities were listed for hearing at court venues in Wales. However, this was rather piecemeal and some cases with a great deal of public interest in Wales continued to be heard in London.[17]

In 2000 a Mercantile Court was opened at Cardiff by Lord Bingham CJ. In doing so he said:

> This court represents the long overdue recognition of the need for the Principality of Wales to have its own indigenous institutions operating locally and meeting the needs of the citizens here. This court is another step towards recognising Wales as a very proud, distinctive and successful nation.

By now, each of the specialist courts in Wales, the Chancery Division, the Administrative Court, the Mercantile Court (now known as the Circuit Court) and the Technology and Construction Court, was headed by a supervising or liaison High Court judge based in London, but each had section 9 judges based in Wales appointed to sit as High Court judges in those courts. However, such specialist cases from Wales could still be, and some were, issued and heard in London.

The Constitutional Reform Act 2005 brought major reforms to the courts of England and Wales. The office of Lord Chancellor was modified. The House of Lords was abolished as the final appeal court and in its place the Supreme Court was set up. The Supreme Court has twice considered a reference by the Attorney General as to whether proposed legislation was within the competence of the National Assembly and on each occasion decided that it was.[18]

The appointment of judges, formerly a function of the Lord Chancellor was transferred to a new body independent of the Crown called the Judicial Appointments Commission.

Despite the creation of specialist courts in Wales, some such cases emanating from Wales continued to be issued and heard in

London. To some extent this continued to be the experience in the English regions. This began to change from 2007 after judicial comments that judicial review challenges against Welsh public bodies should be heard in Wales unless there are good reasons for their being heard elsewhere.[19]

A Judicial Working Group was set up to make recommendations, and as a result of its report[20] the procedural rules and practice directions dealing with judicial review claims were amended so that the general expectation now is that such proceedings will be administered and heard where the claimant has the closest connection.[21]

In 2017, specialist courts in England and Wales were brought under the umbrella of Business and Property Courts, and the Business and Property Courts in Wales, although based in Cardiff, will hear cases in other venues in Wales when appropriate and practical.[22] The section 9 judges based in Wales, and district judges in the north-west and south have been appointed as judges of the court. In addition, High Court judges are deployed to hear cases in Wales, as well as the English Regions, when needed.

7. Tribunals in Wales after Devolution.

It has been said that more recognition of Welsh tribunals was achieved as a side-effect of devolution in 1998.[23] At that time, there remained two main perceived defects in the system operating across England and Wales: the perceived lack of independence from the executive, and lack of coherence of tribunals. A further review on such issues was commissioned. The Leggatt Report[24] did not consider devolved tribunals, although the potential significance of devolution was recognised. Tribunals were seen as judicial bodies which provided an alternative to courts. The recommendations included independence from government, the establishment of a tribunal service and a two-tier structure.

In response to the call for independence, the Lord Chancellor agreed with the UK government that responsibility for tribunals would be transferred from the relevant ministry to the Department for Constitutional Affairs, which then became the Ministry of Justice.

The Tribunal, Courts and Enforcement Act 2007 was intended to address the lack of cohesion in the tribunal system. A Senior President of Tribunals was appointed. A two-tier structure of tribunals was set up. First-tier Tribunals from which an appeal lies with permission to Upper Tribunals are made up of several chambers, and the head of each chamber is a High Court judge. There are a few exceptions to this type of structure, such as the Employment Tribunal and the Employment Appeal Tribunal.

At this time, the administration of the court and tribunal system remained distinct. The former was administered by Her Majesty's Court Service, an executive agency of Ministry of Justice. After devolution, HMCS Wales was created to administer the courts in Wales. Tribunals were administered by a separate agency, the Tribunals Service, but arguments that the two should have a distinct administration were not accepted on the basis that Wales was too small to be administered efficiently, and so instead was administered with the south-west of England. In 2011 the two services combined to form Her Majesty's Courts and Tribunal Service Wales, which operates on the basis of a partnership between the Lord Chancellor and the Lord Chief Justice. Judges based in Wales are appointed to hear cases in both tiers at various venues throughout Wales. As devolved tribunals were not considered by the Leggatt Report, they remain outside the two-tier system implemented in the 2007 Act.[25]

A number of matters in which tribunals operate are now devolved matters, which means that the responsibility for devolved tribunals rests not with the Ministry of Justice, but with the Welsh ministers. These are administered through the Welsh Tribunals Unit, which presently has responsibility for eight tribunals: the Adjudication Panel for Wales, the Agricultural Land Tribunal for Wales, the Mental Health Review Tribunal for Wales, the Registered Inspectors of Schools Appeal Tribunal, the Registered Nursery Education Inspector's Appeal Tribunal, the Residential Property Tribunal Wales, the Special Educational Needs Tribunal for Wales and the Welsh Language Tribunal.[26]

The Wales Act 2017 provided for the appointment of a Senior President of Welsh Tribunals, and the first holder of this office, Sir Wyn

Williams, was sworn in by the then Lord Chief Justice, Lord Thomas, in Cardiff in December in 2017.

The Welsh Language Tribunal was set up under primary legislation passed by the National Assembly of Wales, namely the Welsh Language (Wales) Measure 2011. Thus, this is the first tribunal to be set up by the Assembly. The Measure (as primary legislation by the Assembly was then known – now known as Acts) set up the office of the Welsh Language Commissioner with the power to set standards relating to the use of the Welsh Language. Parties dissatisfied with such standards may appeal to the Welsh Language Tribunal, whose Chair is legally qualified.

8. The Judiciary in Wales after Devolution

Apart from the appointment of specialist section 9 judges, there has been no significant change in the structure of the judiciary since devolution, and judges of the High Court and the appellate courts remain based in London.

However, there have been changes in judicial attitudes and deployment to reflect the process of devolution. This was in large part led by successive heads of the judiciary who took a keen interest in the administration of justice in Wales post-devolution. Lord Bingham was the Lord Chief Justice in 1998. He added the words 'and Wales' to the full title of the office which he held. Previously, the title had been 'Lord Chief Justice of England', which says a great deal about how justice in Wales was then perceived.

Such interest has been continued by his successors, and in particular by the last three, Lord Judge, Lord Thomas and the present holder, Lord Burnett. Lord Thomas was the first Welsh holder of the office (apart from one brief spell over a hundred years ago) and now chairs the Commission on Justice in Wales, of which more below. Each of these have regularly attended and addressed Association of Judges of Wales meetings and other events in Wales.

High Court judges are appointed to be presiding judges, one senior and one junior, on a four-year cycle. The practice has grown of appointing such judges on the Wales Circuit who have some connection with or knowledge of Wales. Each of these judges spends about half of their judicial time in Wales. In addition, as has been noted, specialist High Court judges now readily hear cases in Wales when needed, which is more in line with their colleagues in family, civil and crime. A practice has also grown up that both divisions of the Court of Appeal, civil and criminal will sit to hear cases in Wales, usually twice a year for one week.

On St David's Day 2019 (the patron saint of Wales is celebrated on 1 March), the President of the Supreme Court, Baroness Hale, and the first permanent Welsh Supreme Court Justice, Lord David Lloyd-Jones, announced (in the English and Welsh language respectively), that the Supreme Court would, for the first time, sit for a week's session in Wales. The hearing took place in July. The Supreme Court, which usually sits in London, had previously sat for a session in Edinburgh and in Belfast.

The Judicial Appointments Commission is now also responsible for the appointments of tribunal members. The Commission, with the approval of the Lord Chancellor, has adopted an additional requirement of candidates for judicial posts in Wales, that candidates need to have an understanding, or the ability to acquire the understanding, of the administration of justice in Wales, including legislation applicable to Wales and Welsh devolution arrangements.

The particular position of the judiciary in post-devolution Wales was recognised by the setting up of the Association of Judges of Wales in 2008, after a Welsh member of the Court of Appeal, Lord Justice Pill, sought the views of judges in Wales on such an association and received support for the proposal. There are associations of most tiers of judges across England and Wales, for example, High Court judges, circuit judges and district judges. The Welsh association however has membership from every tier, from Supreme Court Justices to district judges and tribunal judges, including those of the devolved tribunals. Membership is open to all judges who hear, or have heard, cases in Wales. It holds an annual general meeting which the Lord Chief Justice is invited to attend. Its main aims include responding, from a judicial perspective, to consultation papers issued by the Welsh government, avoiding of course any political issues, and to help keep its members updated on legislation passed by the National Assembly. This is an example of how the small size of Wales can be used in a positive way to achieve coordination, which may be difficult to achieve in larger countries.

9. Legal Wales

Another such example is the Legal Wales Foundation Board. This has its origins in the Legal Wales Standing Committee set up in 2002 by the first Counsel General for Wales appointed following devolution, Winston Roddick QC. His aim was to bring together representatives of all legal communities in Wales to promote proposals for action on issues affecting the administration of justice, teaching and research law, and the provision of legal services as they affect Wales. Members of the committee represented barristers, solicitors, employed lawyers, academics, Her Majesty's Court Service, the Tribunal Service and the Crown Prosecution Service. Members of the judiciary attended meetings, initially by invitation. The phrase 'Legal Wales' gained currency when used by the then Counsel General, and then the senior presiding judge in Wales, Mr Justice Thomas, to reflect the growing sense of identity and confidence in legal communities in Wales in the wake of devolution. The Committee inaugurated a Legal Wales conference, which has now become an annual event and is held at venues throughout Wales.

The Committee evolved into the Board, which is now independent of the Welsh government. Its members now include judges. Speakers at the conference include the Lord Chief Justice, Supreme Court Justices and other members of the senior judiciary from London and other jurisdictions such as Scotland, Ireland and Europe.

10. The Welsh Language and the Justice System in Wales

Latest figures published by the Welsh government show that almost a third of the population of three million can speak Welsh.[27] It would be difficult now to find in Wales (although easier in Patagonia) a Welsh-speaker who cannot speak English reasonably fluently. However, in many parts of Wales, particularly in the north and the west, Welsh is the everyday language. Legal proceedings tend to be stressful experiences where the nuance of language may be important, and it is a matter of justice that a citizen should be able to engage in them in his or her first language.

In respect of the Welsh language, the basis of equality of that language with the English language in Wales was established by the Welsh Language (Wales) Measure 2011. The Lord Chancellor has set up a Welsh Language Standing Committee and two judges in Wales act as Welsh language liaison judges. The principle of equality is now embodied in procedural rules for criminal, civil and family cases.

After centuries of the imposition of English as the language of the court, described by Lord Justice Judge (later Lord Chief Justice) in 1999 as 'an outrage',[28] it has been a slow process to encourage some Welsh-speakers to use the language in the justice system if they prefer to do so. There is still some perception, although not based in fact, that to do so may somehow disadvantage the speaker. In areas where Welsh is the everyday language, Welsh-speakers who take part in the local justice system can expect to do so without special arrangement.

By now, about a third of the circuit and district judges in Wales speak Welsh.[29] Her Majesty's Courts and Tribunal Service Wales and the judiciary identify where the Welsh language is essential or desirable, and the Judicial Appointments Commission take this into account in making appointments. The Judicial College now holds seminars every two years for judges who wish to practise or improve Welsh-language skills in the court or tribunal room.

The number of cases heard in the Welsh language is increasing, and for 2017–18 rose to 795. This now includes cases in the higher courts too. A murder trial held in 2005 in north Wales was conducted in the Welsh language. The High Court judge Mr Justice Roderick Evans and Queen's Counsel spoke Welsh throughout the trial, and the judge summed up the case and gave directions to the Welsh-speaking jury in that language too.

In 2014, the first Administrative Court case to be conducted in both languages was heard in Cardiff.[30] It concerned a decision of an agency of the UK Treasury to cease using the Welsh language. This was challenged by the Welsh Language Commissioner. The parties' lawyers used each language as a matter of choice, and the written judgments were handed down in both languages. When the Supreme Court sat in Wales for the first time in Cardiff, that court also handed down judgments in both languages.

In Wales, as in England, a number of judges are appointed to be Diversity and Community Relations Judges. These engage with various communities in Wales to attempt to demystify the work of judges. They visit schools, colleges and other communities, and pupils and students visit courts to observe cases and to take part in mock trials. Such engagement in Wales takes place in both languages.

11. The Divergence of Laws

The National Assembly has passed over 4.600 pieces of secondary legislation since devolution, and 59 primary pieces of legislation since that power was conferred in 2007.[31] Although much of that is similar to that passed by the UK Parliament as applicable only to England, there is increasing divergence between the law applicable in Wales and that applicable in England. By way of example, some of those areas are dealt with in this section.

Two of the first areas in which the National Assembly exercised its new law-making powers in 2008 related to care for vulnerable children and the elderly, and the provision of affordable housing. As Professor Thomas Watkin QC (formerly First Legislative Council to the Welsh Assembly) has noted,[32] it is remarkable that these areas each have resonance with the laws of Hywel Dda. The latter contained provisions of some sophistication dealing with the welfare of children and disadvantaged people and also provisions for the right to acquire accommodation by building on land belonging to others in certain circumstances.

The principal enactment on the rights of children is the Rights of Children and Young Persons (Wales) Measure 2011, which incorporates certain obligations in the United Nations Convention on the Rights of the Child (UNCRC) into Welsh government decision-making. The Social Services and Well-being (Wales) Act 2014 contains a similar requirement of those exercising functions under that Act in relation to children. These have been described as 'Wales-only, made-in-Wales laws',[33] in that the UNCRC has effect in Wales which it does not have elsewhere in the United Kingdom.

The first major piece of housing legislation to be passed by the National Assembly was the Housing (Wales) Act 2014. This provided for a system of registration of rented homes and landlords in Wales, and of licensing of landlords and their agents. A licence can be obtained only by an applicant who is a fit and proper person and has undergone training as to good practice in letting homes. A landlord who is not so licensed may still let out homes, but may only do certain things through a licensed agent. One example is the service of a no-fault notice to quit. The intention was to give greater protection to tenants, for example, from the service of such notices in response to complaints. The Act also contained provisions in relation to housing the homeless which give a greater level of protection.

The second piece is the Renting Homes (Wales) Act 2016. This was in response to the Law Commission of England and Wales Report on Renting Homes.[34] At present the law of England and Wales in this area is complex and not easily comprehendible, with half a dozen or so different types of tenancy and different levels of security or protection for the tenant. The recommendation of the report was that the law should be simplified so as to provide only two types of tenancy, one for individual landlords and the other for social landlords. The recommendation was not accepted by the UK government but was accepted by the Welsh government, and the 2016 Act was subsequently passed by the Assembly. For various reasons, at the time of writing it has yet to be brought into force.

The third example where there is divergence between the law applicable in Wales, and that applicable in England is planning law, in terms of process, policy and substantive law.[35] The twenty-two local planning authorities in Wales, responsible for development plans and planning permissions and enforcement, follow county lines. The structure in England is more complex, with some two-tier processes. The Planning (Wales) Act 2015 gives power to the Welsh ministers to create panels to prepare strategic plans, whereas in England such panels only operate in respect of Greater London. There are no neighbourhood development plans in Wales as there are in England, but the Well-being of Future Generations (Wales) Act 2015 requires well-being plans. Developments of national significance in Wales are the subject of a separate regime. Planning Policy Wales gives more descriptive elements and more detailed statements of key subjects than its English counterpart, National Planning Policy Framework, although the essential aims, including the requirement to ensure sustainable development, are the same. A Welsh Revenue Authority was established by the Tax Collection and Management (Wales) Act 2018. The two main unreserved taxes which it manages at present are land transaction tax and landfill disposal tax.

This divergence is set to increase, which raises questions about the training of judges who sit in Wales. A Wales Strategy Group of judges has been set up to assist in this task, and judicial seminars on various aspects of Welsh Law are now being held.

12. The Form and Accessibility of the Law in Wales

The increasing divergence also raises questions about the form and accessibility of Welsh law. Moreover, the fact that law making in Wales since devolution is still relatively new provides an opportunity to streamline and simplify the law.

The Wales Act 2014 modified the Law Commissions Act 1965 so as to take account of devolution. A protocol was entered into between the Commission and the Welsh government, and a Welsh Advisory Committee was established for the Commission. The Welsh government invited the Commission to report on the form and accessibility of the law applicable in Wales and the then Chair of the Commission, Sir (later Lord) David Lloyd-Jones, accepted. The resulting report was published in July 2016.[36] It contained detailed recommendations for consolidation and codification of Welsh Law. The Welsh government agreed that it was necessary to ensure that the laws in Wales are easily accessible.[37]

In October 2018, the present Counsel General, Jeremy Miles AM, announced at the Legal Wales conference the proposed introduction of the Legislation (Wales) Bill, now progressing through the Assembly. This provides for a programme of activity to improve accessibility of Welsh law and to make provision for consolidation and codification. This led the present Chair of the Commission, Sir Nicholas Green, to comment, 'Wales is one of the first jurisdictions worldwide to enshrine the public importance of legislative commitment to ensuring the accessibility of laws to individuals.'[38]

Welsh planning law was the subject of another Law Commission report in 2017.[39] Its detailed recommendations included a new planning code which should be comprehensive yet simplified. Again, this was welcomed by the Welsh government, who indicated that there is already a bill in progress which implements many of the recommendations.[40]

13. The Future

It is hoped that it will be apparent from this brief account how much can be achieved by a legislative assembly of a country in a relatively short period of time, when allowed to do so. This is despite, but perhaps in some ways because of, the relatively small governance involved.

Yet in this context Wales remains in a position which is nowhere else to be found. The then Counsel General, Carwyn Jones AM, observed in the annual Law Society lecture at the National Eisteddfod at Cardiff in 2008 that he was not aware of anywhere else in the world where a legislature has primary law-making powers but no associated territorial jurisdiction. The debate as to whether Wales should have a separate jurisdiction continues.

It was he who, as First Minister, set up in 2017 the Commission on Justice in Wales, chaired by Lord Thomas, to review the operation of the justice system in Wales. The Commission has been receiving evidence over the last two years from all stakeholders. As a result of evidence given to the Commission, and drawing on a lecture entitled 'Developing Legal Wales' by Lord Lloyd-Jones at the 2017 Legal Wales Conference, the Commission at the following year's conference launched a discussion and consultation paper responding to the demand in Wales for greater cooperation and coordination in the field of law. The proposal suggests a Law Council of Wales, which is not dependent upon further constitutional change in the justice system in Wales. The proposed council would be an independent advisory forum which promotes knowledge and skills, best practice and innovation in the field of law.

As well as announcing the Legislation (Wales) Bill at the 2018 Legal Wales conference, the Counsel General announced other initiatives, including an accompanying draft Welsh taxonomy of codes setting out the subject matter by reference to which Welsh law could be organised. He also announced that the task of updating Welsh legislation – in both English and in Welsh – will be taken over by the Welsh government from the National Archives and that he intends to relaunch the Cyfraith Cymru/Law Wales website. As part of his address, he said this:

> Trying to maintain the single legal jurisdiction, and the reservation of policing and most justice-related matters, is by far the single biggest remaining cause of complexity of the Welsh devolution settlement...
>
> A process has begun of creating a distinct legal infrastructure for Wales. This is a process that won't stop. The process of making laws for Wales won't stop, the divergence in law between Wales and England won't stop. The creation of a Welsh legal jurisdiction and ultimately the devolution of the justice system is inevitable.

Lord Carloway, Lord President of the Court of Session and Lord Justice General of Scotland also addressed the conference.[41] His message was that having a small separate jurisdiction, as now exists in Scotland, has some disadvantages, but also advantages, even if it means formally disengaging from a much larger jurisdiction. He observed that, for a new legal jurisdiction, success depends on the confidence of those operating within it and the perception of those outside it, in Wales and elsewhere, looking in.

The report of the Commission has made seventy-eight detailed recommendations to improve justice in Wales. The overarching recommendation is that justice should be devolved to Wales to align with health, education, housing and other social policies, as the determination of justice policy in London treats justice as an island and not central to the development of Wales as a just, fair and prosperous nation. It was pointed out that the people of England, Northern Ireland and Scotland are not disadvantaged in this way. The recommendations ranged from enabling better access to justice through joining up legal aid and third-sector provision, encouraging innovation in the legal sector and law schools in Wales, and increasing leadership skills in relation to matters affecting justice. Whilst some of these changes need legislation others do not, and the final recommendation was that the Welsh government should begin the process of reform by listing the recommendations it will seek to implement whilst devolution continues, and the Assembly should monitor and review the process of reform. The Welsh government has welcomed the report, but a detailed response is awaited from it and from the UK government.

Notes

1. Medieval Welsh law has attracted a good deal of interest from academics, with over 350 works on the subject, of which the most prolific writer was the late Dafydd Jenkins; see Sara Elin Roberts, 'Dafydd Jenkins – Scholar of Cyfraith Hywel', *The Welsh Legal History Society*, XI (2013), p. 222.
2. About forty manuscripts survive, dating from the mid-thirteenth to early fifteenth centuries; see Sara Elin Roberts, 'The Welsh Legal Triads', *The Welsh Legal History Society*, XII (2012).
3. Demetian Code, Book II.
4. For a detailed exposition of the position in Wales between the Acts of Union and the twentieth century, see Mr Justice (now Lord) Thomas, 'Legal Wales: Its Modern Origins and its Role after Devolution: National Identity, the Welsh Language and Parochialism', *The Welsh Legal History Society*, I (2015), p. 113.
5. *R v. Athoe* (1723) Strange 553. See David Gardner, *Administrative Law and the Administrative Court in Wales* (Cardiff: University of Wales Press, 2016), pp. 1–18 at 2–14.
6. Brian Hutton, 'The Reform of the Testamentary Jurisdiction of the Ecclesiastical Courts', *The Welsh Legal History Society*, I (2001), p. 90.

7. See n. 4, p. 128.
8. The Peel Report, *Report of Royal Commission* (Cmnd 5262, 1936) and see n. 4, pp. 139–43.
9. The Beeching Report, *Report of Royal Commission on Assizes and Quarter Sessions* (Cmnd 4153, 1969) and see n. 4, pp. 150–4.
10. The Franks Report, *Report of the Committee on Administrative Tribunals and Enquiries* (Cmnd 218, 1957).
11. Thomas Glyn Watkin, 'Devious Debates and Devolution', *Welsh Legal History Society*, XIII (2016), p. 114.
12. Empowerment and Responsibility: Legislative Powers to Strengthen Wales (Commission on Devolution in Wales. 2014).
13. Thomas Glyn Watkin with Daniel Greenberg, *Legislating for Wales* (Cardiff: University of Wales Press, 2018), ch. 3.
14. Practice Direction of 16 October 1998 (relating to proceedings in the Crown Court) and Practice Direction of 26 April 1999 (relating to civil proceedings).
15. *Practice Direction (Supreme Court: Devolution)* [1999] 1 WLR 1592.
16. For a full account, see Gardner, *The Administrative Court in Wales.*
17. Examples are *Jones v. Ceredigion County Council* [2004] EWHC 1376, which concerned the provision of free transport to a Welsh-language school in west Wales, and *Community Power Ltd v. National Assembly for Wales & Anor* [2004] EWHC 2186 Admin (planning), where a controversial plan to erect wind turbines near protected and historic landscape in Wales was rejected at a local inquiry but the appeal was heard in London.
18. The Local Government Byelaws (Wales) Bill, which sought to simplify procedures for making local authority by-laws in Wales [2012] UKSC 53, and the Agriculture Sector (Wales) Bill 2013, which aimed to regulate wages of agricultural workers, 2014 [UKSC] 43.
19. *R (Condron) v. The National Assembly for Wales* [2007] 2 P&CR 4 at 68, *per Lord Justice Richards and R (Deepdock) v. The Welsh Ministers [2007] EWHC 3347* (Admin) at para. 20, per HHJ Hickinbottom (as he then was, sitting as a High Court judge). See also Gardner, *The Administrative Court in Wales*, n. 16, para. 2-14.
20. *Justice Outside London.*
21. *Civil Procedure Rules 1998*, Rule 54 and PD 54D.
22. *Business and Property Courts: Advisory Note.*
23. Huw Pritchard, 'Building a Welsh Jurisdiction through Administrative Justice', in Sarah Nason (ed.), *Administrative Justice in Wales and Comparative Perspectives* (Cardiff: University of Wales Press, 2017), ch. 8.
24. The Leggatt Report: *Tribunals for Users – One system, One Service* (London: HMSO, 2001).

25. See n. 15.
26. See n. 23, p. 230.
27. StatsWales as at March 2019.
28. *Williams v. Cowell* [2000] 1 WLR 187 at 199.
29. *The Lord Chief Justice's Report*, 2018, p. 22.
30. *R (Welsh Language Commissioner) v. National Savings and Investments* [2014] EWHC 3283 (Admin).
31. See n. 29.
32. Thomas Watkin, 'The Laws of Wales', *The Welsh Legal History Society*, X (2013), p. 33.
33. Jane Williams, 'Implications for Administrative Justice of Wales's Unique Child Rights Laws', in Nason (ed.), *Administrative Justice in Wales*, p. 33.
34. *Renting Homes*, Law Com 297, updated in *Renting Homes in Wales*, Law Com 337.
35. Graham Walters, *Welsh Planning Law and Practice* (Cardiff: University of Wales Press, 2017), ch. 2.
36. *Form and Accessibility of the Law Applicable in Wales*, Law Com 366.
37. In the response of the then Counsel General, Mick Antoniw AM.
38. See his foreword to *The Law Commission Annual Report 2018–2019*, Law Com 385.
39. *Planning Law in Wales*, Law Com 383.
40. In the response of Julie James AM, the Minister for Housing and Local Government.
41. *The Administration of Law in a Devolved Context.*

PART IV

Judicial Training Reform

9

The Status and Influence of Judges of France and of Common Law Jurisdictions: Recruitment, Training and Reform

Winston Roddick CB QC

Milwyn Jarman focuses on access to justice in Wales; Winston Roddick, by contrast, discusses the importance of adapting the training of judges to the specific features of their own justice system with the prospect of the devolution of the responsibility for the administration of its own justice to Wales. Judicial independence, judicial diversity, access to justice and judicial reform, all four themes around which this book revolves, form part of the major overhaul of justice in Wales recommended by the report of Lord Thomas of Cwmgiedd, *Justice in Wales for the People of Wales*, published in October 2019.

1. Perspectives

His Honour Judge Jarman QC writes with the perspective and experience of a judge familiar with the administration of justice in Wales and with the evolution of Welsh law and as one who is involved daily in the making and clarification of it. My perspective is quite different. It is that of an advocate. I have practised before the courts of England and Wales for a number of years, thirty as Queen's Counsel, during which I became 'Leader' of the Wales and Chester Circuit, one of the six barrister circuits of England and Wales. I have appeared before courts from the lowest to the highest level and have experienced advocates and judges of the highest skills and standing. I have served as a fee-paid judge and as the Honorary Recorder of Caernarfon. I have served in two other public offices, that of Counsel General for Wales (1998–2003), and the police and crime commissioner for north Wales (2012–16). In those offices, I experienced at first hand the radical effects of devolution and the police reform legislation on the UK's unitary system of government and on the administration of justice in Wales.

Wales, an Emerging Jurisdiction

I also write from a Wales perspective as well as a UK perspective. Although Wales continues to be part of the unitary system of the UK, by the Government of Wales Act 1998 it became a devolved nation, as did Scotland and Northern Ireland by their devolution statutes, and its justice system has since become recognisably different in many respects from that of England. Those differences are apparent in the appointment and the working of the judges and of the courts in Wales and are relevant to the main themes of this book.

The Welsh Parliament, Y Senedd, has legislative competence in twenty areas, and many of its laws are different from the laws of England. Since 1999, it has made more than 4,000 statutory instruments, and since 2007 it has passed more than fifty pieces of primary legislation, all in bilingual form. In addition to the High Court and the Court of Appeal of England and Wales and the Supreme Court of the UK, all of which sit regularly in Wales, there are also a number of specialist courts centred in Wales. That one of the contributors to this book is the 'Specialist Chancery Judge for Wales' and that in 2017 there was created a new judicial post, the President of Welsh Tribunals, is proof of this process of change. The President is responsible for establishing the judicial strategic direction for the Welsh Tribunals and ensuring the independence of the Welsh Tribunals.

The Welsh language enjoys equal status to that of the English language in the administration of justice in Wales. A third of all Circuit Judges, a third of District Judges and just under a half of District Judges (Magistrates' Courts) are able to conduct cases in Welsh. Their training is organised through the Welsh Committee of the Judicial College. Processes have been adapted to recruit judges to posts requiring Welsh-language skills. In 2015–16, 570 cases were heard in Welsh and some 600–700 cases in 2017, some 20 per cent more than in the previous year. The Judicial College now produces a bilingual e-letter for Wales. The rights of court users in Wales to speak Welsh in the criminal courts has already been established and Court Rules will be made permitting a similar right to the use of the Welsh language in the Family and Civil Courts. On 24 July 2019, the Supreme Court of Justice of the UK, which was that day and for the first time sitting in Wales, delivered judgment in Welsh, an event of historical significance acknowledging the status of the Welsh language in the administration of justice today. It now stands shoulder to shoulder with the English language as a language of the law and of the administration of justice in Wales.

That those judges are appointed from amongst local barristers and solicitors and are assigned to the courts in Wales, together with the fact that today most High Court judges appointed Presiding Judges of the Wales Circuit have strong professional and personal connections with the circuit, considerably strengthens the local character of the justice system. These links between the judiciary in Wales and the community in which they serve as judges is of inestimable value to their understanding of that community and to the respect of the community for the status of the judges and their influence on the quality of justice.

That this development is taking place despite the fact that responsibility for the administration of justice in Wales remains with the UK Parliament renders it inevitable, in my view, that the responsibility will, to some extent at least, be devolved to the National Assembly for Wales in the foreseeable future. The only uncertainty is when and to what extent. For the reasons I set out in section 4, the *status quo* does not make any constitutional or practical sense.

2. The Judicial Role

As the focus of this chapter is the differences between civil law and common law jurisdictions in their selection and training of judges, and the influence of their judges on the law and justice systems, I will begin by describing the qualities required of those judges and I take France as my example of civil law jurisdictions and England and Wales as my example of common law jurisdictions.

Drawing up the judge's 'job description' and the requirements of the role is not as simple as it sounds, but the following authoritative descriptions when read together provide a sufficiently clear definition of it.

According to Socrates, 'Four things belong to a judge: to hear courteously, to answer wisely, to consider soberly, and to decide impartially.' In their article on the selection and training of judges, Luis Muniz-Argüelles and Migdalia Fraticelli-Torres[1] describe the qualities as sensitivity to social and human problems, hard work, impartiality, honesty, patience, courtesy, being discreet, the ability to distinguish between facts, lies and half-truths, and to make decisions quickly. The judicial oath in England and Wales also provides a good summary of it: 'to do right to all manner of people after the laws and usages of this realm without fear or favour, affection or ill-will.'

Lord Kerr of Tonaghmore, a judge of the Supreme Court of the UK, described the qualities as insight, wisdom, compassion and forward thinking.[2] He no doubt used 'wisdom' as including (as it does in the Welsh word 'doethineb') that most important quality of all, sound judgement.

Lord Steyn, also a judge of the Supreme Court, emphasised independence and impartiality in his description of the role as making 'judgements on matters that affect the way in which we are governed … A neutral arbiter of disputes between citizens, and between citizens and state, is essential to the working the democratic system.'

Lord Judge, a former Lord Chief Justice of England and Wales, speaking at Equality in Justice Day, October 2008, emphasised the importance of the judge being worldly wise, an attribute which comes not with youth but age:

> Many qualities are required of a judge … He or she must of course know the law and how to apply it, but the judge must also be wise to the ways of the world. The judge must have … moral courage …

> a very important judicial attribute – to make decisions that will be unpopular with the politicians or the media and the public, and indeed perhaps most importantly of all, to defend the right to equal treatment before the law of those who are unpopular at any given time … But however you draw up the list, and in whatever order, gender, colour of your skin, religious belief, and social origins are all utterly irrelevant. It is you who is the judge.

3. Selection and Training, very Different Systems

The importance of discerning selection systems and effective training systems is described in the opening paragraph of Luis Muniz-Argüelles and Migdalia Fraticelli-Torres's article as follows:

> The question of how to attract, train, and retrain for the judiciary those to whom we entrust the task of imparting justice has worried people of all ages in all countries. It is natural that this be so. Even the best laws … need an excellent judicial corps to implement them if there is to be a guarantee of efficient, impartial justice. Legal reforms will prove useless unless adequate attention is also given to the selection and training of the men and women who will implement the new laws.

The French system of selection and training of judges and that of the UK could hardly be more different. The difference occurs not so much in their post-appointment training as at the selection stage at which there is a vast difference in the quality of the evidence available to the appointing authorities as to whether the candidate has or can develop the qualities described earlier. What then is this difference and, more particularly, what is the nature of that all-important evidence of the qualities?

Training and Appointment in England and Wales

Whatever the selection criteria were prior to 2006 – some would say something of a 'nod and a wink' – today's formalised appointments system under the management of the Judicial Appointments Commission is open and diverse with merit being the ultimate criterion. The overwhelming majority of appointments are of barristers who have been in independent practice as advocates for more than twenty years and who will have sat, also over many years and on an occasional basis, as fee-paid judges prior to appointment as full-time judges.

My putting 'training' ahead of 'selection' in the subtitle to this subsection is not to put the cart before the horse; it is to make the point that the largest and the most important part of the training of the judges of the UK is acquired as advocates at the independent Bar for some twenty years or so before their appointment as judges. During this 'training period' advocates learn and acquire the skills and qualities of judges through experience and observation. Whilst I agree with the descriptions of the judicial qualities given earlier, I strongly disagree with the description of them as unteachable.[3] Such is the effectiveness of this 'training period', it could be said that by the time the advocate applies for appointment as a judge he/she will have been 'self-selected'. In many instances, suitable applicants will have been identified and will be encouraged to apply for appointment. No jurisdiction anywhere else in the world has a better and more reliable system of training and selection of judges. This 'self-selection' process, more than any other, accounts for the consistent and high quality of the judges of England and Wales. The independent Bar is the cradle in which the judges are brought up. The quality of the former determines the quality of the latter.

As there is an unbroken line between becoming a barrister to becoming a judge, how barristers qualify and train is also relevant to the theme of this book. Therefore, before I elaborate on the training of judges, I will summarise that earliest stage in the training process. To qualify as a barrister, a university degree is the first requirement. In the overwhelming majority of cases, this will be in law. Where it is not, it must be followed by a twelve-month law conversion course at a university or other approved teaching establishment. The second stage is based on the Bar Finals examinations set by the Bar Council. Success in these is followed by the ceremony of 'Call to the Bar'. For those that seek only the title 'Barrister at Law', there the journey ends. Those wishing to practise at the independent Bar must begin their careers as pupils (pupillage) with experienced junior counsel for a period of twelve months, usually divided into two periods of six months with different 'pupil masters'. Here the training process begins. My pupil masters were Francis Ferris, who later became Queen's Counsel (usually referred to as 'QC' or 'silk') and a High Court judge, and Monro Davies, who also took silk and was appointed a Circuit Judge. As they practised in very different fields of law and appeared in different branches of the High Court (Chancery Division and Queen's Bench Division), I benefited greatly from a working introduction to two wide and different fields of law. Reading my pupil masters' written opinions, sitting in with them in consultations with solicitors and clients, and sitting behind them in court observing their performance were all essential learning experiences of the highest value.

After pupillage, the young barrister needs to join a 'chambers' (the unit from which barristers practise), but as the competition is so acute many fail to progress beyond their pupillage. Those who do are then on their own. Every barrister in independent practice is just that – independent. Although they share the expenses of running chambers and are subject to the same regulatory controls and standards, they are not in partnership with other members of their chambers and there is no sharing of profits. Their independence is probably their most important circumstance. It is on this that everything else about the barrister is built and it is the most important attribute they will carry with them throughout their careers and which they will take with them to the bench if so appointed. Hence my reference to 'an unbroken line'.

Returning to the judges and the second of their training stages, only rarely will a barrister or solicitor be appointed permanently as a judge of the High Court, County Court or Crown Court without his or her having previously served as a fee-paid judge. Sitting as such, albeit on an occasional basis, is an important stage as it provides the advocates with 'on the bench' experience and enables the appointing authority to observe and assess their judicial qualities. The fee-paid judges, just as do the full-time judges, attend educational or refresher courses arranged by the judicial College. The third stage is the regular but occasional post-appointment training and refresher courses of full-time judges provided by the Judicial College. From that brief description of the pre- and post-appointment training of UK Judges, one can see that most of it, ironically, precedes full-time appointment and, unlike the long duration of the classroom training of newly appointed French judges, the 'classroom' courses are occasional and of comparatively short duration.

According to the Lord Chief Justice's report for 2017, the College provided 340 courses including induction and continuation training in the core legal subjects, social context and diversity issues embedded through case studies. E-learning is now blended with face-to-face training; It has online courses and reference materials which can be accessed and booked on line through its Learning Management System. It has a Faculty, including external academics, to coordinate pervasive work themes, which are activities, skills and knowledge (rather than the substantive law) that are applicable and common to all judges regardless of jurisdiction. Skills training includes training judges to be trainers; business of judging, which provides opportunities to consider ethics; unconscious bias; leadership and management; appraiser and mentor skills; and judge as a communicator. Separately, the leadership masterclasses were attended by 150 leadership judges. There was a seminar on the Welsh language to assist members of the judiciary undertaking hearings in Welsh. The College also prepared a range of distance learning and training packs for local delivery by magistrates and accredited legal advisers.

Selection and Training in France[4]

The judges of France are recruited through competitive examinations and special qualifications. Whilst they will have the necessary academic qualifications ahead of appointment, most of them will be without any relevant experience of the judicial system. For them, everything turns on the outcome of the competitive examinations and all their training takes place after appointment. They are 'career judges'. Bearing in mind the similarity in the essential qualities required of judges of the two systems, the extent of this difference is surprising. It is summarised by Luis Muniz-Arguelles and Migdalia Fraticelli-Torres on p. 2 of their article:

> Today the English choose experienced, respected elders to be judges. On the European continent, the tendency is to appoint young, easily trainable law graduates willing to accept a prestigious and stable career, if not one as well paid as that of a highly successful attorney or consultant.

I wonder what Plato would have made of the European tendency there described. Did he not say in *The Republic*: 'A judge should not be a youth, but old ... he should have learnt to know evil, not from his own soul, but from late and long observance of the nature of evil in others, influence and authority.' In his address to the Congress of Magistrates, Quebec, November 2008[5] Lord Justice Robin Jacob said in a passage highly relevant in the present context

> The judge must appear more than superficially worldly – he/she should in fact be so ... I suspect very few will challenge the proposition that a bar- appointed judge is likely to be better placed than a career judge. A judge whose only worldly experience is school, law at University, judge school, judicial continuing education and actual judging is not given much of a chance to learn the ways of the world. That is not to say that there are not many fine civil law judges, for there are. But it is surely easier to judge if one has experience of actual clients and of actual case preparation. The best gamekeepers were once poachers; as the saying goes 'set a thief to catch a thief.'

Both Lord Justice Jacob and Plato hit the nail on the head. Applicants for the position of judge need to have acquired the essential qualities by the date on which they are appointed. Of course they will become better through further experience and training but that is simply a process of adding to what is there already. It is what is there already, high standards and long experience as advocates and fee-paid judges, that identifies them as suitable for appointment. Neither the enlarging effect of *stare decisis* (following precedent) on the law-making authority of UK judges, nor the limiting effect of the French constitution on French judges necessitates or even explains these differences in the selection processes.

In addition to providing much better evidence of competence, the selection and training system of England and Wales provides better value for money than the French system in that the costs of the training of the judges falls on the governments of the UK[6] much later, some twenty years later in fact, and for shorter periods than it does on the French government.

Although senior members of the French judiciary participate in the selection and training programmes of new judges, the written examination is autonomous and the oral entrance examination is of a high standard, the successful candidates attend a high-standard residential training programme of nearly three years at the *École Nationale de la Magistrature* (ENM) which is followed by many months as interns in various institutions including 'attorneys', the police and prison services and courts, it is nevertheless remarkable that judges are chosen from applicants with no experience of the judicial system and that their post-appointment courses are of the classroom kind.

Another remarkable feature of the French system which distinguishes it from the system in England and Wales is the close relationship between France's judiciary and its prosecutors. France does not distinguish between them. Quite the opposite, in fact. They are appointed by the same authority and selected through the same competitive examinations. They are both career civil servants. They are part of the same professional body. They are collectively referred to as *magistrats*. They attend the same educational establishment for their post- appointment education, their offices are situated in the same buildings, and they may transfer from one position to the other throughout their careers. Sometimes prosecutors become judges, sometimes judges become prosecutors. Judges and advocates on the common law side of the divide would find this very uncomfortable. It cannot but compromise, or at least dilute, the independence of the judges from the prosecutors. Just as justice must not only be done but must be seen to be done, the judiciary must be seen to be independent of the executive, and especially of the prosecuting authorities. The quality of justice, of which a fair trial is the most essential element, can be tarnished by the appearance of bias or unfairness. Does not the fact that the civil law jurisdiction is inquisitorial and that France has investigative judges sharpen these concerns? Allowing for the fact that the system in the UK is adversarial, if a former judge became a prosecutor and were to appear as such before a judge it would be likely to lead to an objection by the defence based on the appearance of unfairness or bias. I speak not in the abstract here but from actual experience of such a situation. The following statement is not surprising:

> French prosecutors have their office either inside the courts of original and appellate jurisdictions or inside the Supreme Court. Consequently … although they have different tasks (prosecuting and judging), the risk of collusion is said to be higher in the French legal system.[7]

A corollary of the independence of the judiciary of court advocates is the independence of court advocates of judges. In the ALBA Lecture, Lord Steyn said, 'An authoritarian regime cannot easily tolerate a wholly independent body of advocates: it is a substantial check on absolute executive power.'[8] Sir Malcolm Hilbery in the classical booklet *Duty and Art in Advocacy* also refers to the independence of advocates as a duty. After referring to counsel's duty to disclose to the court matters which the client might not wish disclosed, he concludes with the words: '[the Barrister] is an integral part of a system which has been developed for one purpose, and with one object in view, which is to do justice.'[9]

I conclude this section by citing a passage from the 2017 report of Lord Thomas of Cwmgiedd, then Lord Chief Justice of England and Wales:

> The twin pillars of our legal system are an independent, diverse, impartial and incorruptible judiciary and an independent, strong, diverse and effective legal profession. As a nation, we have a long-standing history and well-earned reputation for excellence in respect of each pillar. It is because of this strength that English

> law is so often the law of choice in commercial contracts; why our courts, arbitral institutions and [alternative dispute resolution] providers are so often used in cases of dispute; and, why the UK is able to contribute significantly to the promotion of the rule of law and fundamental rights worldwide. The UK is therefore, rightly, seen as a world-leader in law and justice.

That the laws of England and Wales, its judges, courts and its advocates enjoy a pre-eminent reputation internationally is strong and independent evidence of the quality of the process by which the judges are selected and the common law is made. And it is to that 'law-making process' I now turn.

4. Different Influence and Authority

Similar though their roles are and the qualities required of them, the influence and authority of civil law judges over the development of the law and the administration of justice are quite different from those of common law judges. What are those differences and what accounts for them?

The Constitutions

One very obvious influence on the status and authority of judges is the constitutional framework within which they work. In the case of common law jurisdictions of the UK, the effect of the constitution is to extend the judge's scope for influencing the law and its justice systems, but the constitutions of civil law jurisdictions limit the scope of judges to influence those matters. Both the written constitution of France and the largely unwritten constitution of the UK are made up of the principles of the sovereignty of their legislatures, separation of powers, independence of the judiciary and the rule of law, but they differ in two fundamental respects, both of which account for the very different influence of the judges on the shaping of the laws and the justice systems

One is that civil law codes, especially those of France, adhere strictly to written constitutions which expressly limit the authority of judges to make law. Of equal if not greater influence on the decisions of French judges than their earlier decisions are the very detailed civil law codes, legislators and the specialist lawyers and academics in their interpretation of earlier judgments and their resulting legal principles. Although the French judges follow those interpretations they do not expressly base their decisions on them and their decisions are expressed in more general terms than are decisions of UK judges. They can also reverse prior decisions, even of higher courts.

The other is that in addition to those four constitutional principles I have just referred to, the judges of the UK work to the principle of *stare decisis* which is to the effect that decisions of superior courts shall be binding on lower courts. The superior courts of England and Wales are the Supreme Court, the Court of Appeal and the High Court. Because of their binding effect, their decisions become part of the law until overturned by the Supreme Court or changed by the legislature. This is the foundation of the common law and explains the expression 'judge-made law'. Through this process, common law judges have a very real influence on the substance of the law and on the administration of justice more generally.

It should not be thought that in making law in this way, the judges of England and Wales are usurping or trespassing upon the function of the legislature or are acting inconsistently with the fundamentally important constitutional principle of the sovereignty of Parliament, the ultimate principle of our constitution. The 'judiciary unreservedly respects the will of Parliament as expressed in statutes'.[10] The reason, quite simply, is that as the legislation of the UK is nowhere near as detailed as civil law codes, there is greater uncertainty as to its meaning and application in the particular circumstances of the case under consideration. The judges are doing no more than interpreting the legislation in a way which fills those gaps. It is because of this vagueness or uncertainty in our legislation that the judges have much wider scope and authority than civil law system judges for influencing the development of the law. It is how the common law is made. The purpose of *stare decisis* and the effective reporting of judicial decisions is to ensure consistency in the judges' interpretation and application of both statute law and common law. The description of decisions made under the precedent system as 'judge-made law', more than any other, summarises the difference in the status and authority of the judges of the two systems.

Lord Steyn sat as a member of the Judicial Committee of the House of Lords (the Supreme Court as it is today). The following passage from his 1996 Administrative Law Bar Association (ALBA)[11] lecture describes in clear terms how the judges of the UK work in practice and just how independent they are of other possible influences in arriving at their decisions:

> Uniquely in our society, the judges seem to be the only public servants who do all their own work. The case is heard and decided by a judge … *without any aid or intervention by anybody else*. The parties and the public can be confident that the decision has been taken … *wholly and exclusively* by the judge or judges who heard the evidence and the arguments … And it is important to bear in mind that English judgments are not written in the oracular style that characterises judgments of the European Court of Justice; in an English judgment the reasons including policy reasons for the decision are discursively but fully exposed. (my emphasis)

I do not mean to imply that civil law judges have no influence on the development of the law and that there is no flexibility in civil law codes. Plainly, they do influence it and there is some, albeit little, flexibility in the codes. In the provision of that flexibility in the decision-making authority of judges, the code acknowledges that its draftsmen cannot foresee all circumstances in which a judge might be called on to exercise that authority. However, as the codes are detailed, the scope for exercising that discretion is small and the occasions on which it is exercised are infrequent, so that the influence of the judges on the decision-making process and on the substance of the law is very little. I should also explain that not every part of the decision of the superior courts of the UK is binding on the lower court; it is only that part which was central to the court's reasons (the *ratio decidendi*) for coming to the decision it did. Also, decisions of the Court of Appeal are not binding on itself in cases where the earlier decision is inconsistent with another of its decisions (in which case it must choose which to follow), where the earlier decision is inconsistent with a decision of the Supreme Court and where the earlier decision failed to take into account a matter of high significance. As to the extent to which the decisions of the High Court are binding on itself, there is some uncertainty but history and experience show that in the absence of sound reasons for departing from its earlier decision it does not do so.

In summary, therefore, France's written constitution and the detail in which the codes are drafted limits the scope of the judiciary to develop the law through the decision-making process. In the UK, the judges as well as the legislature make laws, the former through legislation and the latter through the process of *stare decisis*. It is through that process that the judges of the UK have such a large influence on the substance of the law and the administration of justice more generally. The common law is the product of it.

5. Reforms

I have three proposed reforms. Each relates to the central themes of the book. The first is that responsibility for the administration of justice in Wales be devolved to Wales. The constitutional anomaly I described in a public lecture in 2008[12] continues to be a substantial impediment to the good governance of Wales and to the administration of justice in Wales. It can only be removed by the devolution of responsibility of the justice system:

> The principal argument is that including responsibility for the administration of justice as part of a devolution settlement which devolves full law-making powers makes good constitutional sense if the institution which is responsible for making the laws were also to have the responsibility and the accountability for their administration. Is there an Assembly or Parliament enjoying full legislative competence which does not also have responsibility for the administration of justice within its territorial jurisdiction?

Secondly, it would be internally logical, consistent and coherent. Thirdly, it would make for consistency between the constitutions of Scotland, Northern Ireland and Wales, and fourthly it would bring justice closer to the people for whom the laws are made.

In his submissions of January 2012 to the Welsh government's inquiry into the establishment of a Welsh jurisdiction, Professor R. Gwynedd Parry described that argument as

> a mature argument for the creation of a separate jurisdiction because it is necessary if Wales is to operate in a way that is constitutionally valid, and consistent with the pattern generally found within the British state. Indeed, this pattern of having a legal jurisdiction and regional legislature is seen in devolved and federal countries throughout the world, such as Australia and Canada. I would call it the constitutional argument ... possibly the most important argument (paragraph 85) ... [Its core] is that for democracy in Wales to mature and operate in accordance with democratic and constitutional standards seen in devolved regions and nations world-wide, Wales's own legal structures need to be consistent with those standards.

My second proposed reform is that there be established a law reform commission for Wales. The purpose of the commissions, of which there is one for Scotland, one for Northern Ireland and one for England and Wales is to make recommendations for reform and to explain the need for the reform. They are important to the quality and the development of the law. They complement the law-making functions of the legislators and the judges.[13] It is imperative that the legislatures and the judges understand and are well informed of the need for reform and how proposed reforms might satisfy that need. The commissions are independent and objective observers of the need. Their recommendations have led to major improvements. In a devolved constitution like the UK, it is important that the legislators and the judiciary are aware of compatibilities and incompatibilities of the laws of the devolved nations with each other and with those of the central government. Difference may well be justified by the different needs and circumstances of the devolved nations, but awareness of them is nevertheless important. The amount of Wales-only legislation, primary and secondary, produced in Wales since 1999[14] and the sure assumption that the amount is likely to increase makes it imperative that Wales should have a law reform commission (or some such body) of its own. The effective and efficient performance of the legislative responsibilities of its government and the law-making responsibilities of its judges would be considerably facilitated by a law reform commission for Wales. Creating it would be in the public interest and it would bring about better symmetry between the constitutions of Wales, Scotland and Northern Ireland. There could hardly be a more appropriate time for establishing a law reform commission for Wales than during this period of significant constitutional changes.

The third reform is that the prosecution of cases before the Crown Courts and the Superior Courts of England and Wales be conducted by counsel independent of the prosecuting authority. The Crown Prosecution Service (CPS) of England and Wales has responsibility for the prosecution of cases before the Crown Courts and appeals to the Court of Appeal. These are conducted on its behalf by barristers. Until recently, and certainly when Lord Steyn and Mr Justice Hilbery made the statements they did[15] emphasising the importance to the quality of justice of the independence of advocates, it instructed only barristers in independent practice. That has now changed. It now instructs its own employed barristers in many serious cases before the Crown Court and the Court of Appeal. This undermines the advocate's independence of the executive, the quality of the administration of justice, the confidence of judges in the independence of the Bar, the confidence of defence counsel in the independence of prosecuting counsel and the confidence of the public in the independence and integrity of our justice system generally. It is just as undermining in its effect on confidence, if not more so, than is the close relationship between prosecutors and judges in the French justice system. If the barristers who are employees of the CPS become eligible for appointment as judges, the system in England

and Wales will drift towards the French system in which the prosecutor and the judge are from the same stable. Lord Steyn's statement about the importance of advocates maintaining their independence of the executive is one of fundamental importance. The independence of advocates and judges of the executive and the legislature ensures fair and independent dispute resolution.

Losing sight of that principle led to another very significant change in 2013: the appointment of the head of the service, the Director of Public Prosecutions, from within the service itself. The established practice had been to appoint an experienced and skilled barrister from independent practice. The experiment of 'in-house' appointment of the DPP was abandoned after only five years with the appointment of Max Hill QC as DPP. Following his appointment, it emerged that the number of prosecutions in England and Wales that had collapsed because of a failure to disclose evidence had increased by 70 per cent in the previous two years. History has proved the necessity, the durability and effectiveness of the independent Bar to the quality of the prosecution service.

Conclusion

The tradition of codification in civil law jurisdictions, the tradition of judicial law making in common law jurisdictions, the very different processes by which they appoint and train their judges and the different procedures in court (the inquisitorial and the adversarial) all contribute to the very substantial difference in the status and authority of the judges. The difference between their influence on the development of the law and on the administration of justice more generally is explainable on the basis of the different constitutional frameworks within which they function, but those differences in the constitutions neither explain nor necessitate the very substantial differences in the systems by which they are selected and trained. In April 2018, the French Minister of Justice announced that the government planned to submit a bill making quite comprehensive and far-reaching reforms to the country's judicial system,[16] but they do not touch upon those aspects of the French judicial system addressed in this chapter which are fundamentally different from those of the common law jurisdictions. I therefore close this chapter in the knowledge that those differences will continue to distinguish between the civil and common law judges of France and the UK.

Differences though there may be between the status and authority of the judges, the civil law judges also enjoy a high reputation, domestically and internationally. Although I have focused on differences, I conclude by acknowledging their common strengths. Of these, the greatest are their high regard for the rule of law, the independence of the judiciary and the ideals of justice. Above and outside courts of Europe, America, Canada and the UK stands the statue of the Goddess Justitia. That tells us, does it not, that different though our constitutions may be, and differences though there may be between aspects of our justice systems, our courts and our judges are there to achieve justice which, since ancient Greece, is considered not a simple value but a supreme governing principle of human society. The differences between the civil law jurisdictions and the common law jurisdictions are but different routes to the same terminus. Every morning on my way to school in the town of Caernarfon, I walked past the court of justice. Above its entrance was the statue of Justitia with her scales, sword and blindfold. It is no coincidence that I made my career in the justice system she represents.

Notes

1. 'Selection and training of judges in Spain, France, West Germany, and England', *Boston College International and Comparative Law Review*, 8/1 (1985), article 2 at p. 2.
2. *The Times* (28 May 2019), p. 46.
3. 'Selection and training of judges in Spain, France, West Germany, and England', p. 2.
4. I have here put the horse back in front of the cart!
5. Jacob Robin, 'Knowledge of the World and the Act of Judging', *Osgood Hall Review of Law and Policy*, 2/1 (2014), 22–8, *wwwdigitalcommons.osgoode.yorku.ca/ohrlp/vol12/iss1/2*
6. Of which there are three – Scotland, Northern Ireland and the UK.

7. Akila Taleb and Thomas Ahlstrand, 'The public prosecutor, its role, duties and powers in the pre-trial stage of the criminal justice process – a comparative study of the French and the Swedish legal systems', *Revue internationale de Droit pénal*, 82 (2011), 523–40.
8. Lord Steyn, 'The Weakest and Least Dangerous Department of Government', *Public Law* (1997), 84–9 at 88.
9. Sir Malcolm Hilbery, *Duty and Art in Advocacy* (London: Sevens and Sons, 1946), p. 16.
10. Lord Steyn, 'The Weakest and Least Dangerous Department of Government', 85.
11. Lord Steyn, 'The Weakest and Least Dangerous Department of Government', 84.
12. The Ninth Annual Lecture of the Centre for Welsh Legal Affairs, University of Aberystwyth, November 2008, 'The Development of Devolution and Legal Wales'.
13. See section 4.
14. See subsection, 'Wales, an Emerging Jurisdiction'.
15. Subsection, 'Selection and Training in France'.
16. *Compte-rendu du Conseil des ministres du vendredi 20 avril 2018: Projet de Loi, Renforcement de l'organisation des juridictions et programmation pour la justice 2018–2022* (Minutes of the Council of Ministers of Friday 20 April 2018: Legislation Project, Reinforcing the Organisation of Jurisdictions and Programming for Justice 2018–22), *www.elysee.fr* (website of the French Presidency) (20 April 2018).

10

The Declaration of Judicial Training Principles: Judicial Training 'as Part of the Judicial Role'

Benoît Chamouard

The final analysis, provided by Benoît Chamouard, chooses not to contrast the legal systems and legal cultures, but instead shows how bodies that train judges can interact at the European and international level to guarantee high standards of justice and underpin the rule of law.

On 8 November 2017, the International Organization for Judicial Training (IOJT) adopted the Declaration of Judicial Training Principles.

This first text of worldwide scope marks a significant step forward for judicial training,[1] an area that now has clear, simple international standards that are very much in line with the challenges and realities of the twenty-first century.

This declaration follows on from a number of other major texts setting down standards in justice, such as the Bangalore Principles of Judicial Conduct,[2] the Universal Charter of the Judge[3] or the Declaration on Social Justice for a Fair Globalisation.[4] Like the first two of these texts, the Declaration of Judicial Training Principles was not adopted by an international organisation but by a group of members of importance in their field, in this case the representatives of the judicial training institutes. As a purely soft law norm, its purpose is to guide and advise with all the legitimacy of the 129 judicial training schools that make up the IOJT, but without establishing binding legal obligations.

This article looks back at the reasons that led the IOJT and its members to work towards recognition of the principles guiding their action, and at the progress made through adoption of the declaration. Looking to the future, it also proposes possible ways of upholding the standards set out in this declaration.

1. The Adoption of the Declaration of Judicial Training Principles, the Culmination of a Collective Effort

A. An Idea Comes to Maturity

The idea of adopting a worldwide declaration on the principles of judicial training was initiated in November 2015 on the occasion of the seventh conference of the IOJT. A call was put out at the inaugural session of the conference to conceptualise and proclaim these principles. It was accepted immediately by the members of the organisation who scheduled the adoption of the declaration for the eighth conference in 2017. This call came at the same time as reflection was being launched at the European level on the adoption of principles for judicial training, culminating in the adoption of a European declaration on 10 June 2016.[5]

The idea of laying down principles to guide judicial training emerged as judicial training reached maturity. The idea of providing the judiciary with specific training coincided with the opening of the first judicial training institutes at the end of the 1950s. Creations of institutes dedicated to this training accelerated from the 1980s onwards, then again in the 2000s, in countries with a variety of different judicial cultures. The immense majority of countries now have such institutes that share values and practices reaching beyond the specifics of their judicial systems in many ways.

Sixty years on from the creation of judicial training, the declaration consecrates its role and specificity internationally by formalising a consensus that already existed within the community of schools.

It is widely accepted that training of the judiciary constitutes a major democratic factor in the life of a state. Only a properly trained judiciary will have the ability and strength to act independently and impartially, thereby embodying the principle of the separation of powers. In systems where judges are not elected, their legitimacy is based solely on their competence and independence, thus making effective training particularly necessary. Judicial training therefore plays a prominent role in constructing and upholding the rule of law.

This role implies specific features that are accepted by all, but which had not, until now, been the subject of any formal recognition. The governance of a judicial training institute serving to train independent professionals cannot be similar to that of training institutes in other sectors. The training methods, meanwhile, must be adapted to the judicial profession and to modern techniques in adult training.

B. An Inclusive, Pedagogical Approach

From the acceptance of the principle of a declaration in 2015 through to its final adoption in 2017, most of the work consisted in highlighting the values of, and the consensus between judicial training institutes around the world.[6]

An international working group was set up with representatives from four continents and from a variety of legal and judicial systems. Its work was organised in three main stages:

1. compiling a list of national or regional declarations or texts that define the principles of judicial training;[7]
2. writing a draft declaration and circulating it among all IOJT members for their remarks;
3. presenting, debating and adopting the text at the 2017 general assembly.

In order to ensure that the declaration was as broadly representative as possible, yet without renouncing the fundamental values of judicial training, preference was given by the working group to an inclusive approach. The 129 members of the IOJT were consulted at all three phases and had the possibility of expressing their views at each of them. All the remarks on which there was a consensus were included in the final version of the text.

The working group also decided to annex explanatory commentaries to the ten articles of the declaration for the purpose of clarifying the content and scope of the articles themselves, as well as their adaptation to certain national specifics. These commentaries are an integral part of the declaration and were debated and adopted in the same way as the preamble and ten articles of the text.

This inclusive approach and the addition of commentaries provided a balance between asserting values and seeking broad consensus. They resulted in the unanimous adoption of the declaration by the IOJT members represented at the General Assembly.

2. Asserting Common Values

A. The Power of Unanimity

The unanimous adoption of the declaration considerably reinforces its scope. As a *de facto* standard or soft law norm, the weight of the declaration can be based only on:

- the representative nature of the community that adopted it, and
- the extent of the consensus around it within that community.

With its 129 institutions from 79 countries, the IOJT forms the largest network of judicial training institutions in the world. It is the only worldwide organisation that federates regional initiatives. At present, the IOJT is therefore the most representative forum for the community of judicial training schools. The unanimous adoption of the declaration by the General Assembly, which is the broadest body of the IOJT, thus endows the text with the greatest possible representativity in the field of judicial training.

B. Addressing the Different Dimensions of Judicial Training

The declaration is divided into four parts addressing the different dimensions of judicial training.

The first part comprises article 1 and is dedicated to 'principles'. It emphasises notably the essential role of judicial training in the rule of law, judicial independence and the protection of fundamental rights.

The second part addresses the 'institutional framework' (articles 2–5). The four articles refer to the governance of judicial training institutes, each from a different angle.

The administrative organisation and positioning of judicial training institutes are intimately linked to judicial system organisation. They therefore vary considerably from one country to another[8] and cannot be modelled or standardised to any great extent, unlike other areas of judicial training. The declaration therefore seeks to set out the essential principles of the governance of an institute: independence in course design, content and delivery (article 2), the support of the judicial authorities (article 3) and the provision of sufficient human resources and funding (article 4). Article 5 provides a reminder that these principles also apply to relations with any international funding agencies which may provide support to the institutes.

The third part (articles 6 and 7) addresses the place of training in the professional life of members of the judiciary. It stresses that training is not only a right, but also a responsibility for the latter, and that they must enjoy the benefit of both pre-service and in-service training.

Finally, the fourth part (articles 8–10) is dedicated to the 'content' and 'methodology' of training. It states that judicial training should not be limited to the law, but must also cover non-legal knowledge, skills, social context, values and ethics, which means that it should mainly be dispensed by peers using specific and modern techniques.

The fact that these standards were adopted unanimously should not be taken as suggesting that they represent only the lowest common denominator between today's judicial training institutes. Few institutes around the world can claim to apply all the principles that have been adopted, demanding as these principles are. For instance, pre-service training is not always mandatory, in particular in certain common law countries. The institutional rules are not applied in all the civil law countries. In-service training throughout the career of members of the judiciary does not exist in many countries. The adoption of these principles by IOJT members therefore represents a demand for strict compliance with their own principles and the wish to progress together.

Despite their consensual nature, the adopted principles show the way forward and form 'the common base and the horizon uniting judicial training institutions throughout the world'.[9]

3. Upholding the Judicial Training Principles

The adoption of a declaration of judicial training principles is more than a mere expression of values by the institutes, no matter how solemn and important. In order to become genuine standards, the principles set out in this declaration must be recognised, accepted and applied by the judicial world outside training schools. The role of the institutes is not to act alone, and the principles governing their action can only take root if they are relayed by all judicial stakeholders.

It is therefore incumbent upon the members of the IOJT to uphold this declaration nationally by bringing it to the attention of their major partners, having it accepted or adopted by their boards or steering committees, and making reference to its content in their day-to-day action. Internationally, the declaration would benefit from being cited and taken up by the organisations acting in the area of justice, whether funding authorities, international or non-governmental organisations. In many ways, the declaration provides a useful, objective framework for the intervention of these organisations in the field of justice.

Finally, the IOJT is the right organisation to uphold these principles.[10] As a forum for exchanges, the organisation can place itself at the disposal of its members to implement the principles it has adopted.

One concrete proposal that IOJT is considering is a series of regional meetings of IOJT members in the region, probably by teleconference or other electronic means, where members could discuss the challenges of delivering judicial education in accordance with these principles, either because of issues within the institute or within the broader judicial structure. A plan will be finalised in the upcoming months for that purpose, with the support of the network of IOJT regional deputy presidents.

Notes

1. According to the declaration, the notion of the judiciary may 'include prosecutors, defenders/defence counsel, court staff and others, depending on the justice' (commentary to the Preamble).
2. Adopted on 25 and 26 November 2002 by the Judicial Group on Strengthening Judicial Integrity.
3. Text of the International Association of Judges, adopted on 17 November 1999 and updated on 14 November 2017.
4. International Labour Organisation, 29 November 1985.
5. *www.ejtn.eu/Judicial-Training-Principles/*
6. This dimension is written into the preamble of the declaration, which states that 'the declaration sets out guiding principles for judicial training that reflect how IOJT members conceptualize and strive to implement judicial training. The principles are both the common base and the horizon uniting judicial training institutions throughout the world, regardless of the diversity of judicial systems.'
7. After listing the existing texts, the working group based itself mainly on the following documents:
   - 'The 20 Principles of Judicial Education in Canada' – National Judicial Institute, October 2006;
   - 'Judicial Training Principles' – European Judicial Training Network, June 2016, *www.ejtn.eu/Judicial-Training-Principles/*
   - 'European Charter on the Statute for Judges', Council of Europe, July 1998;
   - 'Opinion no. 4 to the attention of the committee of Ministers of the Council of Europe on appropriate initial and in-service training for judges at National and European levels', Consultative Council of European Judges, November 2003;
   - 'Opinion no. 15 on the Specialisation of Judges' (Point 27), Consultative Council of European Judges, November 2012;
   - 'The Bangalore Principles of Judicial Conduct' (see above);
   - 'The Principles of Judicial Training: Towards International Recognition?', Xavier Ronsin, November 2015.
8. The training institution may therefore be totally independent (Italy), under the supervision of the judicial authority (Spain, Romania, common law countries), under the supervision of the Ministry for Justice (France, Tunisia, Egypt, Laos, United Arab Emirates) or even a part of the Ministry for Justice (Senegal, Finland, Austria).
9. Preamble to the declaration.

10. As the declaration expressly indicates, 'the IOJT also encourages judicial training institutions to support each other in the implementation of this declaration.'

Conclusion

This book has examined the challenges faced by the justice system in many countries under both common and civil law in the early twenty-first century. In the last few years, it has experienced a whole series of serious, unprecedented crises, from a decade of austerity with drastic cuts in its budget to the 2020 coronavirus pandemic. These have occurred while the law is still trying to adjust to Brexit and its possible impact on judicial cooperation. The judges, declared Lord Judge in 2008, have shown their 'moral courage', their capacity to adapt, including to new ways of delivering justice as well as their resilience. As the Lord Chief Justice, Lord Burnett of Maldon, said in the introduction to his 2019 Report, 'the judges and magistrates of England and Wales at every level do a remarkable job in difficult circumstances. They are dedicated to the public interest.' This book for its part is yet another testimony of the legal expertise and commitment of those dispensing justice.

Looking to the future, however, justice cannot rest solely on the good will and good practice of judges. They also need substantial financial means to reach the high standards that are expected from them, and a secure environment to perform their mission in the best possible conditions, taking into account their own welfare. This cannot be achieved without a strong political will on the part of governments and the determination to invest more funds in justice. As Lord Thomas of Cwmgiedd recommended in his report on justice in Wales, justice must be placed 'at the heart of government'. This will require funding and will-power.

Modern courts and equipment, access to and training in new technologies, are more necessary than ever under the new constraints imposed by the 2020 'remote justice'. Lately more emphasis has been put on judges' training and awareness of a different social context in areas such as sexual assault, domestic abuse, aggravated by the lockdown introduced in March 2020 by the British government. The additional strain on national economies due to the fight against the coronavirus could, however, lead to new austerity measures to the detriment of the quality of justice. A number of law firms are already struggling to survive – especially those dealing with legal aid and family law. It is vital that they do so, for the sake of equality and social justice.

Another aspect of the current health crisis is that it has revived the controversy about the future of jury trials and the handling of jurors to avoid putting them at risk, whereas an efficient administration of justice, inspiring public confidence, rests on the involvement of citizens. At a time of a recruitment crisis among judges, the contribution to justice of jurors and lay magistrates is even more valuable. They represent – or are expected to represent – a cross-section of society, thus bringing in more diversity as well as preserving identifiable links with society as a whole.

Among the aspects of justice that particularly need to be improved – as shown throughout this book – is indeed the question of judicial diversity. This is an area where there are significant gaps in terms of the representation of women and Black, Asian and Minority Ethnic (BAME) people. While the BAME are seriously underrepresented on the Bench they tend to be overrepresented as offenders within the criminal justice system according to the findings of the Commission on Justice in Wales – which makes it even more urgent to recruit more BAME people on the Bench. There is still a lack of diversity in socio-economic terms. Breaking the mould, avoiding too many people with similar social backgrounds would also diminish the risk of corporatism and conservatism. Matthias Kelly believes that the way forward would be to have more part-time judges. An increase in part-time judges could facilitate the day-to-day relationship between the judicial bench and the advocates, as Lord Judge points out. More flexibility as far as working conditions and hours are concerned, could also encourage more women to join the judiciary.

As for the reform of justice, the codification of criminal law could help judges in their sentencing power – providing them with clearer guidance and more legal certainty. As Victor Bailey explains, attempts were made as early as the nineteenth century to rationalise the structure of penalties to facilitate sentencing by judges. As the Lord Chief Justice pointed out in his 2019 Report, 'complex sentencing law [i.e. criminal law] continues to be a cause for concern and adds to the demand on resources.'[1] A vast project regarding a Sentencing Code has been launched in the United Kingdom – in which Lord Judge is actively involved – to make sentencing procedure and the law regulating it clearer, more accessible and faster. The Sentencing (Pre-Consolidation Amendments) Bill paving the way for such an important code which had reached its report stage in the House of Lords in the previous Parliament (2017–19) was interrupted by the 2019 general election before being carried over in the next Parliament. It reached its second reading in the House of Commons on 18 March 2020, and The Sentencing Act received Royal Assent on 22 October 2020.

There are also important needs in terms of improving sentence implementation – in France a judge (the *juge d'application des peines*) is charged with this specific task. It is particularly urgent in terms of applying jail sentences when there are no appropriate facilities for vulnerable offenders such as women – there are still no prisons for women in Wales – or transgender people. And yet some form of hope might come from Wales following the enlightening report of Lord Thomas[2] – about what justice might look like in Wales in the future with proposals of a much less centralised and devolved type of justice. This report has already received a favourable response from the Welsh First Minister, Mark Drakeford, and the changes it foreshadows would probably not be confined to Wales alone.

The politics of the law are also of crucial significance. For the UK at large, the current government unveiled its programme, including justice, in the Queen's Speech at the last opening of Parliament on 19 December 2019. The measures proposed contain longer sentences for violent criminals and more severe sanctions against people breaching deportation orders. The general trend seems to be on punishment and repression, with less emphasis given to prevention and rehabilitation. The 2019 Conservative Manifesto thus promised to 'put 20,000 more officers on the streets' while 'giving them the powers to tackle crime with stop and search'.[3] In the government's plan to look at the broader aspects of the British constitution, access to justice was explicitly mentioned, yet without providing any detail as to how it would be dealt with.

Finally, a 'virtual' type of justice imposed by the exceptional circumstances in 2020 as the only way of delivering justice in a safe way for citizens could have wider significance. It might lead to a virtual justice from a possible meaning of the word. The result would be a disembodied, more abstract type of justice no longer operated by judges in a courtroom wearing the full regalia but by 'remote' judges. Géraldine Gadbin-George in her chapter, however, warns against the risk of dehumanisation of justice. Technologies and circumstances may change, yet it must not be to the detriment of the fundamental principles discussed in this book – judicial independence, judicial diversity and access to justice – for they are essential to every democracy.

Finally, in his chapter, Lord Judge points out that in the UK 'the attraction of judicial office has diminished'. Does it mean that there is nothing to look forward to for practising judges, and even more for aspiring ones? A good start would be to give judges a better status in terms of salaries and pensions, and also in terms of recognition and consideration. Protecting their independence from undue political and/or media interference would allow them to deliver justice without unnecessary additional strain, and governments should make this a priority. The only form of distancing that one could require – under normal circumstances – for the sake of judicial independence and the quality of justice – is, 'keeping law at a distance from politics'.[4] It is hoped that the present volume offers help in that direction and the proposal of future reform.

Notes

1. The Lord Chief Justice's Report (London: Judicial Office, 2019), p. 15.
2. 'Justice in Wales for the People of Wales', The Commission on Justice in Wales Report (Cardiff, 2019).
3. The 2019 Conservative Manifesto, 'Get Brexit Done'.
4. Martine, Valois, *Judicial Independence: Keeping Law at a Distance from Politics* (Markham, ON: LexisNexis, 2013).

Bibliography

Books

Abel-Smith, Brian and Robert Stevens, *Lawyers and the Courts: A Sociological Study of the English Legal System 1750–1965* (London: Heinemann, 1970).

Arlidge, Anthony and Igor Judge, *Magna Carta Uncovered* (Oxford: Hart Publishing, 2014).

Ashworth, Andrew, 'Sentencing', in M. Maguire, R. Morgan and R. Reiner (eds), *The Oxford Handbook of Criminology* (Oxford: Clarendon Press, 1997).

Bailey, Victor, *The Rise and Fall of the Rehabilitative Ideal, 1895–1970* (London: Routledge, 2019).

Bingham, Tom, The *Rule of Law* (London: Penguin Law, 2011).

Bory, Stéphanie, *L'éveil du dragon gallois: D'une assemblée à un parlement (1997–2017)* (Paris: L'Harmattan, 2019).

Bresler, Fenton, *Lord Goddard: A Biography of Rayner Goddard, Lord Chief Justice of England* (London: Harrap, 1977).

Churchill, Randolph, *Winston S. Churchill: Companion Volume*, vol. 2, part 2: *1907–1911* (London: Heinemann, 1969).

Collini, Stefan, *Public Moralists: Political Thought and Intellectual Life in Britain 1850–1930* (Oxford: Clarendon Press, 2006).

Davet, Gérard and Fabrice Lhomme, *Un président ne devrait pas dire ça …* (Paris: Stock, 2016).

Dicey, Albert Venn, *Introduction to the Study of the Law of the Constitution*, eighth edn (London: Macmillan, 1915).

Fifoot, C. H. S., *Judge and Jurist in the Reign of Victoria* (London: Stevens and Sons, 1959).

Gadbin-George, Géraldine, *Déréglementation et Professions du Droit Outre-Manche* (Paris: Dalloz, 2016).

Gardner, David, *Administrative Law and the Administrative Court in Wales* (Cardiff: University of Wales Press, 2016).

Griffith, J. A. G., *The Politics of the Judiciary* (London: Fontana, 1977).

Huppé, Luc, *Histoire des institutions judiciaires du Canada* (Montreal: Wilson and Lafleur, 2007).

Jackson, R. M., *Enforcing the Law* (London: Macmillan, 1967).
Jackson, R. M., *The Machinery of Justice in England* (Cambridge: Cambridge University Press, 1972).
Jiménez Asensio, Rafael (ed.), *El acceso a la función judicial. Estudio comparado* (Madrid: Consejo General del Poder Judicial, 2001).
Judge, Igor (Lord), *The Safest Shield: Lectures, Speeches and Essays* (Oxford: Hart Publishing, 2015).
Lambert, Édouard, *Le Gouvernment des Juges*, foreword by Franck Moderne, reprint of the 1921 edn (Paris: Dalloz, 2005).
López Aguilar, Juan Fernando, *Justicia y Estado autonómico. Orden competencia y administración de justicia en el Estado compuesto de la Constitución de 1978* (Madrid: Civitas, 1993).
Montesquieu, *De l'esprit des lois*, introduction by Victor Goldschmidt (Paris: Flammarion, 1979).
Nason, Sarah (ed.), *Administrative Justice in Wales and Comparative Perspectives* (Cardiff: University of Wales Press, 2017).
Neira Pena, Ana María, *La Instrucción de los Procesos Penales Frente a las Personas Jurídicas* (Valencia: Tirant Lo Blanch, 2017).
Nieva Fenoll, Jordi, *Derecho Procesal I. Introducción* (Madrid: Marcial Pons, 2014).
Ortells Ramos, Manuel (ed.), *Introducción al Derecho Procesal*, fourth edn (Cizur Menor: Aranzadi, 2014).
Polden, Patrick, 'The Judiciary', in *The Oxford History of the Laws of England*, XI: *1820–1914*, Part Four|: *The Legal Professions* (Oxford: Oxford University Press, 2010).
Russell, Peter, H., *The Judiciary in Canada: The Third Branch of Government* (Toronto: McGraw-Hill Ryerson, 1987).
Smith, Keith, 'Sentencing and Review', in *The Oxford History of the Laws of England*, XIII: *1820–1914, Fields of Development* (Oxford: Oxford University Press, 2010).
Stevens, Robert, *The Independence of the Judiciary* (Oxford: Clarendon Press, 1997).
Stirn, Bernard, Duncan Fairgrieve and Mattias Guyomar, *Droits et libertés en France et au Royaume-Uni* (Paris: Odile Jacob, 2006).
Thomas, D. A., *Constraints on Judgment: The Search for Structured Discretion in Sentencing, 1860–1910* (Cambridge: Institute of Criminology, 1979).
Thomas, D. A., *The Penal Equation: Derivations of the Penalty Structure of English Criminal Law* (Cambridge: Institute of Criminology, 1978).
Thomas, D. A., *Principles of Sentencing* (London: Heinemann, 1979).

Valois, Martine, *Judicial Independence: Keeping Law at a Distance from Politics* (Markham, ON: LexisNexis, 2013).

Walters, Graham, *Welsh Planning Law and Practice* (Cardiff: University of Wales Press, 2017).

Watkin, Thomas Glyn and Daniel Greenberg, *Legislating for Wales* (Cardiff: University of Wales Press, 2018).

Wiener, Martin, *Reconstructing the Criminal: Culture, Law, and Policy in England, 1830–1914* (Cambridge: Cambridge University Press, 1990).

Zedner, Lucia, *Criminal Justice* (Oxford: Clarendon Press, 2010).

Official Documents

Cabinet Manual: A Guide to Laws, Conventions and Rules on the Operation of Government (London: Cabinet Office, October 2011).

Commission on Justice in Wales Report, *Justice in Wales for the People of Wales* (Cardiff, October 2019).

Final Report, Judiciary of England and Wales, *Civil Courts Structure*, Justice Briggs (Lord Justice), July 2016.

Home Office, *Corporal Punishment*, Report of the Advisory Council on the Treatment of Offenders (London: HMSO, 1961).

Home Office, *Digest: Information on the Criminal Justice System in England and Wales* (London: HMSO, 1995).

Home Office, *The Length of Prison Sentences*, Interim Report of the Advisory Council on the Penal System (London: HMSO, 1977).

Home Office, *Making Punishments Work: Report of a Review of the Sentencing Framework for England and Wales* (London: HMSO, 2001).

Home Office, *Sentences of Imprisonment. A Review of Maximum Penalties*, Report of the Advisory Council on the Penal System (London: HMSO, 1978).

Home Office, Research Unit Report, *The Effectiveness of Sentencing: A Review of the Literature* (London: HMSO, 1976).

Report of the Committee on Administrative Tribunals and Enquiries, Oliver Franks (London: HMSO, 1957).

Report of the Royal Commission on Assizes and Quarter Sessions, Richard Beeching (Lord Beeching) (London: HMSO, 1969).

Silk Report, *Empowerment and Responsibility: Legislative Powers to Strengthen Wales* (Commission on Devolution in Wales, 2014).

Index

D

E

J

K